LIGHTING CANDLES

A PARAMILITARY'S WAR WITH
DEATH, DRUGS AND DEMONS

DAVID LESLIE

BLACK & WHITE PUBLISHING

First published 2014
by Black & White Publishing Ltd
29 Ocean Drive, Edinburgh EH6 6JL

1 3 5 7 9 10 8 6 4 2   14 15 16 17

ISBN   978 1 84502 751 3

This book is a work of non-fiction, based on the life, experiences and
recollections of Manny McDonnell. In some limited cases names have
been changed solely to protect the privacy of others. The author has
stated to the publishers that, except in minor respects not affecting the
substantial accuracy of the work, the contents of this book are true.

Typeset by RefineCatch Limited, Bungay, Suffolk
Printed and bound by Grafica Veneta S.p.A.

It has only been possible to tell this remarkable story because of the unstinting and generous help given by Manny McDonnell. Over many, many hours of interviews and meetings, our friendship, which began two decades ago, has grown.

It is at his request that this book is dedicated to two people: his mother, Nellie, whose passion for and loyalty to Ireland never diminished, and to his good friend Billy Kane, murdered in his Belfast home on 15 January 1988, aged just 20.

CONTENTS

Prologue

THE WATCHERS

THE IRISHMAN WAS CERTAIN he was being watched. He knew it didn't take a genius to work that out. Years on the terrifying streets of Belfast had given him an extra sense that sent out warning signals when something was not right, when the routine of the day was out of place. At least he was sure that this time the game of cat and mouse would not end with a bullet in the head. But he was a man who had learned never to take chances, to always assume the worst.

Yet even at this moment of peril he found it hard to stifle a laugh at the antics of the watchers. It might be late summer, but the streets of Benidorm on Spain's sweltering Costa Blanca were still thronged by sweating tourists wearing little more than was needed to allow the Mediterranean sun access to most of their bodies while retaining their modesty.

Mostly their flimsy outfits were soft and gaily coloured. But a handful of visitors looked out of place, attracting not just the interest of the Irishman but also that of scores of bemused sun worshippers sipping cool drinks in crowded street-side bars or peering into souvenir shops. The giggles of red-skinned over-weight women caused their huge breasts and bellies to jiggle and wobble as they gulped beer and shushed cries of 'banana men' from children as the watchers passed.

The pale skins of those who were the subject of his attention marked out the men as new arrivals. No chance though, thought the Irishman, of them suffering painful sunburn. Their heavy waterproof yellow luminous jackets would have been at home on a building site or damp chilly Belfast or Glasgow housing scheme. In Benidorm they were more suited to a fancy-dress parade.

Even without any giveaway lettering on their coats, Emmanuel 'Manny' McDonnell knew a policeman when he saw one. He'd been sniffing out cops, undercover Army operatives, rival para-militaries and touts in his native Ulster since his schooldays.

In Ireland there wasn't merely a daily need to watch for anything out of the ordinary. Eyes and ears had to be on the alert every second of the day and night. Men and women listened and watched and heeded warnings, knowing a slip could cost a life.

Manny had been recruited to beef up security on an operation in Spain that was coming apart at the seams through careless talk and needless bravado. Not so long ago, Volunteers in arms like him had been smuggling guns, bombs, explosives and, on occasion, fugitives past police roadblocks and Army checkpoints in the cause of freedom. Here, the merchandise was a sickly brown substance called hashish and the rewards for sneaking it across Europe came in currency, millions and millions of pounds that gave the holders a freedom not just to live the life of which they had dreamed but to spend that life anywhere in the world.

The ingenuity of the smugglers had to be marvelled at; the lofty reputations of some of the businessmen who had invested in the racket and earned mind-boggling returns would cause astonish-ment had details of their crafty venture reached the ears of fellow members at their Rotary Club lunches or Round Table dinners.

For years, the gang that had hired Manny and his colleagues from Belfast had pocketed fortunes with a carelessness born of a ludicrous belief that the torrent of money would continue to pour into their hands for all time.

The Irishman knew otherwise. From the outset he had realised there were too many in on what was no longer a secret. Too many with loose tongues and outstretched hands pleading, Oliver-like, to those running the show, for more and more. Too many wanting not just a share but an ever bigger share. Too many spending too much money. Too much greed. Such recklessness, he was convinced, would ultimately lead into the pit of disaster; the participants would be forced to swap their luxury villas for grim prison cells. And if they fell, then he too might tumble.

During the Troubles at home he had learned how to sniff out an informant. He was convinced not just that a grass had hinted of this multimillion-pound smuggling racket to the authorities but also that he knew his identity.

And thus he was sure the day of reckoning would eventually arrive. He'd known for some time that detectives in Scotland had called on the help of their colleagues in the Spanish Cuerpo Nacional de Policía, the CNP. He wondered too whether Interpol had been contacted.

Weeks earlier he had spotted a police presence in Benidorm but could not have known then that as far as evidence was concerned the authorities had little that might stand up in a court. Coincidence and suspicion were not proof.

But now the sight of men wearing serious expressions and their ludicrous luminous jackets mingling with package holidaymakers told him that day had come too soon. Had their appearance occurred ten years later, the police would probably have been mistaken for characters in the popular television comedy series to which Benidorm gave its name. But this was no fantasy; there was nothing comical about the likely outcome. Not for him. Not for his friends. Not for those he had been hired to help.

Manny watched the watchers as they watched him. He listened to snatches of their conversations, quickly recognising that the harsh accents were those of Glasgow, aware this was that moment of fear and thrill he had known so often during furtive operations with his unit in Belfast. That tick of time when the unexpected pays a surprise call. That moment for which all his experience and guile had prepared him, for the flash when suddenly danger appears. Now he knew the time of ultimate decision had come.

In Ulster, there was customarily no going back. Too often it was shoot or be shot, kill or be killed. Every operation, every move had to be thought out and planned to the minutest detail. An escape route always needed to be prepared because even the most carefully scripted plan could not take into account the unforeseen. Things could, and did, go wrong.

He had graduated through the violent ranks of paramilitaries dedicated to releasing Northern Ireland from the chains that bound the province to the London government of Britain. Like many, he had served and fought with the Irish Republican Army, had broken away with the group that became the feared Irish National Liberation Army and then joined with the relative few who established the ultimate in terror, the Irish People's Liberation Organisation. Even the IRA believed the IPLO was too violent for the good of Ireland. Along the way he had seen many friends and family members lowered into their graves. Here, among the bustle but relative safety of Benidorm the consequences would not be so fatal, but catastrophic nonetheless.

Even as he zigzagged across the busy Spanish streets, strolled with apparent unconcern through bars, stopped to window shop, constantly checking to confirm he was still being followed, he knew that even at this eleventh hour there might be a way out, a means of fooling the police into believing they might be lurking along the wrong track. That there was an escape that could even allow the smugglers to resume after a reasonable break.

First, though, he needed to convince the men behind the smuggling racket that danger was close by. 'Cops are here,' he warned one of the gang and was astonished by the man's apparent indifference to the threat that was so near at hand. He made a telephone call to Scotland, pleading: 'Do nothing next time. The police are on to you.'

His warnings did not exactly fall on deaf ears. But his arguments failed to get home the message that to continue was a recipe for disaster. He felt like the little boy in the pantomime audience screaming to a hero on stage 'he's behind you' and almost crying in frustration as his warnings went seemingly unheeded.

The old terrorist adage was 'if in doubt, clear out', and he knew that moment had come. It was time to go. As he prepared for his own departure back to the bloodied streets of west Belfast, he reflected that it was annoying how often the obvious was ignored. In Ireland they had been squabbling and killing for more than a thousand years, apparently indifferent to the fact that tongues and not guns would be needed to work out a solution. In packed cemeteries, the victims lay side by side with the killers.

Back home among the killings and bombings he had been at a crossroads where all roads led to despair. Then had come along the offer of work in Spain, one that promised him a new start, the chance to break away from the bigotry that spawned unfairness and poverty. But now, even here, greed had overcome sense. At least, he mused, lives would not be lost as a consequence. But in that, he would be wrong.

1

INVASION

HE WAS ASLEEP WHEN the soldiers came at four in the morning, the favourite hour of the burglar. A time when sleep is deep, senses dull, defences down. The most vulnerable hour of the day. Manny McDonnell, aged 13, woke to the sounds of dogs barking, men and women shouting, cursing, the trundle of heavy wheels, noisy engines, doors crashing, banging and being slammed, and then gunfire, curses and the screams of children. In his drowsy state he wondered if he was dreaming. But this was no fantasy. He had awoken to a living nightmare, one that for so many is as vivid today as it was that early morning of Monday, 9 August 1971.

The soldiers had known there would be little likelihood of meeting anyone up and about at that hour as they at first quietly, then loudly, stormed into west Belfast's Ballymurphy, intent on surprise and shock. It was too early even for a milkman. Few of the residents had any cause to rise early or to rise at all. This was a Catholic area, and Catholics who had somehow managed to find sympathetic employers willing to give them jobs were a rarity.

Ballymurphy was already a byword for trouble. But none of the families living there were prepared for the nightmare that was about to rip through the grim streets. Not even schoolboy

Manny, as he dragged himself to the window of the bedroom he shared with his brothers in Glenalina Road and peered into the morning gloom, looking for signs of friends and neighbours.

But the soldiers, in particular men of the renowned Parachute Regiment, the Paras, had an axe to grind. British Army dead had already reached double figures. One was a victim of a near neighbour of Manny. Another had died just a few hours before Ballymurphy found itself turned into a ghetto in which only the undertakers would thrive. As the body count of their comrades mounted, British troops wanted revenge, even if those who would suffer most were innocents caught up in a war in which words became bullets and bombs.

It is impossible for outsiders to understand the extent of the hatred that had built up between neighbouring Catholic and Protestant communities in and around Belfast. Republican Catholics felt deprived of jobs, votes and rights. In the main, Loyalist Protestants resented those who wanted the north to become part of a united Ireland, suspecting they themselves would then become victims of the same discrimination that so angered their nationalist neighbours. Over the decades, planners and housing managers had inflamed the situation by partitioning families according to religion, perhaps ignorant of the potential devastation their policies would cause. Whatever their beliefs, everyone, even children and teenagers like Manny, were being sucked into the maelstrom of fear and hatred.

Already by that August morning the Angel of Death had reaped the first of what would become a monstrous harvest, and the first signs had been shown of just what lay in store as the seeds of trouble planted years earlier began to flower into appalling tragedies. As Manny was to discover for himself, so much of the grief that corroded Northern Ireland was not only caused by mere religious divide but also by divisions within factions whose members worshipped at the same churches and perhaps even ate at the same family tables.

Catholics loathed the province's police force, the Protestant-dominated Royal Ulster Constabulary. Yet the first police officer to die during what would become known as the Troubles was killed not by a Catholic but by a Protestant organisation, the Ulster Volunteer Force, one of many set up to counter the Irish Republican Army.

Victor Arbuckle, a 29-year-old Protestant and family man, was called into the Shankhill area on 11 October 1969 when angry loyalists swarmed onto the streets protesting against a report proposing the disarming of the RUC. At the time he was shot dead, Arbuckle had been standing next to a Catholic RUC officer, Sergeant Dermot Hurley. Killing a policeman was still then a capital offence and three UVF members, arrested and charged with the murder, faced hanging if convicted. They were cleared but later jailed for other offences. Two years later the IRA shot dead father of five Sergeant Hurley, aged 50, one of his killers later fleeing to the USA after being exposed as a police informer.

Manny recalled his parents discussing the Arbuckle shooting. It had taken place, after all, less than a mile from their home. But it was eight months later that just what terrorism could mean for seemingly ordinary families was brought home by a terrible incident in Derry. The fact that it happened 70 miles away did nothing to diminish the horror.

Tommy McCool was a dedicated and respected Republican, well known to the police and Special Branch, who had served five years in prison after being jailed in 1957 when he was caught with firearms. Within the IRA there were divisions about the extent of the violence that could be justified in being used to bring about a united Ireland, and those calling for sterner action broke away to form the Provisional IRA, the 'Provos' or PIRA. Among them was Tommy, a hardliner who became the backbone of the Provos' Derry brigade.

When it was evident trouble was escalating, Tommy allowed his house to be used for storing and making petrol bombs, but something went wrong in the early hours of 26 June 1970. A huge explosion ripped through the family home, killing 40-year-old Tommy, his daughters Bernadette, aged nine, and little Carol Ann, four. Helping Tommy prepare bombs in the kitchen had been fellow Republicans Joseph Coyle, killed at the scene, and Thomas Carlin, who died in hospital a fortnight later.

Manny had been warned about the dangers of petrol bombs. There had already been rioting in the Ballymurphy area earlier in the year when the Scots Guards were sent in to protect members of junior Orange Order bands who had infuriated Catholics by early morning playing along the Springfield Road. He'd joined those of his pals who wanted to help the older Republicans by lobbing stones and bottles at troops and police, and watched bottles filled with petrol soar into the air to explode at the feet of the men in uniforms cowering behind riot shields.

For most of the youngsters this was little more than a prank. But Manny and a handful of his friends knew otherwise: that they were fighting to protect their homes and families. Not everyone understood that. Out on the streets, he'd listened to men tell how during trips across the water to watch Glasgow Celtic they occasionally despaired of convincing friends in Scotland just how serious the situation in Northern Ireland was becoming.

And it was difficult to persuade a Glaswegian whose only brush with violence was an occasional rammy after an Old Firm encounter, or who maybe had a son, brother or cousin in the armed services, that the men who leapt from armoured personnel carriers and pointed guns at women and children were no longer the 'Army' but the 'British Army', and the hated British Army at that. Like most of the population of Britain, Glaswegians based their assessment of the Troubles on what they saw on television: the riots, bombings and shootings. They were unaware of or failed to understand the very deep-seated causes of the cancer that was rotting the province.

A week after the McCool tragedy, an armoured car had knocked down and killed Catholic Charles O'Neill during a disturbance on Falls Road, inevitably adding to the unrest. But who in Glasgow had needed to dodge a bullet while out shopping or leap to avoid an onrushing Army vehicle? Admittedly the city had its own share of heartbreak to deal with when, at the start of January 1971, 66 football fans died during a crush as a crowd left Ibrox, the home of Celtic's bitter rivals, Rangers. But while the sectarian divide existed in Scotland, sometimes with real bitterness, when it came to a tragedy on this scale Catholics and Protestants joined together in their grief. Yet just over 100 miles away in Belfast, men, women and children were being killed by the dozen because of the consequences of that same divide. The existence of the Irish Sea might make those terrible events seem a million miles away, but Belfast was no more distant from Glasgow than Aberdeen or Carlisle. That's how close the terror had crept.

There were those who actively wanted to extend the Troubles to Scotland and feed off the rampant sectarianism that had grown with the influx of Irish workers to the city during the First World War while Scots menfolk were dying in the Flanders trenches. A picture of how scared the establishment was of this potential spread was about to be painted when staunch Republican John Friel appeared at the city High Court. A fervent Republican, he had left Ireland to seek work and a future.

He had been given a temporary home in a city hostel for the homeless, where he was treated with kindness and generosity, and had moved on to become a successful entrepreneur, owning property and bars. But not everyone appreciated his nationalist views or his work to raise money for the IRA, which he sent back over the water to them. Friel ran the Shamrock Club, which primarily catered for the Irish community, and it was there, after an anonymous tip-off, that police uncovered a secret cache of gelignite and detonators. Friel, a married man with three children, was found to have a loaded pistol and pockets bulging with bullets. The discoveries caused near panic and the authorities made it obvious they were ready for any terrorist attempt to interfere.

When Friel came to trial, armed police had stayed in the High Court through the previous night. During his one-day appearance, police packed the courtroom and surrounding streets. Visitors were questioned and some, suspected of having terrorist connections of either persuasion, were refused entry. Even food was checked and sampled before being served to the judge and jury. Friel was jailed for seven years and the message was that suspected terrorists moving into Scotland could expect harsh treatment: something the young Manny would discover when he was older.

After his release, Friel moved into the lucrative business of buying and selling drugs, a venture he was anxious to hide from his IRA associates in Belfast, who wanted to give the impression that not only were drugs evil, but anyone caught dabbling in them would be severely dealt with.

Manny was already old for his years. In that hate-filled environment, boys missed their adolescence and became men. He knew it was IRA commanders, and not the RUC, who laid down the law and dished out justice in Catholic areas of Belfast. Drug dealers, housebreakers and in particular child abusers were summarily dealt with. In November 1970, Alexander McVicker, a 35-year-old Roman Catholic, had been condemned by the IRA as a criminal and shot dead as he worked outside his home repairing his car.

Of course, not every Republican favoured the IRA. In 1969 at the same time as the Provos had come into existence, so had another breakaway group, which christened itself the Official IRA, or OIRA. All claimed to be the voice of the Catholic population, but the resulting inevitable infighting not only weakened the fight for a free Ireland but encouraged yet other groups to spring up and claim a share of the mandate. In March 1971 Charles Hughes, a 26-year-old member of the IRA, was killed outside his home in the Lower Falls by an OIRA gunman.

The young Manny found it difficult to understand why men who were on the same side should want to kill one another. Surely the targets were the RUC and, more particularly, the British Army?

Each time a soldier or policeman pointed a gun at a Catholic, one more recruit was added to the Republican cause, which dramatically grew in strength until senior politicians, security advisers and British Army commanders decided the roots of the nationalist cause needed to be chopped off. They were determined to return to a regime under which known troublemakers and agitators could be legally taken off the streets and held without trial. It was known as internment and had been used sparingly in the past. Now a plan was drawn up to reintroduce it but only against Catholics. Knowing the inevitable violent reaction that would be a consequence, the job of arresting more than 300 nationalists in August 1971 was given to the pride of the British Army, the Parachute Regiment, their motto 'Ready for Anything', words that were particularly apt.

At four that morning, the Paras, whose proud battle honours included Bréville, the Normandy Landings and Arnhem, added Ballymurphy to the many theatres of war where the Red Devils had seen action. Operation Demetrius had begun. With the dawn had come hell, and what followed would shape the course of Manny's life for the next 35 years.

2

NELLIE

JUST AS THEY WERE PROOF of the age-old adage that opposites
attract, there was a magnetism to the relationship between Nellie
and Paddy McDonnell that many others envied. True, they were
poles apart in nature, he quiet and reserved, she forthright and
determined. And even their backgrounds pointed to them having
little in common. But their love for one another and for the
nine children that would come along overwhelmed their many
differences.

Both were from Belfast Catholic families, Nellie from New
Lodge and Paddy from Falls Road. But while she was a vibrant
and dedicated Republican who passionately believed that if
violence was the only route leading to a united Ireland, then that
was the bloody road which had to be travelled, he was a man of
peace who worried over the consequences of his family being
drawn into conflict.

After marrying they made their home in Glenalina Road,
Ballymurphy, a gathering of housing estates in west Belfast into
which Catholics had been directed. While willing to follow her
husband to Ballymurphy, Nellie never lost a hankering to return
to her New Lodge roots. In Glenalina Road she and Paddy raised
four girls and five boys, Manny being the fourth boy, born in
1957. But these were hard, unfair times and occasionally the

problems spilled over into friction within the crowded household, as Manny remembers.

'Ma and Da had grown up in an environment where Catholics were discriminated against. Very few Catholics could get jobs. I was only a kid so I don't remember how unpleasant that would have been for adults, but I remember my ma telling me about Protestant domination, Protestant government for Protestant people, how Catholics were discriminated against and not even allowed to vote in their own country. I don't remember my da having a permanent job, just being taken on now and again as a labourer. But that was it. Ma was the breadwinner, doing three jobs, working at a school, as a cleaner and on a mobile shop to put food on the table for us. She was the governor. My brother Joseph managed to get a job in a brewery, but he was the exception.

'My uncle John, Da's brother, had been a soldier in the British Army and served in Egypt. He'd been shot serving overseas, and sometimes when things got a bit heated and they were maybe rowing, Ma would tell Da, "Your brother took the king's shilling. They should cut his hand off." Some of my aunts and grannies used to work in a British Army munitions factory in Belfast, but Ma refused to join them there.

'She had too many memories of the British Army being in Ireland when she was young and of the things they had done and the ill treatment of Irish people. I'd never heard of internment, imprisonment without trial, but Ma told me all about it and how it had been used to jail Republicans from the 1920s onwards. Some of her neighbours used to come out of their houses with trays of tea and sandwiches for the soldiers, but not Ma, because she would have nothing to do with the soldiers. She saw them as invaders and hated them with a passion during the whole of her life.

'And her sisters were all staunch Republicans who spoke nothing but Irish in the house. They refused to talk in English. Ma was well known for her forthright views. Many a time she stood up to and went toe to toe with the soldiers, looking them in the eye, and it was always they who backed down. Da, on the other hand, was a very quiet guy who always seemed to be in the background. He was peaceable and always saw the good in others. Ma was just the opposite, outspoken and not afraid to tell anybody what she thought.

'One of my sisters, Kathleen, was just two when she was run over and killed by a coal lorry as it was delivering to our street. It destroyed Da because he had been looking after her and I think that after that Ma held that against him. Da didn't want any of his children to get involved in the Troubles, and of the boys I was the only one who did. I think a little bit of my mother's fierce Republicanism rubbed off on me. All the girls were Republicans and they also probably got that from our mother.'

Just as the McDonnell family struggled against the poverty that was an inevitable side effect of discrimination, so did others. They did not know it at the time, but many of their neighbours would become deeply and at times bitterly involved in the nationalist movement that was increasingly swelling passions. Many of these men were older, but their faces were familiar to youngsters who often saw them in and around the 'Murph'. Manny remembers Gerry Adams, who would become President of Sinn Fein, well known as the political wing of the Irish Republican Army. In his autobiography, Adams recalls, 'At around the same time as we arrived in Ballymurphy, so did the Magees, who came from the country, from Glenavy; they were two doors below us and Joe Magee and I quickly became close friends. Joe and I, our Paddy, Jimmy Gillen, Frank and Harry Curran, the McManuses, the Irelands, the McKees, Dominic Grogan and Desi Carabine all knocked around together. My life really began on the slopes of Divis Mountain, roaming with my gang. But first we had to get past our mothers . . .'

Another who the growing Manny would occasionally see was Pat Magee, who would make worldwide headlines as the

Brighton Bomber. In 1984 he checked into the Grand Hotel, Brighton, under a false name and secreted a bomb with a long-delay timer in a bathroom wall. Three weeks later, while then prime minister Margaret Thatcher was staying at the hotel for the annual Conservative Party conference, the bomb was detonated, killing five people. Among the badly hurt was Margaret Tebbit, whose husband Norman was president of the Board of Trade. Margaret, and others, were permanently disabled.

Sometimes Manny would notice Paul 'Dingus' Magee or see Robert 'Fats' Campbell. Along with Angelo Fusco, Dingus and Fats were members of a team known as the M60 Gang because their IRA active service unit specialised in operating an M60 heavy machine gun. It was used to deadly effect in 1980 when the unit found itself in a house on Antrim Road with an eight-man Special Air Service patrol moving in. Suddenly the M60 spat a burst from an upstairs window, killing Captain Herbert Westmacott, aged 28, the highest-ranking SAS soldier to be killed in the Troubles. Within minutes, Magee was caught trying to organise the gang's escape while the others gave up after being surrounded. Manny knew, though, there were scores of other young men who would grow up to graduate into one of the several nationalist paramilitary organisations to which the Troubles gave birth.

Through listening to his mother, Manny already knew about the IRA by the time he began lessons at St Aidan's Christian Brothers' Primary School in Ballymurphy, but the organisation meant little to a five-year-old. Not for long though. What had been sporadic incidents of trouble between Republicans and Loyalists increased in number and ferocity, and Catholic anger had turned into rage and disgust in 1966 when a gang of members of the newly formed protestant Ulster Volunteer Force, led by a former British soldier, Augustus Andrew 'Gusty' Spence, once a member of the Royal Ulster Rifles and then for a time a military police sergeant, lobbed a petrol bomb into a Catholic pub on

Shankhill Road. Next door lived widow Matilda Gould, aged 77, who died when the ensuing blaze spread to her home. Next day Spence and his men shot dead 28-year-old John Scullion and the following month murdered teenager Peter Ward, simply because both were Catholics. A charge against Spence and two others of murdering John Scullion was dropped. But Spence was convicted of killing Peter Ward.

Incidents such as these demonstrated just how lawless Northern Ireland was becoming, and Manny often listened as Nellie talked with her neighbours of rumours that the British Army was about to move onto the streets of Belfast and Derry to keep the peace. Manny remembers her telling the children one day, 'These streets are ours, they are Irish streets, and once you get the British Army into them it will take an awful lot to get them off the streets again.'

As he graduated to St Thomas's Secondary School on Whiterock Road, he was aware of the sense all Catholics felt of being under attack, not just from the Protestant community and its para-militaries, but even more so from the Royal Ulster Constabulary. Republicans blamed the RUC for beating to death Catholic pensioner Francis McCloskey at Derry in July 1969, after which roadblocks and barricades went up in Belfast. Areas of Ballymurphy were barred to the police, and the following month Nellie's fears came true when Prime Minister Harold Wilson announced troops were being sent to Derry and then Belfast. Once peace was restored they would be withdrawn, he promised. 'My ma was right,' says Manny. 'They were there for 37 years.'

School friends talked enthusiastically about becoming IRA Volunteers, and in fact the Troubles would take a dreadful toll on pupils from St Thomas's. Manny had followed Eamon McCormick from St Aidan's. Eamon was shot by the Parachute Regiment in late October 1971 and died three months later in hospital. He was 17, the same age as Paul Kelly, who was shot dead in 1985 by soldiers from the British Army's Ulster Defence Regiment, the UDR. Paul McWilliams was a year younger, and the eighth in a family of ten boys and a girl, when he was killed by a member of the British Army Light Infantry Brigade in August 1977.

Contemporaries remembered another of their number with little fondness, though. Martin 'Marty' McGartland was an RUC spy who joined the IRA in 1989 so he could pass information to British security-service handlers. When Republicans discovered the truth, a hitman was ordered to kill McGartland, by now living at Whitley Bay near Newcastle upon Tyne. But the spy survived despite being shot six times.

The arrival of troops set off differences within the IRA. Some traditional supporters were disappointed with what they saw as its state of unreadiness to meet the challenge of Loyalist paramilitaries, and the arguing culminated in the breakaway Provisional IRA being set up in December 1969. Such developments meant little to 12-year-old Manny, but his days of relative innocence were fast drawing to a close.

In early February 1971, Robert 'Bobby' Curtis, aged 20, was on foot patrol in New Lodge dreaming of his wife Joan, pregnant with their first child back home in Newcastle upon Tyne. Watching him from a high-rise block of flats was one of Manny's near neighbours, Billy Reid, a staff officer with the IRA 'C' Company, 3rd Battalion, who held a Thompson sub-machine gun. Reid pulled the trigger and the young soldier fell dead, shot through the heart. 'I do not even know what my son died for,' said Bobby's heartbroken dad when the news of his son's death was broken to him. Unionist prime minister Sir James Chichester-Clark went on television to announce, 'Northern Ireland is at war with the Irish Republican Army Provisionals.'

'For some reason, I have always remembered the name of Bobby Curtis,' said Manny. 'I think his is the only name of a soldier I can remember, although we always referred to him as Robert Curtis. I don't know why his name has stuck with me through all the years. As I became older while in the Republican movement, the wiser I was getting. Robert Curtis was a British soldier, but at the end of the day his death, like all deaths, was regrettable. But at the time it happened, I didn't give a fuck, to be honest.'

Some looked on Billy Reid as a hero. But it was not long before his Ballymurphy neighbours were attending his own funeral, because just over three months later he died after a brief gun battle with a British Army patrol. By a remarkable quirk, the spot where he was killed was Curtis Street. A song, 'The Ballad of Billy Reid', was penned about Billy and his Thompson sub-machine gun, and in Glasgow a flute band was named in his memory, the Billy Reid Flute Band.

Ten days after Billy's death, Sergeant Michael Willetts of the 3rd Battalion, the Parachute Regiment, was killed saving civilians and members of the security forces by shielding them from a bomb carried by a Provisional IRA Volunteer in a suitcase and dumped at the entrance to Springfield Road police station. Willetts, 26, was posthumously awarded the George Cross for his bravery. But among his colleagues there were those who felt the man's memory should not solely be left within a medal. The Paras were seething for action against the Catholic population. They wanted revenge, and the opportunity was about to be gifted to them on a plate.

Aided by informers, Special Branch officers and MI5 had been secretly drawing up a list of those deemed to be troublemakers. There were 450 names on it, every one a suspected Republican. The then Northern Ireland prime minister Brian Faulkner ordered them to be interned, and the task of finding these menaces, arresting them and rounding them up was given to the Parachute Regiment. The task was named Operation Demetrius and it would concentrate on Ballymurphy. Shortly after midnight on 9 August, the Paras began preparing to move towards their target zone. They had to be in place by four in the morning, and as the fourth chime rang out from churches throughout Belfast, engines started up and the invasion of the estates began. Manny, on holiday from school, was in bed but was woken up by the uproar in the streets outside.

'Word spread like wildfire that the Brits were marching in, smashing in doors and windows, dragging people out of their beds and threatening anybody who tried to stop them regardless of whether they were children or old folk. At one time I went outside but couldn't see the sky because the Brits had let off so much gas. The troops came in to wreck our homes and take away all our men, dads, uncles, brothers, cousins, you name it.'

As men were being dragged out and thrown into RUC vans, rioting began. Throughout that first day hatred of the 600 troops intensified, and all the time families like the McDonnells were not only hearing horror stories but seeing the homes of their friends and neighbours wrecked. And with the approach of evening, people began dying. Corpus Christi parish priest, Father Hugh Mullan, went to help a wounded man and was shot dead by a British Army sniper. Witnesses said the priest was waving a white cloth; Francis Quinn, aged 20, tried to reach Father Mullan and was killed.

Joan Connolly, 45, whose interests were not politics but knitting and playing bingo, had her face blasted off trying to help fatally injured barman Noel Phillips, aged 20, as he lay dying. Joan was not allowed emergency aid at the scene. She bled to death, leaving her husband Denis and their eight children to grieve. According to onlookers, two soldiers approached Noel, lying stricken, and executed him with head shots. Dad of 13 Daniel Teggart fell after being shot and as he lay helpless a further 13 bullets were pumped into his back. Joseph Murphy, a father of 12, was shot in the leg, an injury from which he could have recovered, and was taken away by the Army. But it was later claimed soldiers beat him so badly he died three weeks later.

Early the next day, Edward Doherty died when a soldier shot him in the back, and the killings continued on the 11th. John Laverty was shot dead, while dad of six Joseph Corr succumbed in hospital two weeks later from bullet wounds. The Army said both had been firing at soldiers, but forensics did not back up these claims. John McKerr was carrying out repairs at Corpus Christi Church but stopped to allow a funeral to take place and while standing outside was shot in the head by a Para; McKerr died over a week later in hospital. Community worker Pat McCarthy was grabbed by a British Army patrol and one soldier was alleged to have put an empty gun into Pat's mouth and pulled the trigger for a joke. Pat suffered a massive heart attack and died.

'That first night, when five people were shot dead, I saw three of them being killed. I was a kid of 13 and it was absolutely fucking horrendous for me and my mates, seeing people blown away.'

One consequence of what was, and still is, known as the Ballymurphy Massacre was that when Manny returned to school, his mind, and that of many of his friends, was made up. They would fight the Brits. Nellie McDonnell had never been really happy in Ballymurphy and the massacre left her determined to return to New Lodge.

'She said that's where we were going, and Da didn't object. He knew that in New Lodge Ma would be happy, and if she was happy then so were all of us, and so we moved to New Lodge Road.'

Manny continued at St Thomas's Secondary School, but at night he'd be out in the streets of New Lodge making new friends.

'With my pals and at school the conversation was all about the British Army and the people that were getting killed. Everybody seemed to know the family of somebody who had been shot by soldiers.'

3

SPYING

'ONE SATURDAY NIGHT at the start of December 1971, I was playing football in the street with my pals. It would be my 14th birthday in a couple of days and I suppose that as a bit of an early present I was allowed to stay out later than usual. Plus it was the weekend and there was no school next day. Ma always told me not to go far from the house and Da worried until all of us were back home. Just before nine o'clock I heard a huge explosion, and we all ran in the direction of the noise to see what had happened. When we got into North Queen Street where McGurk's bar had been, there was just dust and rubble, shouting and screams. British soldiers had joined local people digging among the stones and wreckage, trying to find survivors and get them out. It was a sight I'll never forget.'

The bomb claimed 15 lives, victims who were in the bar and the living quarters above it: Francis Bradley, 61, a dock labourer; schoolboy James Cromie, aged 13; Philip Garry, 73, a school lollipop man; mill worker Kathleen Irvine, 45, a mother of five who had gone to the bar for an evening out with her husband; Thomas Kane, 45, a livestock drover; Edward Kane, 25, married with a family that included young sons Edward and Billy; pensioner Edward Keenan, 69, and his wife Sarah, 58; Philomena McGurk, 46, whose husband Patrick ran the bar, her daughter Maria, 14, and brother John

Colton, 49, who worked part-time at McGurk's; labourers Thomas McLaughlin, 55, and David Milligan, 52; James Smyth, 55, a docker; and slater Robert Charles Spotswood, aged 38.

Official sources and the British Army tried to lay the blame on the IRA, even suggesting Volunteers had been working on the bomb in the bar when it exploded prematurely. But even dogs on the street knew it was the work of a four-man Ulster Volunteer Force squad who had planned to place their bomb at the nearby Gem bar, but on being thwarted by the sight of customers standing outside instead left it at the entrance to McGurk's. However, it was not until September 1978 that UVF fanatic Robert Campbell admitted helping plant the bomb, but he refused to name his accomplices. He was jailed for life.

Manny and his friends watched both in horror and fascination as friend and foe alike, Army and police uniforms alongside men who had rushed out of their homes from in front of television sets, scrabbled in the debris. One of the soldiers digging with his bare hands was Major Jeremy Snow of the 2nd Battalion, the Royal Regiment of Fusiliers. Just 200 yards away Loyalists began cheering and waving flags. An IRA gunman took up a position overlooking the scene. Snow moved in to prevent rioters getting in the way of the rescue operation and at that a shot rang out and he fell with a deadly head wound, dying in hospital four days later with his wife by his bedside.

'I couldn't believe what I was seeing: a man who had been actively digging in the rubble shot dead,' said Manny.

What brought the bombing even closer to home was that the McDonnells were friends with the family of Edward Kane, and more than three and a half decades later, Manny was still being made sadly aware of the consequences of the blast.

In the days following the explosion, two more soldiers were wounded. The trend was to automatically assume that IRA gunmen were to blame, so increasing the hostility of soldiers towards a Catholic population already wholly distrustful of the Army and police.

'Living in New Lodge had turned into life on a permanent battlefield. If the police had been bad, the British Army was worse. It was constant brutality, doors kicked in and then houses smashed up, people who had done nothing wrong or who weren't active or involved being arrested and charged, others just arrested without even getting charged, more and more of the men being hauled away and interned. As a teenager I was now in the streets with the rest of the kids throwing stones, bricks, bottles, petrol bombs, you name it. If my da found out he'd give me a beating, but Ma used to encourage us a wee bit.

'School became a weird place. Even guys of my age were talking about getting guns and killing British soldiers. They wanted to join the IRA, but because you were supposed to be 17 before you could do that, they joined the junior wing of the movement. Bloody Sunday in January 1972 at Derry, when British soldiers massacred 13 civilians, made us even keener to do something to help the fight against the troops. In the junior wing you more or less spotted for the older men, looked out for the Army and police and reported back what you saw.

'A few years later I read about how some teachers had been in prison sharing cells with their pupils, both groups having been locked up for throwing petrol bombs at the soldiers and police. Somebody else who'd been at my school was found murdered in Holland because he'd been involved in gunrunning. At school it was impossible to ignore the shootings and the aggro from Loyalists, and I guess my education mostly consisted of learning how to make bombs and ambush soldiers.

'As a teenager I saw Loyalist mobs coming into New Lodge and they were being led by the RUC, who were throwing petrol bombs. This was the RUC, the police force that was supposed to protect people, leading them in. No wonder I remember New Lodge as being so fucking wild. We took on the British Army and the soldiers didn't like it.'

Just how much the troops did not like it was demonstrated at the beginning of February 1973 during 90 minutes of madness. It began when a car carrying gunmen emerged from a Loyalist area and drove into New Lodge, spraying bullets and killing teenagers James Sloan and James McCann before disappearing. Witnesses said the attack was watched by a British Army Saracen armoured car, which made no attempt to intervene. Stunned and curious local residents poured into the streets and found themselves under fire from British Army snipers.

'Tony Campbell was a friend who lived across the landing from me. Earlier that day Tony had been telling me it was his 19th birthday and he was going out with a group of friends to a discotheque for a party. I wished him "Happy Birthday". They were the last words I ever spoke to him.'

As he made his way home, Tony had found himself caught up in the throng on the streets and died when he was struck by a sniper's bullet. Seeing the youngster fall, Brendan Maguire went to see if he could help and he too was killed. Dad of three John Loughran ran from his home to go to their aid and was shot dead. Ambrose Hardy waved a white cloth as he emerged from a doorway to try to reach the huddled bodies and he too was shot in the head.

There were conflicting versions as to who was to blame. Local people accused Loyalists and the Army of collusion. The IRA admitted Sloan, McCann and Campbell were members of the organisation, but said they had not been on active service. The Army claimed it had come under attack from Republican gunmen, but it admitted killing Campbell, Maguire, Loughran and Hardy and paid compensation to the families of the dead men.

Manny says, 'The British Army just ran amok and shot people. They opened fire on unarmed civilians. Incidents like this caused an incredible degree of bitterness. I know of one victim of a British Army murder whose brother was a soldier. The next day this squaddie was told his brother had been killed, and he not only immediately deserted but as soon as he reached Ireland joined the IRA, took up arms and within 48 hours was firing on his former comrades.'

If he had any doubts as to what he wanted to do next, the massacre of the New Lodge Six convinced Manny, now 15, that his duty lay with taking a more positive role in the fight. He and two friends, we'll call them Matthew and Luke, began spending their spare time spying for the IRA.

Hour after hour in the evenings, day after day during weekends and holidays, they wandered the streets seemingly innocently, but all the time they were watching, timing and carefully noting the movements of British troops and the RUC. They looked for patterns in the routes used to patrol; sought out the locations of hidden snipers; learned when deliveries were made and the names of those collaborating or supplying materials; they carefully wrote down the registration numbers of cars entering and leaving police stations. 'I wasn't yet a fully fledged IRA Volunteer, but by helping to gather all that stuff felt I was doing really useful work.'

They looked like youngsters out for a spot of fun, not unduly attracting attention to themselves. Or so they thought. One day an RUC patrol stopped Matthew and Luke as they rode through Belfast on a motorcycle and a search revealed a bundle of documents showing the results of their sly homework – and the name of their accomplice.

A few hours later there was a knock at the door of Manny's home and he joined the pair in police custody. All three were charged with possessing documents likely to be useful to terrorists. His friends were remanded to Long Kesh prison, a collection of Nissen huts on a former airfield south-west of Belfast, where they joined hundreds of internees along with Loyalists and Republicans imprisoned for a variety of mainly paramilitary offences. The younger Manny was bailed.

The trial of the three youngsters was held in a Diplock court in Belfast, before a solitary judge. In the summer of 1973 the government had suspended the right to trial by jury. Despite their youth, the teenagers knew what to expect.

'The judge was there for one purpose only, which was to jail you. And he duly did that. He gave us two years each. So my pals went back to Long Kesh and me with them. I was put into one of the compounds, I think it was number 14, with what were classed as "decent" criminals, while the other two went off to the compound holding IRA men.

'I woke up next morning and told myself, "There's no way I can stay here." I was with thieves and perverts and wanted out, and I complained to guards I was being kept from my friends, that I was a political prisoner and should be with the rest of the political prisoners. Nothing happened and I fretted over what to do, but in mid-morning the commander of the IRA compound came to the gates of my compound and called me over. "Manny, pack your bag, you're coming with me," he said. I looked at the screw who was in charge of my compound. "Don't worry about him," said the commander. "You're under IRA command now." The screw said nothing. And that was it. I was in the IRA.

'The compound commander interviewed every new arrival. His first words to me were, "What do you want to do when you get out of prison?" I was 16 and told him, "I want to kill as many British soldiers as I possibly can." His reply was, "That's no use to me, no good at all. I need you to read, to become politically aware, learn what this is all about, I want you to get to know why the British are in Ireland, to learn the history of Ireland, what this present situation is all about and why we are fighting." And that's what I did, read, read and read.

'It was a strange path for me. I'd gone in determined to learn how to murder British troops, but here was this very committed Republican making me spend time in the prison library reading about not just the history of my own country but about the revolution in Russia, about Lenin and Trotsky, the different forms of socialism and communism and being tested each night. He insisted everybody in the compound spend at least an hour a day studying.

'In Long Kesh, the University of Terror, you could learn about anything you wished. Everything from stripping down weapons and putting them back together again blindfolded, to marching, ambushing, how to lay booby traps and fix bombs under cars, you name it, there was someone in Long Kesh who was an expert on any subject and who could teach you how to do it. Mainly, though, you were encouraged to become more aware of politics and how they went hand in hand with the military side of things. The theme was all about having the ArmaLite gun in one hand and the ballot box in the other, using the first to achieve fairness through the second. It was compulsory for us to have political as well as military discussions.

'During the 16 months I was held there, I met with men from all parts of Ireland who were being interned, men with lots of different views. We were taught the Irish language, how to use different types of code and semaphore, and we used to pass messages right through the camp. Then the screws tippled what we were doing and brought in officers who could speak Irish.

'There are two different types of Irish language, so we would switch from one to the other and even try to develop our own form of the Irish language. Make no mistake, it was not the authorities but the paramilitaries who ran Long Kesh. Frankly, the screws had no say in what went on. Every month there would have to be a commanders' meeting at which the commanders of the Provos, the IRA, the INLA, the Ulster Volunteer Force and the Ulster Defence Association (UDA) would meet with the governor to discuss how the camp was being run.

'We ran our own educational classes, our own keep-fit courses, physical-education sessions, we detailed our own men for work. The only time you would see a screw was when he was calling you for a visit. Of course, the war continued outside and we had no say on how things were run in the streets. It was the people there, those on the front line, at the sharp end, who had the final say, because after all they were the ones doing the fighting and taking the risks. There were four battalions on the outside, but the prisoners became known as the 5th Battalion and we regarded ourselves as prisoners of war. And all the time we were trying to escape, trying to dream up ways of getting out, trying to fuck the Brits' heads up, keeping the war going inside.

'In the early days at Long Kesh, one of our officers, a very much respected man named Paddy Joe McKenna, taught us that sectarianism was a British invention intended to take advantage of a voting system deliberately engineered to ensure Protestants in the nine counties would always win and thus portray the Catholic minority as the troublemaking element. What he said about sectarianism stayed with me. He said Protestantism was a very highly respected religion and Republican organisations had once included Protestant leaders.

'We learned about Wolfe Tone, who was born into a Church of Ireland family but became a committed Republican, James Connolly, Constance Markievicz and Henry Joy McCracken. I realised that in the early days the Republican movement wasn't about Catholics or Protestants but about Irishmen. "Don't get dragged into the sectarian argument," Paddy Joe told us. "If you do then you play into the hands of the British government."

'He was a man of real vision. He said, "There will come a time when the Protestant government will have to sit with us and negotiate, because we are not going away. One day Catholics and Protestants will live peaceably together, form a government together and run the country together. But if you are determined to fight, then you first need to know why you are fighting." And he always stressed, "You are only a Volunteer. Volunteers can withdraw their services at any time. We may have commanders, but we are all Volunteers at the end of the day."

'Paddy Joe was a farmer-type guy from the country, an older man who had gone through the suppression of Republicans through internment operations in the 1950s and 1960s, so when he spoke about how history had gradually led to the violence in which we were now involved, he knew what he was talking about. He'd take us younger Volunteers to one side, walk around the compound with us, talking in a voice that was both soft and yet authoritative. He was a devout Republican. But he stressed that while he was committed to the military side of the war, politics would, in the end, decide the outcome.

'In the 16 months I was in Long Kesh he changed my views on just about everything. I'd gone in with the sole ambition of killing Brit soldiers but emerged knowing and understanding there was so much more to the way the war had to be run than just shooting those who weren't on your side.

'One evening we were watching the television news when there came an item about two British soldiers being killed. Everybody began cheering, but he ordered us to shut up. "I'm ashamed to hear this," he said. "Two guys are dead, let them rest in peace." And he was right. All deaths are regrettable. He was doing 12 years for attempted murder, and how that came about was weird.

'With him in Long Kesh was his second in command, a young man with hair so grey, almost white, that it made him seem old. The two had planned to kill a farmer, a member of the Ulster Defence Regiment, by planting a bomb on his tractor. The idea was to kill him and then make the bomb go off to give the impression he had died in the explosion. It was dark as Paddy Joe's number two crept through a field to fix the bomb to the tractor, and in the pitch black he fell down a well the farmer had been digging. It was about 20 feet deep and there he was, helpless, his limbs broken and the bomb lying right next to his head, wondering if it might go off at any second. That's where he was found in the morning, and arrested. He'd had black hair when he climbed into the field and overnight it changed colour.

'The UVF prisoners were in the next compound to us and Gusty Spence was their leader. At one stage he'd been in charge of the UDA contingent too, but the two groups had fallen out and the UDA chose their own commander. Just like Paddy Joe, Gusty made his own men learn to speak Irish and how to use weapons. My only visitor was my ma, who was anxious to know what I wanted to do when I was released. "Keep going," I told her.

'I came out of jail a better man than I had been when I went into Long Kesh. Of course, the Troubles were still going on, and the IRA asked to meet me and wanted to know what I was going to do. There was no pressure at all put on me; they said they would go along with whatever I wanted to do. "Are you going to report back, or pack it all in?" was the only question. I took two or three weeks off just to think about it, but then reported back, encouraged by Ma.

'Da was totally against the Troubles. He really was peace loving, and his health was deteriorating. He tore into me every time he could, arguing against my getting involved again. I'd say to him, "Da, you've been brought up in it, you were born an Irish Catholic, you're not allowed to vote, you can't get a job, you can't get a house." But he maintained talking was the only way forward, and maybe he had a point, because at the end of the day the IRA called a ceasefire and wanted to talk.

'What I could never understand was why the Protestant community could not see just what was happening among themselves. They too ended up killing one another, and if they'd just talked when it all kicked off then it could all have been avoided. But they didn't and so I went to war. We were just friends and neighbours, people who grew up with one another, trying to become an Army.'

4

MOVING CAMP

'I WAS STILL A KID when I left prison, but I knew what I wanted for me and for Ireland. That was to fight the Brits. In Long Kesh the talk was increasingly about a ceasefire. There were about 150 young bucks like me, keen guys, raring to go and get at the Brits, and the attitude of most of us was, "Fuck this ceasefire crap." We just didn't want to know about it. We wanted to go to war.

'I'd gone into prison a sectarian bigot, wanting to fight for the wrong reasons. When I came out I was no longer a bigot, I was absolutely against sectarianism. Now I felt I understood what the fight was all about, and it wasn't about killing somebody because they were Protestant. It was about killing those who invaded our country and who opposed a united Ireland.

'When I had convinced officers of the IRA's 3rd Battalion in Belfast I was committed to becoming a Volunteer, I went along to a safe house one evening to join up. I was given advice on matters such as security and how at some time it was probable I would be arrested by the police. The advice was good. In summary, it was to keep a low profile, never to discuss Army business in public, especially in bars, where police and British Army spies were lurking and listening to conversations, and if I was arrested to say nothing. That was something I never forgot, no matter what the police tried.

'So I put on a beret, held the tricolour and read out the oath, "I do solemnly promise to uphold and have belief in the objectives of the IRA and obey all orders issued to me by the Army Council and all my superior officers," and I was sworn in to be an IRA Volunteer.

'About an hour later I had my first taste of combat, but it wasn't with soldiers or the police. When I got home there was still a mark on my head left by the beret, and Da asked, "What's that mark? Have you been wearing a hat or something?" When I didn't reply he tippled and said, "Don't tell me you've gone and signed up," and gave me such a beating. My ma wasn't happy about that. But I was a full-time Volunteer and my aim was to eventually have my own unit.

'The threat of informers infiltrating the movement was ever-present. IRA officers had long ago recognised the danger of touts. In a company of say 30 men, it was difficult to weed out an informer. He could be any one of the 30. So they introduced the idea of small units of, say, five men, each working independently of one another. That way you narrowed the chances to one in five instead of one in 30. Of course there would always be touts, but smaller units meant less chance for them of remaining unsuspected for long.

'One day I was having a drink with friends in a club in the city centre when I was introduced to another Volunteer, Sean Caldwell, who lived about half a mile from me and very close to the Loyalist area. It was a dangerous spot to be in and I didn't envy him. We got on well from the very start. Sean was right into the music, Irish folk stuff. I found him a great guy and we are friends to this day.

'I was young and eager, and not impressed by the increasing talk of our leaders calling a ceasefire. As I saw things, there I was, relatively fresh out of prison for serving a sentence as a result of doing work for the cause, just starting to get into gear and now pricks were wanting to stop fighting, despite all we'd suffered with the massacres of Ballymurphy and New Lodge alone.

'At regular conventions of Volunteers, we were being asked how we felt about a ceasefire and our reply was that we didn't give two fucks for the idea. As far as we were concerned, all the talking had been done during the previous 1,200 years and hadn't taken us any further. It was time now for action, but we were being told to listen to people who had been involved in the movement in the 1930s and '40s. Things were so different now. Some of them seemed like dinosaurs to us, old farts out of tune with what most of us felt. I believed we had the Brits on the run; if not, then why were they making overtures for peace? If you are fighting and the other side indicates it is willing to talk, then it means you are doing something right. I thought we were in a position of strength.'

While Manny was in Long Kesh, talks had been held between the Westminster government and Republicans. These had been the culmination of three years of discussions as to how the deadlock could be broken. Just when these discussions seemed to be going nowhere, a meeting was organised in County Clare between the IRA and Protestant churchmen. When the Garda got wind it surrounded the hotel meeting place, but the IRA representatives had already left. However, a report on the talks was sent to Westminster. As a goodwill gesture, the IRA called a ceasefire over Christmas 1974 and this led to it declaring a formal truce in February the following year. The aim was to secure the withdrawal of troops from Northern Ireland, a move that enraged Protestants, who were accused of stepping up attacks on Catholics with the aim of scuppering peace talks.

Among the worst offenders in these attacks was a murderous group given the name of the Shankhill Butchers. This gang, led by a bully named Lenny Murphy – often thought to be embarrassed by a surname more likely to be associated with a Catholic background – and mostly comprised of Ulster Volunteer Force members, came to the notice of the police and Republicans in October 1975 when it entered Casey's Bottling Plant, a Belfast bar, and on discovering that the four staff were Catholics shot them all dead. The victims were Marie McGrattan, 47, Frances Donnelly, 35, and 18-year-olds Gerard Grogan and Thomas Osbourne. The massacre was the start of a terrifying campaign by the gang in which barman Robert 'Basher' Bates, like Murphy born and bred on Shankhill Road, was an eager lieutenant of ringleader Murphy.

The crew roamed Belfast streets in a seemingly innocent black hackney cab in search of more Catholic victims. On occasions they were joined by the Scottish girlfriend of one of the Butchers' members, a woman from Glasgow who would be one of a number of killers to escape retribution. Even looking like a Catholic was as good as a death sentence, because among those to be killed would be Protestants mistaken for Catholics. Some of the dead had their throats slashed; others were beaten, others shot and yet others poisoned. The existence of the gang meant even hardened veterans of guerrilla street warfare had to be vigilant. Many of their faces were known to paramilitaries of both sides from appearances in riots and rallies. Manny knew Bates, and suspected the reverse applied.

Not long after leaving Long Kesh Manny had been visiting a Republican club one night when, as he was leaving, he met pretty Sally Giles. He'd known Sally through her brother Eddie, a 'cracking guy', according to Manny, and a fellow Volunteer whose membership of the IRA brought him constant death threats.

Sally invited Manny back to the home of her grandmother, a Protestant who had turned Catholic, and from then on the pair became inseparable. She realised, from his close association with her brother, that her new boyfriend was an IRA Volunteer, but, in the fashion of the womenfolk from New Lodge, neither asked about his ties nor expected to be told of them. The pair fell in love, but one late-night date with Sally brought him into a close encounter with the hated British Army while another almost cost him his life.

'Sally's grandmother was a lovely woman. She was blind and didn't like people being in her house when she wasn't there. Sally and me often met at her home, and we were there one night chatting when her grandmother arrived back. As soon as I heard the key turn in the door, I knew I couldn't go past the old lady to the door, so the only alternative was the back window. I shoved it up and jumped out into the back yard then over a wall and almost literally landed slap bang on top of a British Army patrol. Fortunately the soldiers burst out laughing and I just legged it. I could still hear them laughing when I turned the corner at the end of the street.

'Sally and me hit it off from the very start. We saw each other most nights, and while we loved being in each other's company, whenever we were out I was constantly looking out of the corner of my eye for the RUC, a British Army patrol or some other paramilitary group to appear, and now for the Shankhill Butchers. We knew they were operating from a black taxi and dragged unsuspecting victims into it and cut their throats.'

One night the young couple had been enjoying a meal in Belfast city centre and decided to walk the mile or so home to New Lodge Road. Their route took them partially along Donegall Street, the scene in March 1972 of a horrific car-bombing when a device left by the Provisional IRA exploded just before noon in an area packed with shoppers and a party of schoolchildren. It was later claimed by the police that a series of telephoned warnings deliberately gave the wrong location of the bomb and by the time a caller gave it as Donegall Street it was too late to evacuate the area. Seven people died and 148 were injured, many losing limbs and eyesight. Manny and Sally had reached St Patrick's Catholic Church, half a mile from Shankhill Road, when fear gripped them.

'I saw a black taxi pulling up and two guys getting out of it. Right away, I recognised one as Basher Bates. I said to Sally, "These cunts are going to pull us," and told her, "Run, Sally, run, just get away," and she ran as if her life depended on it, which it did. The two cunts came running across the road trying to cut me off, but I managed to get away. A couple of hundred yards away I found a cop car parked up and two cops sitting in it. They must have seen what had happened and I said, "Listen, Basher Bates and that mob are running about." One of the cops looked at me and said, "It's a pity they never got you." Fortunately I managed to catch up with Sally and we made it back safely.

'Afterwards some of my friends wondered if the cops had tipped off the Shankhill Butchers that I was on the street, because they would very likely have known who I was. But it was a close thing, and I realised just how frightening it must have been for the people who didn't get away. It was scary, but to be honest the fear thing was happening all around you. It was like part of the daily norm.'

Not long after the escape, Sally and Manny were married in church and moved into a flat in New Lodge, where they awaited the birth of their first child. Manny had had occasional jobs but, like the majority of Catholics, knew there was little hope of permanent work, and in between casual jobs he and Sally survived on social security. Few employers were willing to take on a known member of a paramilitary organisation. IRA Volunteers were liable to be targeted by other groups, even including Republicans, as a feature of the Troubles were the unceasing internal feuds both causing and resulting from breakaways. The Volunteers themselves knew and accepted the risks, but employers saw it as unfair that non-combatants should be drawn into the dangers.

'I had one job at a community centre where my boss was a woman. Not long after I'd started she told me, "Wash my car." I told her, "Wash your own fucking car. Who do you think you are?" She shouted, "Who are you?" The "who are you?" exchanges pitter-pattered across her desk like a table tennis ball. He smashed one of her returns by telling her, "Wash your fucking car? What do you think I am, your fucking slave?" and walked out.

'Half an hour later she called me back into her office, said she had investigated my circumstances and was happy for me to clock in and then right away clock back out: "Mr McDonnell, it will be okay by me if you start at eight in the morning and then clock back out at five past and go home. The others here don't want to work with you because there are so many people trying to murder you." And so that's how it was for a year, start at eight, finish at five past and collect the wages on a Friday. It was mad. Then they told me the job no longer existed and it was back on the dole.'

Meanwhile, he was increasingly disillusioned with the decision of the IRA hierarchy to call a ceasefire. Differences in ideology and the extent to which violence should be used to respond to the outrages inflicted on the Catholic minority by Loyalist groups had already led to the formation of the Provisional IRA. Now the mutterings among those who remained intensified.

Some Volunteers had already either been kicked out of the IRA or left of their own accord because of their opposition to the softening of its approach, and in December 1974 these traditionalists formed the Irish National Liberation Army, the INLA. Just as Sinn Fein was regarded as the political wing of the IRA, so was the Irish Republican Socialist Party, the IRSP, to the INLA.

Among the early members of the INLA was Gerard Steenson, a sort of modern-day version of the Wild West gunslinger-turned-lawyer John Wesley Hardin, in that his love for violence began in his early teens. He was only 14 when he joined 'C' company of the IRA, and two years later he defected to the INLA and immediately became embroiled in a vicious feud between the two organisations. His first known victim was a high-priority figure, Billy McMillen, commanding officer of the OIRA Belfast brigade. Steenson shot him dead in April 1975 as he was out shopping, McMillen dying in the arms of his wife, Mary.

Tit-for-tat killings followed, and in the middle of the bloodshed Manny attended a regular meeting of IRA Volunteers. His friend

Sean was with him. The subject was the way forward, whether to stay or go.

'Sean approached me and asked which way I was going to vote. Straight away I told him I wanted to break away from the IRA because it had become too political. He said, "Between us Manny, I'm breaking away myself." And so we both joined the INLA.

'I'd already discussed moving to the INLA with Ma, as loyal a Republican as you could find. She was an IRA woman through and through, brought up to believe in achieving the aims of the IRA by peaceful means, and didn't really want me to switch camps because she believed a ceasefire was coming and that at least meant the various sides talking. But I thought the talking was over and it had got us nowhere. However, she had made up her mind to stick with backing the IRA. At the same time she wanted me to keep going with anything to get the Brits out. But she told me, "Do whatever you feel comfortable with, you know you've always got a bed here. I'll always come and see you if you are in jail, I'll always come and see you if you're on the run."

'The decision to join the INLA wasn't really a difficult one for me because I was still a young man with plenty of fire in my belly. The INLA was a smaller group with about 200 members in Belfast, but it was much more ruthless than the IRA. And those who joined were dedicated, prepared to sacrifice themselves. We had people wanting to join up, strap themselves with explosives and walk into a police station. It was our view that if the Army and the RUC were going to be ruthless then we should be even more ferocious.

'A lot of people, especially outside Ireland, were under the misconception that this was all about being a Catholics versus Protestants thing. It wasn't really as far as we were concerned. Our objective was a free Ireland, a 32-county socialist republic. Things like Loyalist organisations were distractions, taking us off the road we wanted to be on. They were shooting Catholics from the start, whereas we had no real interest in shooting Protestants just because of their religion. To be honest, I was never into that, but if we got the chance of a UVF or UDA man we would take him out.'

Initially, Manny found himself in the INLA's 'A' company.

'The problem was that we just didn't have enough men, even though we were calling ourselves companies. Then I joined a unit, not as leader but as a member. Loyalists were always attacking New Lodge, and one night they came in with the RUC, as was often happening. I was armed, firing at these people and trying to kill them, my first experience of shooting at somebody.

'It was a ferocious gun battle, and during one stage I ran down an alley and almost collided with an old guy who must have been in his 80s. He was waving a pistol, an ancient thing, and wearing an old Army trench coat that came down to his ankles. "I'm going to kill some of these bastards," he was shouting, but he was so old he could hardly walk. You had to hand it to the old guy, even at that age he was willing to die to protect his home and the people he loved.'

As he dodged through the streets seeking targets, Manny came under fire and was hit in the back by a rubber bullet.

'It was painful, but the real suffering was having to put up with the sarcasm of comrades who pointed out that if you were hit in the back then that meant there was only one direction in which you were going.'

5

ON THE RUN

THE FIRST PROBLEM FOR the fledgling INLA was how to get its hands on weapons and explosives. It had come into being because Volunteers wanted more aggression shown, and this necessitated a steady supply of arms, which required money: a difficulty resolved by means of bank and other robberies. But the question remained of where to buy hardware.

In the minds of most Republicans there was little doubt the various Loyalist groups were being supplied with guns and explosives with the connivance of the British security services and RUC, the former arranging for the UDA and UVF in particular to receive materials from South Africa. However, the attitude of the British government to Republican groups receiving weaponry was decidedly different.

The bulk of the arms used by the IRA came from North America and Libya. When British agents learned that a boatload of arms and ammunition was on its way from Libya to Southern Ireland in 1973, they were certain that once it was landed it would be smuggled to the north. British security officials tipped off their counterparts in Dublin about the boat. But to ensure the Republic was seen to act on the information, Britain also secretly passed on details to the *News of the World* newspaper. Journalists were even supplied with dramatic photographs of the arrest of the vessel, the *Claudia*, off County Waterford. On board five tons of materials were discovered.

'We in the INLA had to start from scratch,' said Manny. 'We managed to get weapons and explosives from the Middle East and from Spain. I wasn't involved in that part of it, so I don't know how it was arranged, and as a Volunteer on a need-to-know basis I would not ask. The less anybody knew, the less they could tell others.'

The INLA hierarchy did not want to risk escalating the feud with former IRA comrades by approaching its suppliers and so set about making contact with terrorist groups mainly in central Europe, such as Baader-Meinhof and the Basque separatist organisation ETA. This resulted in the forging of links with the Palestine Liberation Organization and others, with arms coming from the Middle East via the established drug-smuggling routes through Turkey and Greece. However, the McDonnells had their own arms filled.

With the birth of their first child, a son, Sally felt she needed the security of having her man at home. 'You've done your bit Manny,' she pleaded. 'Pack it in for our sake.' He thought over her words for a while and agreed. But his own personal ceasefire was short-lived.

'The cause of a free Ireland was in my blood. I was fighting for my family too, for their future, for a fairer future. I think my involvement took most of my own family by surprise because they were and are all peaceable folks who had never been in trouble, not one of them was ever in a courtroom. I suppose I was the odd one out.

'This was a highly dangerous time because the INLA Volunteers were under fire from Loyalists and from the sections of the IRA. It was no secret that there was collusion between the police and Loyalist death squads. I was regularly questioned by the police, often on the grounds that they simply needed to bring their files on me up to date. When I asked why I was told that my files had gone missing. Of course they hadn't, they'd been handed over to Loyalists, who would know where I lived and what my movements were and details of my contacts.'

As the McDonnell family expanded, they moved out of the little flat and into a house in nearby Spamount Street. Like virtually everywhere in New Lodge, the street had seen tragedy. Just a few years earlier, the Ulster Freedom Fighters, in reality the Ulster Defence Association, planted a bomb at the Spa Inn in Spamount Street, killing harmless and likeable Hugh Devlin, aged 82. As the Troubles ground on, Spamount Street would feature in a particularly controversial tragedy.

Like Sean, Manny was eventually given his own unit and the responsibility of looking after the lives of the four Volunteers serving with him. During a typical operation, the unit might have an extra man added, but normally it consisted of two gunmen, a driver, a quartermaster who looked after the weapons, and a fifth who spent 24 hours a day looking for targets.

'He would come in with a target, I'd have a look to see whether it was practical to take it on, and as unit commander I would then note down the details, what would be required in the way of weapons, then take it to my bosses, who would look at it and either reject it or give it the green light, and arrange for the unit to be supplied with whatever was needed. Then the operation would take place. The crucial element to any operation was good intelligence.

'Most people think of terrorists and paramilitaries as simply planting bombs or shooting victims. But the gathering of intelligence probably occupied 90 per cent of the time and resources. It was no use going to the brigade and asking for the approval of any operation without every single detail of the target and what was to be involved being to hand. The unit received £30 a week expenses, so because we needed money mainly for travelling around we had to go out and rob, steal, you name it, but always in another part of the city from where we stayed.

'Once a month we had a commanders' meeting at which about 20 of us would meet at a safe house, always wearing hoods and gloves so we didn't know which unit was discussing what operation. We'd wear these throughout the meeting and then have a one-to-one discussion with a commander about what we had been doing and what we were planning. A different safe house would be used for each meeting. There was a safe house in each area, and I would visit my area safe house up to three times a day to find out whether any messages had been left there for me. The details of where the next commanders' meeting was to be would be left here.'

Manny believes he is morally still bound not to discuss specific operations carried out by his unit. However, a fellow Volunteer has said, 'If, for example, we were going to shoot a UDR man, first of all we'd have to find him, then look at his movements, his route, work out whether he could be isolated, then get the right people in to do it when the time was right. Planning the killing could take months or it could be done in 24 hours depending on the circumstances of, say, how easy it was to access the target. One operation to execute an employee of the Northern Ireland Prison Service took 13 months to plan and put into effect. [This is a reference to the murder of David Teeney, aged 25, who was shot dead in November 1979 as he waited at a bus stop shortly after leaving Crumlin Road jail in Belfast. Another needed nearly 40 Volunteers, which was unprecedented.] The main targets were the RUC; they were top of the list.

'The night before an operation, the two gunmen, their driver and, if it was likely the vehicle being used would have to be burned afterwards, the guy responsible for doing that, would all meet at a safe house where they would stay without access to a telephone or being allowed to leave for any reason until the time came to set off. Next morning we'd hijack a car, take the driver to a club, a bar or a house, tie him up and blindfold him, tell him his car was going to be used in an operation and that when he was released he could go to the police and report it. We didn't have any problems with that so long as that was all he did. He'd be warned we'd be taking the details of his licence and his address. After the operation the gunmen would be taken to safe houses and kept well out of the way for a time.

'People think it was a sectarian war, but that wasn't how we saw it. We didn't mind if we shot dead a Catholic policeman or a Protestant policeman. As long as he wore the fucking uniform, we didn't care what religion he was. Frankly, any copper would have done us. Soldiers in the British Army were another legitimate target. We were small, but we were trying to fight three different wars: the military war; the economic war, in which we used to firebomb buildings, knowing it would cost the government money to repair the damage; and the propaganda war. And we were learning all the time.'

Manny said, 'We had successes, but failures too. Over the years we lost an awful lot of men, but then there were a lot of bodies strewn along the way, not just ours but those of British Army soldiers, the RUC and Loyalists.'

At meetings of commanders, despite the disguises, Manny would recognise from his voice Steenson, dubbed the 'Boy General' because of his youthful looks. The police had another nickname for him, 'Doctor Death', because of the number of murders ultimately attributed to him. Manny might exchange pleasantries with another of the INLA leaders, John 'Jap' O'Reilly, Ronnie Bunting the Protestant turned Republican or Hugh 'Cueball' Torney, so named because it was said while held in Long Kesh before joining the INLA he had a penchant for attacking opponents with snooker balls inside a stocking, or even with snooker cues. Or he would look forward to a chat with a particular friend, Jimmy Brown.

Because it was relatively small, when compared with the 2,000 or so IRA Volunteers or the several thousand members of Loyalist paramilitaries, police intelligence units found it easier to identify and monitor members of the INLA. And they were determined to take out active members at any opportunity using whatever grounds. And so it was that when explosives were found hidden in a derelict house next to a well-known New Lodge drinking hole, the Earl Inn, detectives said they had intelligence linking them to the INLA. Not just that, but it was claimed a forensic examination had revealed traces of Manny's fingerprints.

Tipped off by other INLA members that the RUC was about to swoop, he was given an address in Dublin where a safe house awaited, bade a hasty farewell to Sally and the infant daughter who had now arrived on the scene as a sister to his son, gave instructions for them to follow him and fled over the border into the Republic.

He had been instructed to make for Ballymun, a vast, sprawling housing scheme to the north of Dublin and close to the city's airport. Dominating the skyline were the infamous Ballymun Flats, built in the 1960s to provide homes for families forced out of Dublin slums. Some locals claimed that having to give a Ballymun address to a prospective employer was equivalent to a 'no' even before an interview. Indeed, it was said that the only busy employers in Ballymun were drug suppliers or fences handling the proceeds of thefts. Disease was rampant among those forced to live there. There were decent families too living in the Ballymun Flats, but they had no choice but to suffer the crazed behaviour of neighbours who ought to have been housed in cow byres.

'We had INLA sympathisers in lot of places, in every major town, so there was always somewhere to stay. It really shook me when I heard the coppers were trying to tie me into the explosives find. But I knew the movement would look after me until everything was sorted out. We had plenty of safe houses and could nip over the border any time we wanted. Finding a safe haven was no problem, but in the Republic, people needing to get out of the north for a time, for whatever reason, usually headed for Dublin or Dundalk. In fact, one of the running jokes was that there were more people on the run in Dundalk than there were full-time residents. The cops used to call it Dodge City. If the police were looking for you, you could actually stand on one side of the border and they'd be 20 yards away on the other side, and you could shoot at them but officially they couldn't touch you.

'I'd heard of Ballymun and the Flats. It was where everybody on the run seemed to go. And within a few minutes of getting there I knew I'd drawn the short straw. What a dive. The worst place I have ever been to. It was so bad that at one time I was thinking of giving myself up just to get away. Sally came a few days later with the kids. She stayed one night and that was enough for her. "This is terrible, just give yourself up," she told me. "The cops know you had nothing to do with what they found. They just want an excuse to interrogate you." And off she went back to Spamount Street.

'I ended up sharing a flat with nine other guys who, like me, were staying away from the police. It was a brutal place, so bad that people were jumping off the balconies and killing themselves just to end their misery of being there. Eventually Sally and me organised things for her to come down with the children to visit me. There was a Butlin's holiday camp near the border and we used to meet there. But there was no way she'd move back into the Ballymun Flats.

'There was a pub in Ballymun, but every cunt in there seemed to be on the run. There were Volunteers from the IRA, Provisionals, the INLA, you name a nationalist group and there was somebody there from it. How did we all get on together? At the end of the day we were all Republicans. That was the number one thing about it. And also, at the end of the day, we all had the same beliefs. Where we all differed was what way to take to achieve our aims.

'I stayed in the Ballymun Flats for something like 18 months and I'd certainly have been better off in jail. But what really peed me off was that I knew that if they had found fingerprints on the explosives then they couldn't have been mine, because while I had no problems handling guns, I never went near explosives for the simple reason that I didn't like them, they terrified me. And the police knew that. So I had to hang around there doing little or nothing. Apart from the bar, the only other recreation was watching young kids riding about on horseback, no saddles, just up and down this big road running through the scheme and trying to work out which of them was going to fall off first. Then, finally, word came through that somebody else had been done over the explosives and it was okay for me to get back to New Lodge and carry on where I'd left off. I felt like a man who'd just been told he could leave prison.'

In November 1978, Albert Miles, the deputy governor of the Maze prison, Belfast, was shot dead in the hallway of his house. Prison officers and staff were frequent targets for snipers and bombers. But the murder of the 55-year-old would have a special significance, not only for Manny and his family but for many in the Republican movement.

Reports said English-born Mr Miles had been at home with his wife Rene and son Alan, a university student, when she answered a knock at their door. As she spoke to the caller, Mr Miles joined her and was immediately shot in the head, dying before an ambulance could get him to hospital. A huge manhunt was ordered throughout the province, and there were calls for the restoration of the death penalty for killers of police or prison officers, but the finger of suspicion was immediately pointed at the Provisionals.

The murdered man had been given special responsibility for the Maze 'H' Block, where hundreds of Republican convicts and internees were held. They had been insisting they were entitled to prisoner-of-war status, and when their demands were rejected there had been a series of angry protests and even a march past the jail in support of the prisoners. Mr Miles had refused the offer of both police protection and a permit to carry a gun. His heartbroken wife said later, 'Bert was a bit of a fatalist. He knew that if anybody wanted to get him, they would.'

In their hunt for the gunman, police spared nothing. Scores of known activists found themselves dragged from their beds, thrown into police and British Army vans, and taken to Castlereagh, the police interrogation centre in east Belfast. It was a place Manny knew well and it would become even more familiar as the Troubles continued. Suspects dreaded being taken there for questioning, and their complaints of sleep deprivation, beatings, kickings and torture were dismissed by senior police officers. It was alleged that even low-ranking detectives were given a hard time by their bosses, who threatened and humiliated them if it was felt they were not giving interviewees a sufficiently unpleasant grilling.

One detective would eventually admit that Detective Chief Superintendent Bill Mooney would gee up his teams before they went into an interview room by asking, 'Are you men or mice? Get in there,' and if a confession was not extracted in double-quick time, Mooney would warn, 'Have I got to get in there and do it myself?' It would take many years, but claims of ill treatment would eventually be admitted by some officers.

6

PLAYING GAMES

MANNY AND HIS COMRADES in the INLA knew a major action was needed to raise the profile of the organisation, which vied for support from the Catholic communities with the IRA. It came in March 1979 with the sensational murder of Shadow Northern Ireland Secretary Airey Neave. The politician, who had escaped from the German prisoner-of-war camp at Colditz Castle, was driving his car from the House of Commons car park in London when a bomb attached to the vehicle went off. He died in hospital from his injuries.

Admitting it carried out the bombing, the INLA accused Mr Neave of wanting 'more repression against the Irish people'. His death gave the organisation a massive propaganda boost because not only had it proved its ability to build complex explosive devices – the bomb was fixed to the car by magnets, with a wristwatch starting the timer – but it had penetrated the very heart of the Westminster government with which it considered itself to be at war. Only senior commanders of the INLA had been in on the attack on the MP.

'When we heard the news about the killing, the feeling among members was "Happy Days". It really put the INLA on the map because his escape from Colditz had given him a reputation as an English hero and he was the blue-eyed boy of Margaret Thatcher, who was just weeks away from becoming prime minister. Everything just worked out lovely. It was so well planned. Margaret Thatcher called us "corner boy thugs" but this was the work of brave and skilled Volunteers.

'Gradually we were getting better equipment, better people. What we had at the start was a big group made up of all sorts of people, but we whittled it down, getting rid of thugs and deadwood until we were left with an organisation that was dedicated, people who were not there for self gain or financial gain.'

It was as if the IRA and PIRA were stung by the success of an outfit it saw as a comparative sprat in an ocean of sharks. Now its commanders felt the need to flex their muscles, and they did so with terrible consequences on an August day five months later when first a bomb exploded in a fishing boat off County Sligo carrying a party led by the Queen's cousin Lord Louis Mountbatten, killing him, his 14-year-old grandson Nicholas Knatchbull, crew member Paul Maxwell, 15, from County Fermanagh and the Dowager Lady Brabourne, aged 83; and then a few hours on at Warrenpoint, close to the border with the Republic, 18 British soldiers in an Army convoy were blown to pieces by two massive bombs. The IRA admitted the attack on Lord Mountbatten, reasoning it brought 'to the attention of the English people the continuing occupation of our country'. The blame for the Warrenpoint disaster was laid at the Provisionals' door.

Manny knew incidents such as these would only increase the pressure and dangers faced by him and his fellow Volunteers.

'We used to wake up in the mornings with the UVF, UDA, Red Hand Commandos, UFF, British Army, RUC and UDR looking to take us out. All those people wanted us dead.

'I slept with a pistol under the pillow and a shotgun in the coal bunker. Our house had a gate directly behind the front door, a gate at the bottom of the stairs, a gate at the top of the stairs, and steel on the bedroom floors in case soldiers, police, Loyalists or anyone else broke in and fired up through the ceilings. That was how we had to live. That was the life I chose. We were Volunteers with the right to withdraw our services at any time. It wasn't good for my son and daughter, but we had an unwritten agreement with Loyalist paramilitaries to keep the families out of it as much as possible because women and children were regarded as non-combatants.'

But it was the police who were forever over him like a rash.

'Over the years I was questioned by the police dozens of times. I must have been taken to Castlereagh interrogation centre itself at least 50 times. Nearly every week the police would turn up at my home and haul me off, or they'd just pick me up off the street. I was questioned about all sorts of things: armed robberies, murders, kidnappings, extortions. But these accusations and allegations were really just an excuse to try to recruit me as an informer.

'Sean was usually picked up at the same time. We met more often at Castlereagh than in New Lodge. Sometimes the RUC kept you in for seven days and released you. But just as you got to the gate and thought you were on your way home, they'd rearrest you and march you back inside. You knew then you were in for another seven days, and this could go on three or four times, so you might spend 21 or 28 days there, often in solitary.

'I was well known to the opposition, the British Army and the police, and was being picked up under a policy the RUC called "screening" – when they spotted me they would stop and take me away for screening. One day the cops actually kidnapped me. I was walking along New Lodge Road on my way to town to pay some bills and suddenly the police screeched up alongside me in an unmarked car, jumped out, threw me in the back, sat on top of me and drove off.

'It was done so quickly and there was no one around so nobody could know anything. They told me, "We can kill you and nobody will have a clue as to what's happened to you or where you are." And I honestly thought they were going to do just that. I couldn't see out of the windows and didn't know where I was being taken.

'But we ended up at Castlereagh and I was there for four days. It was only on the fourth that word was leaked to Sally about my whereabouts. One of the incidents they questioned me about was an operation that had ended up like something out of an American gangster movie.'

This incident involved an attempt on the life of a Northern Ireland MP by an INLA unit. The organisation had been monitoring his movements for months and finally a high-level decision had been taken to kill him. The murder would guarantee to increase the profile of the INLA among the Catholic communities, on which it relied for backing.

'It was a rush job because the target had been spotted in Oldpark Road, and the unit, which had been on standby, was dispatched immediately. When the guys got to Oldpark Road they saw the MP but also discovered his bodyguards sitting in another car on the other side of the road. It was decided to still go ahead, and a shot was fired at the politician, but it missed and the MP's driver screeched off. The unit went after his car but were then followed by the bodyguards in their motor. It was a crazy car chase, probably more suited to the days of Al Capone's Chicago, with people shooting out of car windows and tyres screaming as motors went around corners on two wheels. In the end, nobody was hurt or arrested.

'I never forgot the lessons I had been taught in my early days with the IRA about how to handle police interrogations. And as time went on, the INLA Volunteers learned their own tactics, so that eventually when we'd inevitably be dragged into Castlereagh by police wanting to question us, we would turn the sessions round so it ended with us interrogating them.

'My interrogators were usually a couple of Special Branch detectives. I'd been told by the IRA to just stare at police asking questions, and that's what I did. I'd look straight into their eyes and then concentrate on one and say to myself, "He's got blue eyes, brown hair, a moustache, he's got a scar on his left cheek, he's got a wedding ring on and he's about 40." If you did that long enough, he'd be the one to react first. "What are you fucking doing, you're studying me?" It was reverse psychology, and when I'd finished with him I'd start on the other one.

'While they were quizzing us and we were studying them, we'd say, "I know where you live." And just go back to being silent again. This tactic worked a treat. The cops liked to play tricks, but then so could we. One day I was sitting in an interview room in Castlereagh when the police left the room, but the door didn't fully close. It was clearly designed to get me wondering whether something had just happened and to ask what was going on when they came back in. But I didn't wait, I sneaked up to the door and could see two cleaners outside and hear them talking about a wedding.

'From what they said, I worked out one of the copper's daughters was getting married and the women were gossiping about it, saying things like, "He's a lovely lad, great job, he's perfect for her," and mentioning her dad's first name. Then I picked up snatches of where the wedding was going to be and where the newlyweds were going for their honeymoon. I made a mental note of everything. I was released, but a few days later was brought back in for questioning by the same cops, who were using each other's Christian names, and so I was able to work out which of them was having the wedding. After a time, they started shouting at me, glaring into my face and yelling I was this and that, everything evil. Things like, "You think you're a paramilitary? A paramilitary? Fuck off. You're nothing but an ordinary criminal, you fucking bastard."

'The guy whose daughter was getting married was called Peter. I said, "Listen, Peter, can I say something?" And he says, "It fucking talks. Yes, feel free." And I said, "Well, I'm really fucking annoyed with you." He asked, "Why is that?" I said, "Because you never invited my unit to the fucking wedding." His jaw dropped, but it dropped even more when I told him the name of the hotel where they were having the reception. I said, "I'd loved to have gone," and I also proceeded to tell them where the honeymoon was to be. He was raging, furious because he couldn't understand how I knew all that and was now worried something might happen.

'Being released after interrogation wasn't the end. We always had to report to our security officers. They would hood us, take us away and make us tell them everything that was said in any interview from day one. We'd have to describe the people doing the interrogation just in case we had them on file.

'We weren't stupid, but we wanted the coppers to think we were. That way they were more likely to let their guards down and let something slip. The more you know about your enemy, the better armed you are. We used to send things to their houses, like wreaths. It was an ongoing war in every department. So we knew the RUC didn't feel safe and we exploited that.

'I was always very conscious of the need to be on the lookout for ambushes whenever I was on an active operation with my unit. So many people died through walking into the unexpected, but I'm proud that my unit was never caught out. Every time I went out on an operation, though, through my mind ran the prospect that I might not come back, might not see Sally or the children again, that I might be killed or captured and sent to prison for a long time, that the action might have been compromised by an informer in our midst. Did the violence scare me? Oh yes, but I tried not to let myself get used to the constant threats on my life. I don't think there is anybody, including me, who couldn't say that fear didn't play a big part. That applied to men in all organisations.

'The police were always playing games. Sometimes they'd actually come to the house and admit my files had been found somewhere in a Loyalist area and were in the hands of Protestant paramilitaries. Then they'd play the part of being sympathetic and helpful, advising me to change my routine and wanting to know what I'd be doing to protect myself. But I told them nothing, because I knew if I had said anything it would be passed onto the UDA or UVF.

'Most paramilitaries had an arrangement with the social security office that meant we didn't have to show up at a regular time but could appear whenever we wanted. Despite all the hassle and the scares, I was still as committed to the cause as ever. All of us were. We still wanted the Brits out, lock, stock and barrel. We just didn't want the British Army off the streets; we wanted anything with a British interest or influence in Ireland to go. And the tactics of the British Army only made that ambition firmer by the day. For example, we used dogs to give warnings. Once you heard a dog going mad, it meant the Brits were about. So the soldiers started to kill the dogs. One time they chopped a dog's head off and drove about with it on top of their Land Rover just to antagonise us. And that led me on to one of my scariest operations.

'The Brits were generally people of routine; most soldiers are. We used to watch them to see how they behaved when they were searching houses. Generally they would turn up at a house in force to do a search, go inside quickly and then close the door so the street looked normal, as if nothing was happening. Once or twice, Volunteers had gone up to a door, looked through the letter box and spotted an officer standing in the hall directing things.

'What we wanted was a guy to go up, knock at the door and as soon as it was opened shoot the soldier standing there. We asked, "Who's up for this?" because it needed plenty of balls. One of my comrades volunteered. Up to the door he went, lifted the letterbox, saw the soldier inside, rapped the door, guy opened it – and the fucking gun didn't go off. Our man ran off up the street with the Army firing at him and he zoomed into a derelict house to hide. The interior walls were made only of breeze blocks. He was on one side and the Army was on the other. One of the soldiers must have heard a sound, because his patrol literally just walked though the wall and piled on top of him.

'Another that had my heart in my mouth came one day when we were waiting to ambush an Army patrol in New Lodge. The unit had two AK-47s, and when the patrol reached a T-junction we were going to hit them from different directions. As we sat waiting behind a wall, we heard English voices on the other side. Then we realised they were more soldiers and they were two doors away searching a series of houses. We hadn't even known they were there, and what was scary was realising that had they spotted us, they could have taken every one of us out.

'There were shootings, bombings and riots every night. The British Army, the RUC and the Loyalists were trying to kill us and we were trying to kill them. So if Loyalists killed one of us, we really didn't complain about it, and when we killed one of them, generally they didn't complain either to be fair. It was a case of, "They've got one of ours, let's move on, but we'll be back."'

The tit for tat applied to the British Army. In May 1980, the M60 Gang, which included Angelo Fusco, 'Fats' Campbell, 'Dingus' Magee and Joe Doherty, had ambushed an SAS squad and killed Captain Herbert Westmacott. The murder rankled with his colleagues, and when in October that year one of Manny's comrades, Ronnie Bunting, was assassinated, the SAS was accused of having a hand in it. Bunting, son of a British Army major and a founder member of the INLA, had become leader of the organisation, but a gang of gunmen burst into his home in Lower Falls and killed him, along with fellow INLA man Noel Lyttle. The UDA claimed responsibility, but Manny and the INLA were convinced the SAS had helped.

As if in a show of defiance over the death of Bunting, the INLA used its connections to Baader-Meinhof to plant a bomb outside the British Consulate in Germany. It failed to go off properly and nobody was hurt, but the blast was a grim warning that the INLA could spread its tentacles far from Ireland. More was to come. In

1982 Manny was told that Dominic 'Mad Dog' McGlinchey had been thrown out of the Provisional IRA and had joined the INLA as operations officer for South Derry. His wife, Mary, also joined. He was soon chief of staff and made a dramatic impact.

In December that year a bomb went off in the Droppin Well discotheque at Ballykelly in County Londonderry as it was packed with soldiers and local young folks. Seventeen people – 11 soldiers and six locals (five young women and a teenager) – died. Saying it carried out the massacre, the INLA warned, 'We believe it is only attacks of such a nature that bring it home to people in Britain and the British establishment. The shooting of an individual soldier, for the people of Britain, has very little effect.' Just over a fortnight earlier Lenny Murphy, leader of the Shankhill Butchers, had been riddled with bullets and slain as he arrived at the home of his girlfriend. Manny had often wondered whether Murphy had been there the night he and Sally had their frightening encounter with 'Basher' Bates.

7

MR BIG

LIKE LOTS OF OTHER VOLUNTEERS, Manny would sometimes use watching Celtic football team as the excuse for travelling to Glasgow. It wasn't necessarily the real reason for his trips, though. The club had been founded a century earlier by Brother Walfrid, a Marist monk from Sligo who wanted to raise cash to help feed starving Irish families in Glasgow.

The team's ground, Celtic Park in the east of the city, was commonly known by fans as 'Paradise'. It and the nearby Celtic Supporters' Club in London Road were often used for discreet meetings between Republicans from various parts of the north and south of Ireland during the Troubles, and for talks between paramilitaries and supporters living in Scotland. Members of the various Loyalist organisations, in particular the UVF and UDA, had strong backing in the west of Scotland, and Protestants too journeyed over in big numbers when their side, Glasgow Rangers, the other half of the 'Old Firm', was in action.

Fans came by road in cars or, most often, by bus. Sometimes they'd treat themselves to a flight to Glasgow airport. Catholic and Protestant coaches leaving Ireland carrying supporters were monitored by police along their journey and generally landed in Scotland at the busy ferry terminal at Stranraer. As buses streamed from the ferries into the little Wigtownshire port, police would regularly board them to search principally for known activists, who would be ordered off and told they were not being allowed to continue on the final 90-mile leg of the trip to Glasgow.

There seemed no pattern to these searches; rather, the detaining of these men appeared to be a matter of pot luck. But Manny knew on those occasions when he was allowed to continue, police did so simply in the hope that in Glasgow their surveillance of him would lead them to his contacts in the city. He knew Scottish police held information on him provided by the RUC. Airport security was much keener, and for that reason football coaches were the favourite means of smuggling money and weapons back into Ireland, yet searches on the return trips were spasmodic, careless even.

'I used to follow Celtic a lot, supporting the team was probably my only interest outside working for the Republican cause. But I was always under scrutiny by the RUC and Special Branch detectives who travelled over on the boats in plain clothes, although we could tell they were policemen. They were known as "spotters" and were always looking for known faces. Many a time I never even saw a match because I'd be held at Stranraer or Glasgow airport. I was stopped about 20 times over the years.'

Neither Republicans nor Loyalists had taken the war directly into Scotland or Wales for that matter.

'The INLA didn't carry out any operations in Scotland, and neither did the IRA, because we believed we were all Celtic nations, Ireland, Scotland, Wales, and we had no beef with Scotland and Wales.'

While the same argument was less applicable to Loyalists, both sides were reluctant to antagonise support in Scotland, especially because it was from there that around a tenth of their funding came. The UDA had a particularly heavy reliance on Scottish money.

A strange quirk would lead to Manny becoming friends with one of the UDA's most determined supporters. At a young age, the engineering brilliance of Colin Campbell had earned him a prized and well-paid post as a foreman in a factory on the outskirts of Glasgow manufacturing domestic appliances, including vacuum cleaners. Eager to do his bit for the organisation, Colin joined a group of friends in a plot to rob a post office in the east end of the city, at Mount Vernon. The proceeds would be handed over to the UDA.

It was a disastrous exploit. The haul was just £995 and one member of the gang was recognised. Police raided a house in the Calton area and found explosives and detonators. In 1974, the robbers were jailed. Malcolm Nicol, said in court to be a high-ranking UDA officer, received the longest sentence, of ten years. Colin went down for six years. The escapade never diminished his faith in the Loyalist cause, but it destroyed his career and his life.

While serving part of his sentence at Perth jail, Colin met up with an old friend, Thomas 'Tam' McGraw, a leader of a highly successful team gang of robbers known as the 'Barlanark Team', as most of them came from that area of Glasgow. One of the reasons why the gang was so effective and able to evade capture for most of its existence was the meticulous attention to detail paid by McGraw when planning jobs, using careful surveillance, teams of observers, engineers to cut telephone wires and disable security systems, and when painstakingly working out escape routes. Among police, there were many who observed these operations were run along near military lines, not unlike those of well-organised paramilitary operations in Northern Ireland.

McGraw was on remand awaiting trial for a spate of shop break-ins and opening lockfast places, for which a court would decide his spell behind bars on remand was nearly sufficient punishment. He was sent home with a £350 fine, a still considerable sum at the time. As a teenager, Colin had occasionally worked with the Barlanark Team. It would be as a result of eventually becoming a close friend of McGraw that Manny would get to know and like Colin.

There were others at this time in Glasgow growing rich from underworld activities, and none more so than Arthur 'The Godfather' Thompson. Thompson ran a string of rackets, including protection, money laundering, extortion and drug dealing. He was highly respected by gang bosses in London, in particular the Kray twins, who occasionally used Thompson to 'sort' difficult rivals.

It was Thompson who arranged for a foot soldier to telephone the information in 1963 that the Glasgow to London mail train had left on time, allowing thieves in England to hold it up and rob it of a staggering £2.6 million in what is still known as the Great Train Robbery. But Thompson had one activity details of which he was determined should never reach others in the city underworld, because had it done so he would probably have joined those whose early graves were the result of orders given by him. That activity was gunrunning. And it was dangerous. It needed nerve, but that and courage were facets which the Godfather had in spades.

His links to the Krays had brought him to the attention of Special Branch officers who decided to take a closer look at this tough Glaswegian. Their monitoring, which included tapping the telephone of his sprawling Glasgow home, known behind its owner's back as the Ponderosa because of its vague resemblance to the ranch house featured in the highly popular television series *Dallas*, indicated links to Northern Ireland. What did these links concern and what did they lead to, the listeners wondered? Thompson thought that secret would die with him, but it was finally revealed by the *News of the World*. The newspaper reported that he was a low-profile arms dealer who ran a thriving racket supplying guns, including some made by his son, also named Arthur, to Loyalist gangs in Ireland. And after an informant told undercover British Army officers about regular meetings between Thompson and senior figures in the Ulster Defence Association, he was discreetly shadowed.

Senior spymasters were keen to acquire reliable information about UDA activities, and the tall Scots gangster fitted the bill as a potential mole. But he firmly rebuffed an initial approach by detectives in Scotland and refused to help, claiming, 'I don't grass, ask anybody.' Then, in 1968, Thompson was arrested in connection with a £3,000 warehouse robbery. As he languished in the cells, he was again targeted by the intelligence services.

Once more he was visited, but this time by representatives of MI5 who made it plain they were not prepared to take no for an answer. They put to him an offer he could not refuse, showing him a detailed dossier on his Irish dealings. The information it contained would have been enough to put him behind bars for a very long time indeed. It would also have made him a prime target for Republicans, many of whom he did business with in Scotland.

Thompson was told that if he cooperated, he would be spared another long jail stretch once the robbery case had been dealt with. 'What do you want me to do?' asked Thompson. 'Just carry on doing what you do now, but give us regular reports on what you do and who you meet,' he was told. It was more than a get-out-of-jail card; it was unwritten permission to make boatloads of money. And there was further good news to come. His past record had meant he was facing a very long sentence for the robbery charge, but after he agreed to help the spooks he was sent down for just four years, and was out in two.

While he was in prison, his security-service handlers paid him occasional visits to remind him of their deal, and once released he resumed his arms dealings, passing on titbits about the UDA in particular during trips to London when he met his new spy friends. Some of his material concerned Scotland. It was filtered back to police there, but they were never told where it had come from.

Thompson and his government handlers were sure the secret of their relationship was safe. But then an IRA plant within the UDA reported on the Scots godfather who supplied weapons. It was as good as a death sentence. In 1970, IRA executioner Cyril McFeeley was told to track down Thompson and give him an ultimatum: that unless he stopped selling to the UDA immediately, his life would be forfeit. But before he could give the warning, McFeeley was spotted by police and sent back to Northern Ireland. Thompson carried on working, but whispers in the province about his UDA support abounded, and eventually Manny would be asked to get the Godfather in his sights.

Around the time the INLA was celebrating the death of Airey Neave, a young man in Glasgow was beginning to make a name for himself. Paul Ferris had been born in the east of the city in 1963 to a Protestant father and Catholic mother, and was raised as a Catholic. Ferris and a close friend, Ian 'Blink' MacDonald, operated a thriving racket raiding jewellery shops.

The method needed a cool nerve and involved one of them walking in posing as a customer, distracting an assistant and running off, invariably in broad daylight and through busy streets, to a getaway car. It was highly risky but also lucrative, and the team went on to hit target shops in England. Eventually Ferris would become an enforcer for Thompson and an ally of McGraw and Manny. And, like Thompson, he would come to the notice of MI5 and others through a gunrunning exploit.

The rackets operated by gangsters such as Arthur Thompson gave them comfortable lifestyles. But a trial in 1981 set operators such as him and McGraw thinking. Nor was the story that led to a courtroom lost on paramilitaries constantly seeking money to finance arms deals. It would have a major impact on the thinking of crime bosses and on the course of the hostilities in Northern Ireland.

The story revolved around a remarkable New Zealander, Terrance John Clark, who would go on to assume a number of aliases, including Terry Clark, Terry Sinclair, Alexander James Sinclair, Tony Bennetti, the Australian Jackal, the Power Man and Mr Big. We will stick to the moniker by which he became best known to police in Britain: Alexander Sinclair.

While in his 20s, Sinclair became involved in drug smuggling. He teamed up with Christopher Martin 'Marty' Johnstone to import high-grade white heroin from Johnstone's Asian base into Australasia. The profits were staggering. While other criminals were regarded as successful for ventures that netted a few thousand pounds, Sinclair and Johnstone pocketed millions. Sinclair began expanding the operation worldwide and set up a branch in Britain. Former Scots Guard Jimmy Smith, from West Lothian, was at one stage earmarked to take charge of the Scottish end of the racket.

Greed inevitably took a hand. Buyers complained Johnstone was diluting heroin to make even more cash. Clark called him to Britain on the pretext of discussing the European end of the business and suggested a meeting in Scotland. The pair had been warned that if they wished an easy path for the operation, then they would need to give the Godfather a sweetener. Thompson would have to be offered a percentage of the proceeds.

In fact, Sinclair had decided his founder partner had to go. He was getting the organisation a bad name. When Johnstone set off to a purported meeting in Glasgow with Thompson, accompanied by Smith and another ex-Scots Guardsman, Kingsley Fagan, from Airdrie, he was shot and stabbed in a Lancashire lay-by, his body taken first to a lock-up garage, where the hands were cut off and his face disfigured with a hammer in an effort to prevent identification, should he ever be found. Before being dumped in a quarry lake, his stomach was ripped open, to make the body sink and not float back to the surface. Then the killers threw their victim into the lake. The gun used in the shooting was buried near Airdrie and one of the victim's hands was later discovered in a brown envelope in the River Almond, near Perth.

But the murderers had made a crucial mistake. By chance, police decided to use the same quarry lake to train their diving unit. Amateurs too practised there, with the result that the body was found a few days later. Still confident they had got away with the perfect murder, because no one knew the identity of the victim, the killers were drinking champagne a few days later in a hotel when a waitress joked, 'Are you the ones who killed the man found in the quarry?' They failed to see any humour in her comment and had even less to laugh about months later when Johnstone's mistress reported him missing. She gave sufficient information for police to put a name to the mystery body in the mortuary, and the gang were rounded up and given long prison sentences.

It is impossible to overestimate the significance of the Sinclair case. At his trial it was revealed his share alone in the profits of his worldwide syndicate was a staggering £25 million, more than enough to fund an army. Now it was clear just how much money was to be made from large-scale drug smuggling, and that was not lost on a host of major criminals and on some paramilitaries in Northern Ireland. Because whereas the Troubles had begun over the right for ordinary men and woman to live in their own fair society, now allegations of drug dealing and racketeering would seep into the equation, souring the perception of many about the leaderships of organisations such as INLA and the UDA. The involvement of Sinclair's syndicate in drugs had led to infighting, murder, feuding and mistrust, features that would threaten to rip apart Loyalists and Republicans alike.

Drugs had been smuggled into Scotland on a small scale, sometimes in cars driven to southern Spain, where the occupants collected relatively tiny amounts of Moroccan hashish and risked checks by customs officers at French border crossing and more stringent examinations at ports and airports in Britain. Men like Thomas McGraw knew of these exploits. He had shown little interest and would continue to do so, but around the back of his mind floated pound signs, 25 million of them. Another event would ultimately convince him the massive rewards justified the risks, but that was in the future.

Manny McDonnell had no interest in drugs. But as time passed he would become drawn into a terrible feud partially caused by them in his home town, and then into a mind-boggling smuggling operation that would threaten to wreck dozens of lives.

Sinclair didn't live to enjoy the utopia his millions promised. He died of a heart attack in Parkhurst prison on the Isle of Wight two years after being jailed. So he never knew the influence his racket had on Ireland, a country he never visited. Long after his death, though, he did achieve worldwide notoriety when his character – they used the Terry Clark alias – was featured in the Australian television series *Underbelly: A Tale of Two Cities*.

8

BLANK CHEQUE

THROUGHOUT NORTHERN IRELAND, Republican and Loyalist families had debated which of the organisations they should associate, support or join. There was no shortage of choice. The INLA, IRA, Provisionals, Cumann na mBan (sometimes known as the Irishwomen's Council), Na Fianna Éireann, Saor Éire, Loyalist Volunteer Force, Red Hand Commando, UDA, UFF and UVF all sought the backing of their respective communities.

The British government had declared them all to be illegal. Joining one or more meant risking a fine of up to £5,000 and, worse, ten years in jail. The list would grow longer, with additions that included the Irish People's Liberation Organisation, Continuity Army Council, Orange Volunteers and Red Hand Defenders.

Manny had opted for the INLA, while others among his relatives, although not immediate family, had committed themselves to the IRA. And from time to time the INLA, IRA and Provisionals found themselves at deadly odds. He recalls one family gathering when the potential of this discord struck home.

'Two of my relations were with the IRA, and one in particular was a very active Volunteer. He asked me, "Manny, what am I going to do if I'm told to come and get you?" and I had to reply, "Well, it works both ways. What if I'm told to go and get you?" I

Neither of us gave answers, but we knew what they were. With others it was brother against brother: scary, but that's the way it was for years.'

Whatever versions of the argument they chose to adopt, the McDonnells were united in their hatred and distrust of the British, their army, their government and their media, and the manner in which the British appeared to manipulate the RUC. But the ferocity of their loathing was as nothing compared with their feelings towards the English and their prime minister, Margaret Thatcher. That was the sentiment of most if not all Republicans, who saw her as the Hand of Evil guiding the welding torch as it made ever stronger the barrier dividing the north of Ireland from the south. But just how far the McDonnell family would be allowed to show their dislike was about to be tested.

At the beginning of the 1980s, the ferocity of the Troubles had deepened when a number of Republicans went on hunger strike in what was popularly seen as a show of their defiance against the policies of Mrs Thatcher and her government. As the hunger strike continued, worldwide media interest in those bent on sacrificing themselves exploded like a terrorist bomb. Would either side back down before the Grim Reaper added to the already horrific toll of dead in the province? The answer was no.

During the strike, one of the protesters, Bobby Sands, was elected the Member of Parliament for Fermanagh and South Tyrone at the age of just 27. He died on 5 May 1981, having refused food for 66 days. Others who followed him to the grave were Francis Hughes, Raymond McCreesh, Patsy O'Hara, Joe McDonnell, Martin Hurson, Kevin Lynch, Kieran Doherty, Thomas McElwee and Michael Devine. All had lasted more than two months without eating. O'Hara, Lynch and Devine had been fellow members of the INLA with Manny. All the dead were still being mourned in the McDonnell home when Nellie dropped a bombshell.

'One of my sisters had moved to London, where she met and fell in love with an English guy. And that was a problem, because

Ma announced my sister was bringing him home to New Lodge to meet her family. Clearly this wasn't going to be a very sociable meeting and there were a few mutterings. It sounded very much like a lamb being brought to the slaughter. But Ma ordered everybody to be on their best behaviour for the arrival of the English guy.

'We were sitting around wondering what to say and expect when he arrived with my sister from the airport to join us for a meal. It was slow at first, everybody was being polite and careful as to what they said, and then the conversation began going very smoothly until something came up about Thatcher.

'There was a silence, and Ma looked at the visitor and told him, "That name is not allowed to be mentioned in this house. She's murdered ten hunger strikers and if you have anything more to say you can get your fucking coat on and get to fuck." It was something of a conversation-stopper. Gradually the chat got going again, but Thatcher's name never again came up. We all agreed our visitor turned out to be an absolutely cracking guy, one of the best you could ever meet, a real gem. I thought that if I had to pick somebody to marry my sister it would be him. Happily, he did, and they went off to live in Australia, which is still their home.

'I suppose the Troubles had left all of us with a distrust of strangers, and not without good reason. What some people failed to grasp was that we were in an out-and-out war, fighting for our lives. We learned from friend and enemy alike. We understood the value of having educated, bright people on our side as well as fighters. We encouraged people to go to college, to study subjects like economics, and when they had qualified to come back and report to us and help us. But often their studying meant these were people who had been away from our community for long periods; could they be trusted when they returned? I suppose, in the end, we were suspicious of everyone, even friends, because there were such a lot of grasses – touts – around.'

Manny had special cause to despise those who told tales to save their own skins, or simply for money, or both. In February 1983, Harry Kirkpatrick, whom he had met on a handful of occasions at gatherings of INLA commanders, was arrested on a whole series of charges, including murdering two policemen, two UDR soldiers and a Catholic member of the Territorial Army. Faced with spending the rest of his life behind bars, Kirkpatrick began spilling secrets, implicating a plethora of his former comrades. Not even the kidnapping by the INLA of his wife, sister and stepfather could stop him talking, although all were released unharmed. Among 27 people who would ultimately be convicted as a result of Kirkpatrick's testimony were Manny's friend in the INLA Jimmy Brown and his acquaintance Gerard Steenson.

In nearly all the cases the convictions would later be quashed, but Kirkpatrick sparked off an atmosphere of doubt and suspicion that would have dire consequences for the INLA and Manny. That atmosphere accounted for the INLA Volunteer Eric Dale, aged 43. Two months after Kirkpatrick's arrest, Dale was questioned by police about an explosives find. Then in May he was abducted by his former comrades, and later his hooded and trussed body, wrapped in plastic, was dumped along a remote roadside. He had been shot and badly beaten. The INLA said Dale had confessed, under interrogation, to giving police details about two other Volunteers that led to their being killed by the RUC. But the dead man's family denied he was a grass.

Detectives had remained baffled by the identity of the killer of Maze deputy governor Albert Miles. But then Christopher Black, a father of four and member of the IRA Ardoyne active service unit, was arrested and found himself facing many years in prison. Black did a deal with police that earned him freedom in exchange for grassing. And one of his victims was Manny's brother-in-law, IRA member Charles McKiernan, whose role as the organisation's top hitman was now no longer a secret. As a direct result of what

Black told police, McKiernan was convicted of murdering both Miles and a UDR member. A judge, wearing a bulletproof vest and with an armed policeman by his side, sentenced McKiernan to two life sentences one day and a further 407 years the next.

'Our biggest fear, our number-one fear, was informers, because we just didn't know who they were. Even when going out on an operation, you didn't know if there was an informer within your own ranks, perhaps the man standing next to you. Normally it took someone six or seven months from volunteering to joining an active service unit and in that time we'd hope to filter out touts.

'It wasn't easy to get into a unit. You had to go through a series of interviews at which you would be asked if you were prepared to kill somebody. Not everybody was willing to kill and we wanted a guy to tell us if he felt he could not take a human life. There was no shame in not being willing or able to kill. If someone did say they couldn't go down that route then we would have a lot of respect for his honesty and there were plenty of other tasks he could do. And all the time you were wondering, "Is he a grass? Has he been planted on us by the coppers or the Loyalists or MI5?"

'We knew that, going on the law of averages alone, we must have been infiltrated by grasses, but wondering as you set out on an action whether you were walking into an ambush or if you'd be coming back, on top of the fear of death or going to prison, convinced us we had to do something. We weren't alone; all the paramilitaries went to a lot of trouble to try to weed out informers. Because of the damage done by Kirkpatrick and Black, the IRA wanted to know what happened to a tout once he turned super-grass and came up with a plan under which a guy pretended to turn informer and became a double agent. They had to make his cover convincing and so his family in Ballymurphy were burned out. They didn't even know what he was doing; even his wife and kids had to genuinely believe he had betrayed them and become a grass.

'The IRA security people were sure that if the Brits fell for it, then they would be able to learn where the Brits took a grass, how they treated him, who were his contacts, his handlers, what safe houses were used, what bank accounts and so on. So one day the guy contacted the British, said he'd had enough, was frightened for the future and wanted to talk. And his story was believed.

'At the end of the day he was taken to Cyprus for debriefing. He had been given the names of people who the IRA was willing to sacrifice, and these were passed on. The British security services told him about court cases where he would be expected to give evidence and gave lessons on how to behave in court. When the agent was back on the streets in Belfast, he was able to reveal to his officers how the Brits had got him out of the country, how he had been treated and everything that happened to him. It was invaluable information.

'We had our own problems. It was an ongoing battle against touts. There were a lot of them about. In one five-man INLA unit in Derry it turned out two of them were informers and one of them grassed on the other to us. Sometimes the RUC and Special Branch would play tricks on you. It was like walking into a room full of mirrors and trying to work out which face was the real one. Sometimes they would deliberately sacrifice one tout just to save another. It was ruthless, but we were fighting a dirty war. Some touts were deep-rooted sleepers who had been undercover for years without being active. We knew our lives could depend on finding them.

'If we had five operations in a month and four of them went wrong – for instance you arrived at a certain location to find a heavier than usual British Army or police presence and had to call the whole thing off – then you might put that down to bad luck. If it happened regularly you knew the odds were that somebody had grassed, and in that case we'd go to our commander, who would ask for the names of everybody involved in the operations. It was then a process of elimination: who had known about all the failed operations, who had shown signs of having a few quid more than anyone else.

'The initial reaction was just to murder the culprit. But like the IRA we wanted to know what made a tout tick. We knew everybody had a breaking point. Sometimes people gave away information not because they wanted to but just because they reached the point where they could no longer handle the threats, the beatings and the torture dished out by the police and soldiers.

'We told all our Volunteers, "If you break under interrogation, when you are released tell us what you've said so we can limit the damage. Just be honest with us and we won't kill you." But there were others who did it for money, just because they were skint, and that was no excuse. We were all in the same boat, but we didn't sell our souls and our friends down the river. Over the years I lost more than 30 friends violently, but I will never know how many died as the result of grassing by others they trusted.

'We had our own security department, whose job it was to trace and deal with traitors, and it was decided that the next suspected informer to be caught would not be executed or beaten right away, because most guys would tell you anything to avoid a bashing. What we had normally done was to torture a suspected grass to get everything out of him and tape-recorded him confessing to being an informer before he was dealt with. The tape recording would then be handed to his family so they would know why he was being punished.

'But now we came up with a plan to use the next informer to educate us so we could understand why he turned grass on his friends and comrades. When we caught the next one, we took him to a priest and in front of the priest told him, "We're not going to kill you provided you are honest and tell us everything you've done." To the priest, we said, "Father, you are a witness to our promise." After the suspect was interrogated, he was told,

"You are going to live, but you have 48 hours to get out of Ireland and you'll only return when we give you permission. That might not be for another 20 years."

'I personally knew a guy who turned informer, a petty criminal named Tim Gregory. He was not involved in any active service units and wasn't even a Republican, but he got a job working behind the bar in a Republican club in Belfast where he could listen to what the customers were talking about and pass on snippets to his handlers. It mystified me how a known thief was allowed to get a job in a Republican club. We found out what Gregory was up to and were about to murder him when suddenly the British Army took him away to safety. Maybe another tout had tipped them off.'

One day around 1984 Manny was picked up off the streets and bundled into an unmarked police car. 'What's up?' he asked two detectives sitting in the front. 'You okay, Manny?' they asked, and despite their morose expressions they seemed unusually amiable. That told him this was not the normal pick-up procedure that customarily resulted in a three- or seven-day lie in at Castlereagh under detention orders allowing suspects to be held without trial for extended questioning. 'Castlereagh, is it?' he asked, and the nod of the man in the passenger seat confirmed his suspicion. He wanted to know why but was told only, 'Look, Manny, there are some people who want to have a wee chat, that's all we know. It's nothing to worry about. We know as much as you.'

Castlereagh, home of the regional crime squad, could be a scary place to someone not used to the ways of the interrogators, with their veiled threats to and actual abuse of prisoners. But today the atmosphere seemed less tense. He was shown into an interview room and two senior detectives who introduced themselves by their first names joined him. What followed was a routine they had practised scores of times. A success rate of one in 20 would have satisfied the pair and their seniors. They were about to try to turn Manny, to induce him to become an informer.

'I knew right away from their attitude, asking about the family, how everybody was, letting slip names of other Volunteers just so I'd know they had a lot on me, where this was all leading. I'd heard it from others. It was the "here's a blank cheque, just fill in how much you want" approach. My reaction to those people was as I had been taught all along: "Don't speak to them, don't give them your name, your age, where you live; give them fuck all."

'I listened while they talked about all the guys who had been killed and were getting killed, what it must be like for Sally and the family, how a new start could be just around the corner. They were saying things like, "There's a blank cheque on the table. Fill your own price in, whatever you want, write it in yourself, we'll give you a new passport, we'll put you in any Commonwealth country, rehouse you, relocate you, we'll give you a new National Insurance number, buy you a house, we'll pay your mortgage, get you a job, open a bank account for you, you'll have a steady income and no worries. Just put whatever amount you want in that chequebook. At the end of the day, you and your people aren't going to win, so why not get something out of everything you've given? It's either this or you're going to end up in prison or dead."

'I said nothing. Not for one second did I ever consider their offer. It wasn't about money to us. We weren't being paid. That's what the coppers couldn't get round: that we weren't doing it for money. I grew up on a giro. I was happy enough with that. I'd seen others go down the road of taking the blank cheque, having it filled in for them, people who betrayed us. But they walked away into no life. Outcasts, snakes, they and their families shamed for all time. Even to this day, if I got my hands on them I'd put a bullet right through their heads without any qualms.

'The police knew from my silence they were getting nowhere and eventually let me go. I told my bosses what had happened and gave them a full account of what had been promised. They didn't even ask if I'd been tempted.'

9

IRISH LUCK

'ONE OF MY CLOSEST FRIENDS in the INLA, a man with who I would have trusted my life, was a unit commander who I'm going to call John. John ran a taxi depot in Belfast and obviously that was very useful when we needed cars, if for some reason we hadn't been able to hijack one, for instance.

'John and I had a good pal who served in the Irish Army – an tArm – and who was sympathetic to the INLA. Our soldier friend had been part of a unit that had come across an arms dump in the Republic, and while confiscating the pile of weapons and ammunition found in it, he had managed to hide one of the guns.

'He telephoned us to say we'd need to collect it. Now, like all the paramilitaries, we were always short of hardware. Usually we had to pay over the odds for anything and so the offer of a free gun wasn't to be sniffed at. So John told me he was off to get it. I offered to come with him, but he said it was just a straightforward trip down, over the border, make the pick-up and get back, no problems.

'It all appeared to be going well, but either the RUC had been tipped off about what was going on or John had triggered something when he crossed the border, because the anti-terrorist people in the Republic were on to him and he was caught with the gun and remanded. He found he was sharing a cell with Dominic McGlinchey.'

McGlinchey was a prime target for the British Army, who suspected him of organising the Droppin Well Inn bombing that had taken out so many soldiers. He regularly flitted between Northern Ireland and the Republic, and on one of his trips to the south had found himself in a house in County Clare surrounded by gun-toting detectives. He tried escaping by climbing onto the roof armed with a machine gun. When he was spotted, he sprayed bullets at the officers, who returned fire.

McGlinchey was slightly wounded, and when he realised the situation was hopeless gave himself up. He was extradited and jailed in the north, but that conviction was overturned on appeal and he was returned to the Republic and jailed for firearms offences. While he was in prison, his wife, Mary, an active member of the INLA, was assassinated by two gunmen at the home in Dundalk she shared with her two children. The killers were believed to be fellow INLA Volunteers and her death was in retaliation for the murder by her husband of a man from South Armagh.

'John and McGlinchey used to have a good craic together while they were banged up, before John was eventually released on bail, but a bail condition was that he remained in the south and reported daily there to the police. That meant his INLA unit in Belfast was without its leader, and it began running wild, shooting at anything that moved and generally putting not just itself but other Volunteers at risk. Something had to be done. We wanted John back to resume control and get a grip on the unit.

'So I sent word to him that he was needed. Almost every day his absence was being missed more and more. I told him, "You'll have to do something to get these people under control. They are causing so much trouble, fouling up other ongoing operations, blazing guns around as if they're in some Wild West town, and their antics are bringing in the Brits, helicopters, the SAS. There are roadblocks everywhere; it's getting so crowded and harder and harder to move about because of these four fucking maniacs. Fuck sake, you'll have to get back here somehow."

'Our bosses called me in and said they wanted me to get down south and bring him out. He was in Dundalk, Dodge City, staying with friends, and we met up in one of the local pubs. There was no problem about him getting out of there because he only had to report to the cops every 24 hours. I thought the difficulty would be in getting him across the border without us being stopped by one of the British or Irish Army patrols, because just about every crossing was being manned or regularly checked.

'We had a few drinks and John said, "Listen, Manny, I've found a way we can get home across the fucking border with no problems. This way is guaranteed. You go up over this road. The locals here say it's called Egg Nog Road, or something like that. I've already tested it. We drive out of Dundalk, follow a track, go up over a hill, get onto Egg Nog Road, and when we come to the end of that, we're in the north. Bingo. Dead easy."

'I said, "Right, we'll have another few beers and then fuck off." It was after midnight when we decided, "Right, off we go."

'So there were him and me in the car and we drove up through this midden till we came to Egg Nog Road. We were driving merrily along, no problem, getting closer and closer to the north, till finally we reckoned we'd crossed the border. That was when we noticed lights in the road ahead, red lights signalling us to slow down. It was an Army roadblock. "Fucking hell," we told ourselves and I thought, "We've got ourselves to the middle of nowhere and we're dead fucking meat. It's as simple as that." I reckoned we were getting buried because we were in the wilderness and then we realised from the uniforms it was worse than the British Army: it was the fucking UDR, the hated UDR.

'I was driving, so I slowed and wound down the window. A big head loomed out of the darkness, came in at the window, had a look at me and John, and asked, "Have you got anything in the car that you shouldn't have?" It was a bit of a stupid question.

We're hardly going to stick our hands up and say, "Right, we've a big bomb in the boot," or "Okay you've caught us bang to rights: we've kidnapped the Irish president." But there didn't seem much point in antagonising this guy, and I was feeling a bit merry after the beers, so I tried to break the ice and said, "Aye, him," pointing to John.

'Now the guy at the window was holding a gun and evidently not up for having a joke, because all he said was, "Right, the two of yous, out of the fucking car." So we got out and he said, "Right, names, addresses, the usual." So we had names and addresses – false, of course – already prepared, which we gave him, and he told us, "Right, wait there while I check the pair of yous out. Don't fucking move."

'Off he went to a wee hut, and while he was away I said to John, "You know what's going to happen here, don't you? Once they find out who we are, each of us is going to get one in the head from him and his pals, then they'll drag us out into the middle of that field and bury us. End of story. Nobody will know where we are or what's happened." John asked, "What do you reckon we should do, run?" I said, "Run fucking where? There's just nowhere. We are nowhere." He said, "Well, we can't just stand here and get fucking shot. Will we fucking run?" I said, "No. Here he's coming back anyway."

'So this big cunt plodded back. "These details you've given us," he said, "are you 100 per cent sure they are accurate?" I said yes, and he gave us a look as if to say, "You think I'm a fucking idiot?" and then asked, "Well, have you got any ID on you?" I told him no, at which he had another look over us and then said, "Wait there for another fucking minute. I'm coming back," and went off to consult with his mates again.

'We watched them talking to each another in the torchlight, pretty sure we knew what they were saying. I said, "These cunts are going to shoot us, John. We're fucked. You're a stupid bastard, anyway. Dopey fucking Egg Nog Road." He said, "I didn't know there were soldiers along it," and I told him the obvious, "Well, we're bang in trouble."

'The guy came back again and told us, "Right, go." I asked him, "What? Go where?" He said, "Just go, fucking go, get into the car and drive." I reckoned John was thinking the same as me, that as soon as we got in the car and started to move away the firing would start and later on they'd claim we'd tried to escape or assault them. But it would have looked even more suspicious if we'd argued, so we got in, started the motor and drove off with our heads down, all the time expecting the noise of firing and bullets smashing through the windows and into us.

'We gave huge sighs of relief when nothing happened and we saw the lights of their checkpoint vanishing into the distance. John kept telling me, "Manny, I know that big fucker's face," and when I asked him from where, he could only say, "I'm trying to remember. I definitely know him."

'The UDR were only part-time soldiers with jobs outside the British Army. John was wracking his brains and kept saying, "I'm certain I've come across him before." Then the penny dropped. "I know where I've seen that cunt. I'm sure we tried to kill him," he said, and then it all came back and he told me the story: "We were on an operation to track down a UDR bastard and I'm sure it was this cunt who just stopped us. That guy was a farmer with his own place, and we took along Jim MacDonald the shooter."

'I knew who John was referring to and haven't given his real name. The Volunteer was a good friend to both of us.

'"The UDR guy had been under surveillance for a fair time, and the information from the monitoring team was that he was an early riser and was out very sharp every morning, ploughing his fields and looking after his cattle. So I told my unit I wanted them up at four in the morning when we'd go and shoot the bastard. We set off in a car. Jim and the unit went to sleep, and when we arrived, sure enough the guy was out on his tractor ploughing his field. I parked on a lane running alongside the field, woke Jim up and told him, 'Away you go and shoot him while he's busy ploughing. Make sure you get him. He's UDR.'

' "While the rest of us sat there waiting in the car, we heard three shots and naturally assumed Jim had killed the guy. But next thing Jim falls through the hedge screaming, 'That bastard just fucking shot me in the arse.' Apparently Jim had crawled through the field towards the tractor and pulled out his pistol, but the farmer had seen him and pulled his own gun out.

' "When Jim saw this he started to run away, and the farmer fired and shot him in the backside. I had to think what to do. His trousers were soaked in blood and I couldn't take him to a hospital in the north, because the doctors were bound to call the police and we'd all get lifted. So I decided to take him to a hospital about 120 miles away down in the south, and throughout the whole of the journey, Jim was screaming, 'My fucking arse, my fucking arse, the bastard.' That bastard is the guy who's just let us go."

'I'd heard Jim had been shot but had never known why until John told me the story. I wondered whether to ask Jim when I next saw him if he'd ever been sent on any bum jobs, but decided maybe it was best not to take the mickey out of a hitman.'

The farmer had been lucky. But his good fortune was as nothing when compared to that of a Belfast businessman builder.

'Workmen were carrying out renovation work in Spamount Street, and it meant that day after day lorries and vans were trundling in and out. There was dust and muck everywhere and I'd just bought myself my first car. It was only an old banger, but I was like everybody else who finally manages to own their own motor: I was forever nipping out to clean it and make sure it was okay.

'One of the workmen dropped a door on my car and scraped the whole side. It was an accident, but I wasn't amused and went out and asked the guy, "What's the script about this?" He told me, "It's an accident, mate, here's the phone number of our boss: phone him and he'll sort it out. It's our fault, but he'll sort it out."

So I rang this character up. His name was Pat and I explained to him what had happened to my car. "Who are you anyway?" he asked in a very cheeky way. I said, "You'll fucking well find out who I am if you don't give me the money to repair my car." He said, "Well, mate, you'll have to take it out on my chin."

'So I rang up John, told him what had happened and said, "Come and pick me up and go with me to see this Pat character." We drove over to the guy's office. It was in a Loyalist area, and when we walked in his secretary was sitting at her desk. I asked her, "Is Pat in?" and she said, "He's in his office through there," pointing to a door, "but he's busy, you'll need to wait." I told her, "Wait? I don't think so," and we walked straight in. He was sitting in a swivel chair behind a desk. As soon as I was inside, without a word, I grabbed a kettle that was on his desk and before he could speak smashed him right across the head with it.

'Then I grabbed him by the hair and started bouncing his head off the desk. When I let go, John took this character's wallet from his pocket and opened it. The guy was groggy. He was still face down on his desk and asked, "What's happening?" I said, "What's happening is this. You asked me who I was; well, this is who I am. You're not being robbed, but I'm taking the money you owe me to get my car put right." When John and I left, I told Pat's secretary, "I think he needs a cup of tea but you'd better buy a new kettle."

'I reckoned that was the last I'd see of Pat, but about a year later he got a major contract in a strong Republican area to replace every single window and outside door in a huge housing scheme that included blocks of high-rise flats. When I heard who had got the job, I told one of my pals, "I know this cunt and I'm going to see him again. He'll remember me." So I phoned him and he agreed to meet me. We met in a pub and I said, "Listen, Pat, you've got yourself a big contract. I'm going to tell you who I am for real. And then I'm going to tell you what's going to happen. And take it from me, it will happen whether or not you like it, because you have no say in the matter. Sit there and listen." He was a smarmy cunt, tanned and cocky, and we'd done some checks on him. It turned out he had been born in a Republican area, worked hard, made good and got himself a big house in another part of Belfast. That was fair enough.

'I told him about my position with the INLA and said, "Pat, this is what's going to happen, mate. The last time you worked in a Republican area we were having a look at you." He asked why and I went on, "Because we are talking about one of the highest areas of unemployment not just in Belfast but in the whole of Ireland. You were driving in every morning with people from outside, probably some of them Loyalists, but not from where you were doing the work. On this job, you're going to hire local labour."

'Fair play to the guy. He said, "I don't mind doing that, because I'm from this area myself and I've still got family living here." He mentioned their name and I told him I realised I knew them. I said, "That's fine, but I'm here about getting work for local people. That's my only interest." He said, "You've got it. I'll hire 20 men." I told him, "No you won't, Pat. You'll hire 50." He said, "I don't have work for that many," so we negotiated and settled on 30 jobs. And it turned out that the labour exchange sent me along to get one of them.

'So I became a window fitter, even though I'd never fitted a window in my life. Now one day I overheard some of Pat's own people talking about a police station and how every time it was blown up it was Pat's company that did the repairs. He was offering guys £20 an hour to work on these jobs, really big money then. But there was no way we could have this prick doing this. He knew, as did everybody else, what the penalty was for working on police, British Army and British government buildings. We decided to whack the cunt.

'While we waited for the contract we were busy with to be completed, we put him under detailed surveillance until we knew everything there was to know about him: where he lived, where he drank, what time he started out for work, when he finished, how he had a boat he sometimes sailed. We found out he had everything, this guy, but that wasn't going to save him from being wiped off the face of the earth. And yet he turned out to be the luckiest man in Ireland.

'When we were ready to take him, we explained everything to our bosses, how he was working on police stations, and the plan to execute him was passed. "Shoot the cunt" was the order. A unit was called in, shown where he lived, in a really plush area of Belfast, and was left to work out an escape route. There would be two shooters, so two revolvers were delivered, and the next morning off they went to shoot Pat. When they came back an hour and a half later, surprisingly early, I knew something had gone wrong. I asked what had happened and they told me, "You're not going to believe this," and when I heard the story I found it hard to take in.

'They had parked in the street a little way back from where the target lived, so they could see his house without being too near to attract attention. The guys who would be doing the shooting were lying down on the back seat so nobody driving past could see them. After they'd been there a wee while, the driver turned around and said to the two guys in the back, "Here, look at this." They asked, "What is it?" and he repeated, "Look at this."

'The driver had noticed a schoolkid walking down the road, just a wee girl, and then a motor slowing down and pulling alongside her. The geezer at the wheel had put the passenger window down and they saw him gesticulating to the kid. "He's a fucking paedophile trying to pick the kid up. What the fuck do we do?" asked the driver to the gunmen, who were in no doubt what to do next. "We make sure the kid's all right," they said. As they watched, the child went over to the motor, and in an instant the passenger door was open and she was inside. "Fuck this," decided our team, who started up, pulled alongside the stranger's car, wound their windows down and demanded, "Hoi, what the fuck's happening with the wee one?"

'The man asked, "Who are you?" at which the two gunmen sat up and produced the pistols, telling him, "This is who we are." It was at this point that the kid piped up, asking, "Daddy, who are these men?"

'The stranger and his daughter drove off and pulled in at the house next to Pat's. Our unit had to clear off; the job would never be done, because the RUC were sure to tip off Pat that two gunmen had been seen in his street and it wouldn't take a genius to link that to his work for the police. The child had appeared five minutes before Pat was due to show up. Five minutes later, and he would have been dead.'

10

DRUNKEN CABBIE

THERE WERE OTHER TIMES when things did not go according to plan. Looking back more than two decades on, Manny can see the humour in some of the situations in which he found himself. But at the time, it was a deadly serious game in which the losers often ended up dead.

'Getting hold of cars when they were needed for operations was never a problem. Sometimes folks were even glad to have a motor taken off them by a paramilitary organisation, because they knew they'd be recompensed by the British government. I've known car owners who almost begged active service units to steal their motors so they could stick the value up and get a better replacement.

'Our policy was that if we needed to hijack a car for any operation then we would take both motor and driver. A couple of Volunteers would be told to look after the driver while the operation was carried out. This could sometimes need a fair bit of discretion, especially if the motorist wasn't happy at having their car borrowed. What you could not afford was the driver making a beeline for a telephone to tell the police. The solution was very often for the Volunteers to take the person whose motor had been hijacked to a bar or social club where we were known and which was sympathetic to us. The Volunteers would sit with the man or woman, get them a couple of drinks, do their best to keep them happy, and then when we had finished our business we'd telephone them and the owner would then be told they were free to go.

'But we always made sure they knew that we knew who they were. They understood it was in their interests not to give the coppers information about us. And mostly people went along with that. We'd tell the driver if the motor had been used in an operation and maybe even what that operation was, and similarly, if it hadn't been used in something active, perhaps just used for driving us around on surveillance, then we'd tell the motorist that too. "Nothing's happened to your car that you need to worry about," we'd say. "You're quite safe to get back in it and drive it. There are no explosives left in the boot, anything like that."

'I never liked explosives; I had a fear of them and did my best to keep well clear. With explosives, you were either an expert or a menace to everybody around you. Every unit had access to somebody who knew what they were doing with this stuff, and one day one of the INLA units was asked to dispose of some explosives that needed to be used up pretty quickly. They were sweating, getting into a dangerous, unstable state. The unit commander was sent a message telling him to pick up the stuff but was warned, "Listen, you want to get rid of this pretty fucking sharpish." Somebody had been looking after the explosives and making sure they were kept cool. It was once they heated up and sweated that they became really dangerous.

'Rather than waste it, the unit commander decided to put it to good use by blowing up a police station. That required a car, and so a couple of Volunteers were sent out and ordered to hijack one. Sure enough, they did. The driver was a woman who was taken back to one of our social clubs, settled down with a couple of drinks, reassured everything was okay from her point of view, that nobody was going to threaten or touch her, and she was told why her car was needed. She was told she would be staying with people from the unit until the operation was complete and all Volunteers were safely back to base. "No problem," she said. "No problem."

'All appeared fine and well, no reason for things not to go smoothly. Unfortunately, the Volunteers hadn't fully appreciated what it could mean when the driver was a woman. Never thinking there could be any problem, they went off to collect the explosives, which had by now been packed into a bomb, and the device was placed in the car boot ready to be detonated. And then they set off for the police station. On the way, the engine spluttered and stopped. They couldn't get it started again and were asking themselves, "What the fuck's wrong?" when they realised, "There's no fucking petrol in the thing."

'We always drummed it into Volunteers: "If you hijack a car, make sure there's fucking petrol in it." No wonder she was telling us there was no problem as far as she was concerned. She must have thought she'd get her motor back with a full tank of fuel.

'They were a mile short, in the middle of a Loyalist area, when the car conked out. There was nothing for it but to start pushing. There they were, known INLA Volunteers pushing a broken-down motor with a bomb inside through the middle of enemy territory. And while they were at it, an RUC car pulled up alongside asking where they were going and if they wanted help. The coppers obviously assumed these guys were Loyalists. Our people told them, "No thanks, we live just around the corner," and the cops went off laughing.

'That was enough for the Volunteers. Next time they might not be so lucky. So they left the motor by the side of the road and caught a bus home. We never knew what became of the car or the bomb, but the owner was advised to tell the police she didn't know where her car was. This doesn't exactly sound like a well-oiled killing organisation at work; in fact, it was pretty pathetic, and people laugh about it now. But if you were one of those Volunteers shoving that motor and praying nobody recognised you, take it from me, you didn't think there was much to smile about.

'The Volunteers were lucky. Nobody spotted them and their faces didn't even ring bells with the coppers who stopped. But moving around Belfast wasn't always that easy. The RUC had their own way of finding out things, and sometimes the only way some of the guys could travel from one side of the city to another was to dress up as women.

'My mate John was high profile and very well known to the RUC, the British Army and Loyalists. Like me, he was forever being pulled into Castlereagh for questioning. If either of us was seen anywhere out of New Lodge by British Army or police patrols, they'd want to know where we were going. We'd never tell them, of course, but there might be an important reason for being away from home territory, involving a meeting or even an operation, and so we couldn't afford to be stopped. Having a shave and sticking on a wig was one way around it. The Brits didn't get on to this one and we were travelling freely across Belfast in high heels and miniskirts. Of course, you couldn't stick in expenses for the cost of gear or make-up; the wives had to cough those up. But there were occasions when extra expenses were paid.

'One day, two Volunteers were told to hijack a car, take the driver to a club, buy a few drinks and make him or her comfortable. They were given £20 to cover the cost of drinks and were reminded to hand back any change. It turned out the only motor they could get their hands on was a taxi that they brought back to a rendezvous with the other unit members. The two hijackers were left to guard the cabbie and, armed with the money, they headed to a Republican club where they knew no questions would be asked and where there would be plenty of help on hand if it was needed to make sure the driver didn't try doing a runner. The other Volunteers headed off on an operation, telling the pair they'd be as quick as security allowed.

'In the club, hijackers and hijacked found themselves getting on famously. The cabbie was having a great time, knocking back free drinks, and rather than be accused of being unsociable his hosts were happy to join him. And all the time other drinkers were watching the three.

'After a couple of hours, the Volunteers had to tell the cabbie, "Sorry, mate, that's us skint, we only had 20 quid." But that didn't put the taxi driver off. He was enjoying himself so much he wanted to carry on boozing. He reached into the bag where he kept his takings and pulled out a fistful of loose change. "You're all right, I've got a good few quid here," he said, and the three of them got legless. By then, the operation using the taxi was long done, and the Volunteers had been telephoned at the club and told to let the cabbie know he could have his motor back. It was parked outside the club. If they had passed on the message, it had been drowned in drink, because I got a phone call from the guy running the club, who told me, "Listen, Manny, you better get up here. Two of your guys are in with a stranger and the three of them are plastered. They're even challenging everybody in the club to play them a game of pool for £100."

'So I called on John and the two of us shot up to the club, and right enough the three of them were absolutely steaming. We told the taxi driver, "Go and get your car, mate, and go home," but John pointed out, "You can't let him drive, he's totally legless." The cabbie said, "Fuck you, I want my fucking motor," and off he went. We couldn't believe it but weren't surprised when the Volunteers said that as they were walking home they saw the cab had pranged into another motor and somebody had called an ambulance. Evidently the cabbie ended up in hospital, although he wasn't seriously hurt. Incidents like this were funny. But sometimes tragedy was just around the corner. People died, and that's not so funny.

'Another incident that wasn't very funny at the time, although it's since been the subject of a good few laughs, concerned a

Volunteer, John M., who had the nickname "Huck". I never found out the source of that tag. He had the letters H, U, C and K tattooed on the fingers of one of his hands.

'Huck had followed the same route as me, originally joining the IRA and then transferring to the INLA. One day, his unit was told to plant an incendiary bomb intended to blow up one of the Belfast Loyalists. The team hijacked a car, and while the driver was being minded, the rest set off to track down the target. As they were travelling, Huck sat in the back seat with the bomb under his feet. The route took them around a lot of bends and the road wasn't too even, with the result that the bomb was wobbling around on the floor. One of the Volunteers said to Huck, "Put your hand on it to keep it steady. We don't want the fucking thing going off in the car. But be bloody careful."

'Huck put a hand down to hold the device, and as he did so he triggered the detonator, blowing all his fingers off. The organisation managed to get Huck to a hospital across the border and he was there for a while. Not long after he had returned to Belfast, cops knocked at his door and told him he was being arrested on suspicion of planting a bomb. Huck protested, but they took him off, and on the way one of them spotted Huck's bandaged hand and asked him what had happened. Huck said he'd had an accident at work, which was, in a sense, true.

'At the cop shop he was seated in an interview room and a couple of detectives gave him the usual about having reason to believe he'd been in a car in which a bomb had prematurely exploded. They wanted to know about the intended target and who else had been with Huck. He feigned complete ignorance of any wrongdoing and so one of the cops told Huck, "Look, we have evidence that you were there." Huck asked, "What evidence?" and the copper pulled a plastic bag out from a drawer. "This evidence," he said, and when Huck asked, "What is it?" the copper emptied the bag out on to the table between them, and out dropped Huck's fingers. The copper neatly arranged them to form the letters HUCK. "We found them in the car," he said. "Want them back?" Huck said, "Fuck you."'

Another bomb plot that didn't quite work out showed just how ingenious Volunteers could sometimes be. The British Army set up points on the roofs of a number of high-rise flats. It was from one of these that snipers had shot at innocent civilians during the New Lodge massacre. Divis Tower was another block on which the British Army had built an observation post. These posts were a major source of irritation to Republican paramilitaries, who wanted to be able to move about freely and unobserved.

'It didn't matter which organisation you were in: everybody wanted something done. It would be difficult to attack them from the ground because of the risk of causing casualties to people living in the flats. We relied on these people for help and support, and we believed we were there to protect them. The posts were well guarded too. The Brits had taken over the top two floors of the Divis Flats to prevent anyone getting near, and allowed their personnel to stay up there indefinitely. We had them on the go; they were so worried that they had to take their men in and out by helicopter, and bring in supplies like food the same way, because it was too dangerous for them to come on to the streets.

'We asked ourselves, "How can we get these cunts off these roofs?" And then one of the Volunteers came up with a brilliant idea. He reckoned it was possible to strap a small bomb onto a model aeroplane and with the use of a remote control fly the thing right up to the top of the tower blocks and crash-land the plane, detonating the bomb at the same time. The theory was good and he was given the go-ahead to do some trials.

'The idea worked: he found the plane could carry a lightweight package. We tried one plane with a grenade strapped to it and it got half way up a high-rise block, but then went out of control, hit the outside wall and blew everybody's windows out. The people inside went ballistic, so we abandoned that plan. And when he tried using even a small bomb, the weight was too much and the toy crashed – fortunately on the ground, without causing damage or hurting any civilians or Volunteers. In the end, we just had to suffer the posts through the Troubles.

'Most units carried out, on average, two operations a month, sometimes more. These were mostly sniping and setting booby traps. Then we went into a phase where we believed it was just as important to attack the British economy as to bomb and shoot its soldiers. So we started an economic war, targeting stores owned by big English firms.

'One of our guys had this bright idea of how to destroy or at least cause major damage to a big superstore without having to plant an explosive device, as these often injured innocent Republican civilians and sympathisers. So one day he went into the store to the clothing department and asked to try on a suit. The assistant was most helpful, and suggested he try on the jacket first, which our man did. While he was parading up and down, looking at himself in the mirrors, he slipped an incendiary bomb into the inside pocket. Then he handed the jacket back to the assistant saying he wasn't quite sure and would maybe come back with his wife for a second opinion.

'As he was making a hasty clear-off from the shop before the incendiary went off, the assistant, about to hang the jacket back on the peg, must have noticed the jacket was on the heavy side. He patted the pocket, felt a bulge and went dashing after the Volunteer, shouting, "Sir, sir you've left something in the pocket." Our man shot off like a turkey spotting the butcher's van at Christmas.

'Speaking of Christmas, one year one of the Volunteers had been out in the city centre having a beer when he met up with an old pal, and the meeting had some bizarre consequences. His wife had told him to get a turkey for the Christmas dinner. He did and was carefully carrying it home when he got caught short and nipped into an alley to relieve himself. While he did so, he put the bag with the turkey in it on the ground. He heard a noise, and when he looked up it was to see bag and turkey disappearing down the street in the teeth of a dog owned by a local family.

'By the time the Volunteer caught up with the dog the turkey was a mess, and when the man got home his missus gave him a right old ear-bashing. He was furious and at the next unit meeting said he had something special he wanted to bring up. He told the story of the runaway turkey and then astonished everybody by demanding, "I want this fucking dog shot." We thought he was kidding, but he got really hot under the collar: "It's no laughing matter; the dog has to be shot."

'We tried telling him not to be so daft, but he insisted. It was a matter of honour, he said. Running off with the bird was the equivalent of stealing, and the dog should be treated like any other thief and shot. Somebody jokingly asked if the dog should be kneecapped. "I don't fucking care what you do, just shoot it," he said. "I you don't shoot it, I'll shoot it." It was pointed out that this would antagonise the dog's owners. Eventually the dog was granted an amnesty, but the Volunteer never forgave it.'

Elsewhere in Belfast, another dog was determined to make a name for himself. Johnny 'Mad Dog' Adair's intended career as a hard man had hardly got off to an auspicious start when as a teenager the UDA threatened to kneecap him for assaulting an old-age pensioner. Eventually Adair was allowed into the UDA and joined C8, an active unit that was part of the West Brigade's 'C' Company. Adair would never be taken seriously by Republicans or by many on the Loyalist side, but his path and that of Manny would eventually cross.

11

MISCHIEVOUS MA

MANNY CAME TO LOOK UPON spells at Castlereagh interrogation centre as an occupational hazard. But the centre would list another McDonnell among its list of inmates: his mother, Nellie. Until the end of her days, she remained as devoted to the Republican cause as ever, never wavering in her distaste for those denying her the right to live in a united Ireland. She was well known in New Lodge as a lady never afraid to offer her views on the situation that had ripped Belfast apart.

One night, while sitting quietly at home, she was unaware that close by was an active service unit, mostly likely belonging to the IRA, that had attempted to ambush a British Army patrol as it drove through New Lodge. The plan was to detonate a bomb at the moment the soldiers passed, but the device was not yet in place when the patrol arrived and the attack failed. However, the unit was spotted and British soldiers gave chase, the Volunteers fleeing on foot and dispersing among the back streets, hiding in gardens and yards. One of them still carried a detonator. To be found with it would certainly result in at best a long jail sentence, at worst being shot. And so as he rushed down a back lane he simply lobbed the detonator over a wall.

Soldiers began searching for men and weapons and discovered the device. The name on the rent book for the occupant responsible for the yard was Nellie, by now well into her 70s. Her name quickly rang a bell with the RUC. She was the mother of a known INLA activist. Despite her age and the protests of her family and neighbours, police arrested Nellie, accused her of conspiracy in the bomb plot and drove her off to Castlereagh. It was a decision they were about to regret. Nellie would remain at the centre for two nights, nights of misery for her captors.

'A few of the family were sitting in her house wondering what to do when there was a knock at the door and a copper was standing there. "We want your ma's St Christopher pendant, her copy of the Prayer to Saint Anthony, her copy of the Prayer to Saint Bernadette, her copy of the Prayer . . ." He held up a long list. We looked them out, handed them over and off he went. A few hours later, the same guy was back. "She now wants her headache tablets, the pills she takes for her legs, her heart tablets . . ." and again he held out a list. "How's it going?" we asked. The guy looked thoroughly pissed off. "We're just getting fucked around," he admitted.

'Next day the papers had stories about a woman pensioner being arrested. A different cop came to the door. "Your Ma wants her reading glasses, her . . ." and showed us another list. "It's not fair putting an old lady through this," we told him. "Not fair on us, you mean," he said.

'Ma came home after a couple of days. The cops knew full well she had nothing to do with a bomb or any detonator. They probably took her in to upset me, but it backfired not just on the RUC but on the IRA. She buttonholed one of their guys who lived in New Lodge and told him, "I was locked up at Castlereagh by the coppers for two days because of yous. I want compensation for loss of liberty. I'm entitled to some money for being a political prisoner." She kept on badgering the guy but didn't get anything. At least the coppers never came back.'

As one McDonnell went home, another would shortly pass through the doors of Castlereagh. The INLA had issued a blanket threat to murder members of any British sports teams visiting Northern Ireland, but many chose to ignore the warning. In February 1985, the organisation planted a bomb close to Windsor Park, Belfast, where the Northern Ireland soccer team was playing against England in a World Cup qualifying match. An hour into the game the device exploded. Nobody was hurt and the INLA acknowledged responsibility. Manny and other Volunteers were arrested and taken to Castlereagh for questioning.

'While we were sitting in one of the interrogation rooms, a copper came in and said, "We're going to bring in somebody right now who can identify you from the point where you get out of your car right through to planting the bomb, walking away, getting into another motor and driving off. She's outside and will come in to point you out." And in walked this fat woman who pointed to me and said, "Yes, he's the one, I saw him."

'It turned out she worked at Castlereagh and it was just one more trick by the coppers, hoping I or somebody else would be shaken up through having been taken to the centre and would just own up and confess. We burst out laughing. There was no way they could pin that on anybody and they had to let us go. We might have lived on our nerves, but that applied to the cops all the time. When they finished duty they were on their own, and even at home they had to sleep with one eye open, never knowing whether if they answered a knock at the door they might open it to find themselves looking into the barrel of a gun.'

Two years later in a near carbon-copy attack, the INLA left another bomb near Windsor Park. It was defused after a warning was telephoned. But the message was clear: that the threat of two years previously still applied. 'It was incidents like these, the dragging away of Ma and the blatant attempt at trickery, that kept my commitment to the cause. We still wanted the Brits out, not simply British Army off the streets; we wanted anything with a British interest or influence in Ireland to get on a boat or plane and go.'

Some sports teams from Britain called off planned visits as a direct result of the bomb threats. But just as the INLA and other Republican organisations had successes, there were failures too. At times these setbacks could be directly put down to information passed to the RUC and British Army by informers. Touts would always be a tumour that must be rooted out and dealt with. The treatment of them was ruthless. Even friends were not spared.

In 1983, Gerard 'Sparky' Barkley was suspected of passing information to the police about the family of supergrass Harry Kirkpatrick. Barkley was invited to a meeting at the home of then INLA mastermind Dominic McGlinchey, and as he sipped tea with McGlinchey's wife, his host crept up behind and blasted him in the back of the head.

Two years later, INLA Volunteer James Burnett from South Dublin was lured to a meeting with other comrades and killed. It was said after his bound and hooded body was discovered dumped by a roadside that he had admitted 'under interrogation' to giving information about past, ongoing and planned operations, the locations of arms dumps and safe houses, and the names of other members. After his murder, the INLA offered a seven-day amnesty, promising not to kill anyone who came forward to confess. The alternative, it would seem, was death.

On occasions, touts passed on tips to police and British Army handlers that had dire consequences. In December 1981, two IRA Volunteers were shot dead when they walked into an SAS unit waiting at an arms dump in Coalisland; a Volunteer was killed in July 1984 during an attack on a factory in Tyrone; two others died in December that same year trying to murder a UDR reservist in Londonderry; three Volunteers died after being ambushed at an arms dump at Strabane; and in 1987, an eight-strong IRA active service unit was wiped out as it attacked Loughgall police station, County Armargh. In each case the SAS was responsible, acting with the help of informers. There were never more than 20 SAS members in Northern Ireland at any one time, but just their presence was enough to set the nerves of paramilitaries jangling.

'My unit decided to take a wee break because we got word about the SAS being in town, and when they arrived, we left, because they weren't to be fucked about with. One of our guys was shot in the stomach and leg after going to an arms cache at a lock-up garage in Hillman Street and finding two SAS people waiting and jumping down from the rafters. We were in a car waiting for our man to come back when these two cunts came haring out waving guns. So when word came that the SAS were about, we left, because we knew they were there to do somebody and they didn't mess around. We decided to go on a fishing expedition, the whole unit, five madmen in the car.

'We ended up near a village just outside Cork and set off to fish. We found this river and had settled down with the rods, fishing happily away, when this character came up from behind, a fucking Englishman, and asked what we were doing. "You are fishing in my river," he shouted. "Pack up your stuff and go." I turned around and asked the guy, "What do you mean your river? You're a fucking Englishman. How can an Englishman own a fucking river in the middle of Cork?" He said, "If you don't leave this land, I'll get the police." So there we were, sitting pondering whether to do him or leave.

'We couldn't believe an English guy was telling Irishmen they couldn't fish in a river in Cork. We ended up by just leaving because he was ready to phone the cops. The poor guy didn't know he was talking to a full active service unit. But it was the attitude of arrogant twats like him that caused so much antagonism towards the Brits.

'We could have dealt with him, of course, but would that have furthered our cause? In any case, there were others who deserved punishment all the more. We knew there were people out there who were purely and simply thugs, who would go out and break people's legs with baseball bats. We didn't like these sorts of people and called them tyre crushers. They were the types who had tried to join an active service unit but had been knocked back and then had become some sort of civil police force, going about snapping kids' legs for stealing cars, self-styled vigilantes. We had our own people who took care of housebreakers and drug dealers, paedophiles, abusers and muggers. I was brought up to believe that being a Republican meant being totally against drug dealing, but we knew we had drug dealers in our ranks and were trying to weed them out.'

Criminals learned to expect no mercy, as John George, a 26-year-old Catholic, discovered. George had been warned by the INLA to behave. When he ignored threats, a gunman burst into his Belfast home in April 1984 and shot him dead. The crime rate in the area dropped.

Manny left these matters to others. His bosses regarded him as too valuable to risk on such relatively trivial matters. They had other plans for him. The INLA had already expanded its fields of activity outside Northern Ireland. It had blown up Airey Neave in London, exploded bombs in Germany, and delivered an incendiary parcel bomb to Margaret Thatcher's Downing Street office, injuring an employee. Now it decided to hit London even harder by attacking British businesses and government centres there.

Manny was sent to the capital to look for potential targets. He went alone but did not stay long, and the story put out among New Lodge neighbours was that he had gone to England to look for work. It was important to build some sort of cover because it would not be long before his absence from the streets was noticed by the RUC or the British Army and before informers would be contacted and asked to find out where he was and what he was up to.

It was a responsible role, but his commanders had total faith in him. He had been one of their youngest unit leaders when appointed and had more than earned his spurs. In London, he was met by Gerard Mackin, who he knew from Belfast. At the time, Mackin was thought of as a small-time crook with a history of petty crime and normally would have been an ideal terrorist-organisation sleeper. As in the case of hundreds of other Irishmen, there was no reason for the police or Special Branch to doubt the story that Manny had gone to London searching for work. It meant he had freedom to move about London without arousing suspicion.

Manny's initial visit lasted only a couple of weeks. He needed to return to Belfast to reinforce his cover. He found temporary work as a painter on building sites in Cricklewood and Southwark and accommodation with other Irishmen in Cricklewood. But the natural thing would have been to return home to discuss with his family whether they wanted to move to England with him.

That would be the story his family and friends would spread, intending it to reach the ears of the RUC. It would also leave the door open for him to head back to London. He did so, staying once more only a couple of weeks before going back home, where he was able to meet up with and report to his INLA commanders.

But his disappearances from Belfast had been noticed. Where was he? Security services began making routine searches of arrivals at English ports and airports. It was clear his arrival at Heathrow, probably on the second occasion, had ticked warning boxes, his name already having been passed to security-service watchers. It was again flagged up when he returned for a third time, and now he was placed under intensive surveillance.

'In London I went back to working on the building site. Sally and the children had still stayed behind in Spamount Street, so when I wasn't at work I had plenty of time to look around. But Special Branch had obviously been watching when I came through the airport and I was followed back to the flat I was sharing with six others in Cricklewood. One morning the coppers just came straight in through the doors and windows. They had a map of the house showing where each bedroom was and who was in each bedroom. By sheer chance I was upstairs visiting somebody else and they were expecting me to be downstairs, but they went through the whole house and found me.

'They put plastic bags over the hands, feet and hair of everybody there, presumably looking for any traces of weapons or weapons having been discharged. They knew who they were looking for and eventually arrested three of us and took us to Paddington Green police station, where they put us in silent cells, so we could not communicate with one another.'

Paddington Green was the number-one high-security police station in Britain. It was where anybody suspected of being involved in terrorism was taken for questioning. The station had been specially adapted to make it impregnable to attack, and the silent cells to which terrorists were allocated were separated from the rest of the complex, making them effectively a police station within a police station. One purpose of this segregation was to intensify the feeling among prisoners that they were wholly cut off from the outside work and thus to make them more vulnerable to unburdening themselves of secrets and information.

'We were questioned for five days and it was obvious they already knew everything about us. We'd been watched. They were right on top of us. We had been looking at people and places who could have been potential targets, and the interrogators went through every one of my movements, demanding to know why I had been to such and such a place at such and such a time. I was used to questioning. I'd sat facing interrogators often enough at Castlereagh and knew the rules of the game. They threw the dice and I ignored the numbers that came up. I said nothing.

'As the time drew near when they'd either have to charge me or let me go, they simply decided that I was a member of the INLA, a proscribed organisation, and made me the subject of a banning order. I was taken to the airport and told that if I set foot in England, Scotland or Wales again during the next seven years

I would be automatically arrested and jailed. Then they put me on a plane back to Belfast. The other two guys held with me were released without charge or any form of ban being issued.'

His cover blown, INLA commanders appreciated it would be risking, time, money and the loss of a top-class resource by sending Manny back into England through another airport or even a port. The organisation had been encouraged by the publicity its attacks in West Germany, at Hamburg and Herford, had achieved. The realisation that the INLA's tentacles stretched so far from home increased pressure on British government security resources.

At another meeting of commanders, Manny was briefed about a further special mission. This time his destination was Bonn, which was to be a base from which he would scout out new targets in West Germany. The plan was for him to find work on one of the many building sites in the area hiring foreign labour.

But his visit to Germany was over from the moment he arrived. He had been spotted at Belfast airport and the Germany authorities were warned to expect him. As soon as he entered the Bonn airport building he was stopped, taken to one side, placed in a small interview room, and told he was unwelcome and would not be allowed to enter. Eight hours later he found himself back on an aeroplane, this time heading home. He arrived back to find himself in the middle of a major paramilitary war – between his fellow INLA Volunteers.

12

THE LONG MATCH

HAVING FAILED TO SCORE in London and then having been red carded even before kick-off in Germany, Manny decided a brief holiday in a new field of play was in order, so he thought it was time to renew his relationship with Glasgow and Paradise by travelling to watch Celtic entertain Aberdeen. His trip would have a dual purpose in that it would give him the chance to meet up with some Republican sympathisers. It was a match that would end with a very lengthy stretch of extra time.

He was not alone in coming to the notice of the police. Paul Ferris had been given a three-year jail sentence for possessing a shotgun. Ferris had then, and still does, strenuously deny the prosecution version that he had been looking to buy guns to start a new right-wing movement. This bizarre allegation was the result of claims made by a UDA armourer and supergrass. It had resulted in Ferris being the subject of detailed surveillance by the security services.

The tout was Andrew Robertson, a one-time Glasgow University student from the Bridgeton district of the city. Robertson had been arrested on a theft charge and, according to the prosecution at his trial in 1987, attempted to wriggle out of this by doing a deal with the police. Among the songs he sang to local and Special Branch officers was one of how Glasgow Rangers supporters travelling to attend the Skol Cup final in October 1986 between the Old Firm had smuggled explosives back with them on the ferry from Stranraer, and which were to be used for terrorist acts in the Republic. His lyric continued with claims these materials had been bought from members of the Territorial Army in Scotland.

The outcome of this was that police found plastic explosives and detonators buried in a field in Easterhouse, in the east end of Glasgow, and then discovered guns in a canal. As a consequence, Robertson was jailed for 12 years, and five men he had grassed up also went to prison for terms ranging between a few months and nine years.

The trial judge described Robertson as 'dishonest, determined and unscrupulous', a description with which many others agreed. Paul Ferris was among them and made his feelings known to Robertson. According to his book *The Ferris Conspiracy*, Ferris recounts what happened when he and Robertson were both on remand in Glasgow's Barlinnie jail awaiting their respective trials and another inmate pointed Robertson out to him: 'Waiting till he came up the landing, I pulled the grass into an empty cell and gave him the most severe barehanded beating I could muster, making sure he knew who I was. Minutes later, the riot bell sounded. Robertson was in the hospital wing with a broken nose and other injuries.'

Lots of others hoped they would have the same opportunity for an encounter with Robertson. But his deal with the police included being given protection in prison – he would spend most of his years in solitary confinement for his own protection – and a new identity when he was eventually released. One aspect in which Robertson and Paul Ferris shared a common view was that both said they had been set up by the police, a not uncommon theme echoing around the landings of Barlinnie and other Scottish nicks.

Manny, meanwhile, without realising it, was on his way to join them.

'Having been sent back to Ireland from Germany, I went straight back into my old routine. But then one of my brothers convinced me I needed a break and should join him on a supporters' coach going to Glasgow for the Skol Cup final. Looking back, I was stupid to even think of attending because I was now the subject of a blanket banning order that applied to Scotland just as much as it did to England.

'We went over on the Friday and were booked in to a hotel in Glasgow overnight. I was so confident that I'd be able to sneak in and out of Scotland that I'd made arrangements to take Sally out the night after we got back from the match. But I never even got to the game; in fact, I never even got to the landing, as I was arrested as I stepped on the gangplank of the ferry at Stranraer. The police were waiting. Obviously I'd either been clocked when the bus boarded the ferry in Belfast or by one of the coppers who always came over on ferries to eye up who was on board. Then they would have radioed ahead to their mates at Stranraer.

'They stopped me and demanded to know my name. I told them I was Edward Peter Giles and showed documentation that actually belonged to my brother-in-law. When I gave that name, one of the coppers burst out laughing. I was taken to the local police station and then remanded in custody in Dumfries jail while my brother got straight on the telephone to Sally to tell her I'd been arrested and probably wouldn't be back that night.

'Eventually I appeared before Stranraer Sheriff Court charged with committing a breach of a banning order made under the Prevention of Terrorism Act, and carrying false papers. I noticed three cops sitting in the courtroom and recognised them. They were from Belfast and had travelled over just to make sure everything went as they expected. They came over while we waited for the sheriff to come to a decision and told me, "Manny you're getting two years." I'd expected a slap on the wrist and to be put back on the boat again. I'd even got a message to Sally to tell her I'd be home to finally take her out.

'But it was a put-up job. Just as the coppers had said I would, I was jailed for two years for breaching the banning order and for six months for claiming to be Edward Peter Giles. I thought the sentence was very harsh indeed. It wasn't nice at all. For an offence like that it was ridiculous. If it had been for some serious criminal offence then okay, but not for something like going to watch a football game. It goes without saying that the coppers were quite happy about how it ended up: as I was being taken out of the courtroom I noticed they were smiling.

'After I was jailed I went back to Dumfries and was then moved to Barlinnie, where I was treated like some sort of special case. A report on me must have followed me to the Bar-L because I remember meeting a governor and he said, "You're the real deal." I asked, "What do you fucking mean?" And he said, "We've a lot of fannies in here calling themselves IRA men and INLA men, but apparently you're the real thing, the real deal." I was still on the top of my form and I said, "Listen, I don't recognise you or any of this gang here; as far as I'm concerned I'm a prisoner of war, I have been captured by you people. I am not going to cooperate in any shape or form, I am not going to wear your fucking uniform, I am not complying with your fucking rules, I am just not cooperating, and you can put that in your fucking pipe and smoke it and do what you want with me. But if you do give me any grief or hassle and I get close to the phone I will get you sorted."

'Throughout the time I was in prison, I was in regular contact with my Republican comrades. Sally had been disgusted by the severity of my sentence and came over to visit me once every three months. It was a real trek for her, but at least her expenses were paid for. When she arrived we had the visiting room to ourselves with at least ten screws wearing riot shields, helmets, body armour and so on in a circle around us. Even so, she still managed to smuggle in what we called 'coms', notes written on cigarette papers. She used to pass these to me all the time. These were basically reports of what was going on, what sort of things the Volunteers had done, what type of things they were up to, what the plans were for me when I got out, what things had changed and how. Knowing I hadn't been forgotten helped my morale.

'At one time in Barlinnie I was getting hassle from a particular screw. I was told he was ex-Army and when he found out my history he went out of his way to give me a hard time. So I reported this back to my comrades in Belfast. They rang up Barlinnie and told a social worker to pass a message on to this idiot that I was a Republican prisoner and if he kept up his hassle and harassment he would be shot dead.

'His bullying stopped, but I was then moved to Shotts, where I told a governor there exactly what I'd said to his colleague at Barlinnie. I wanted to make sure he knew where both of us stood. "You can hold me here for two fucking years. I don't give a fuck about your poxy parole or your poxy good behaviour. You can take every single day of remission I'm entitled to away from me; I just don't care, because what you can't do is stop me getting out after two years. And remember this, when I am out, neither you nor anybody else can stop me coming after you."

'By the time I reached Shotts, Paul had already been transferred there. I was sitting in my cell one day when a screw opened the door and said, "Paul Ferris wants to see you." I asked him, "Who the fuck is Paul Ferris? I'm not being told to see anybody, I'm not going to see any cunt. I'm not going to see any Paul Ferris. I don't know who he is." But Paul kept sending over messages day in day out asking would I go and meet him and so eventually I did. He was on the verge of getting out by this time. He seemed all right, but I still had my Republican hat on and viewed everybody with suspicion.

'What was unusual about Paul and me being in Shotts was that it was supposed only hold guys who were doing at least four years. But he was on a three and me a two. In other nicks, that might have pointed to us having committed offences that meant we needed to be protected from other inmates. But that was certainly not the case with either of us.

'I didn't think a lot of him the first time I saw him. He was a skinny wee runt in a pair of pyjamas. But a nice enough guy all the same, pleasant and very helpful. The fact was, though, that I was a Republican and he was a criminal, and back home those didn't mix.

'He told me his name was Paul Ferris and said, "Anything you need, just ask and I'll get it for you. If there's any hassle, let me know and I'll sort it out." He said he was a Republican and after hearing a member of the IRA was in the jail wanted to meet him to see if he could help in any way. I was sceptical because so many people came on with that, but Paul was as good as his word.

'We got to know each other and spent a lot of time talking. He used to tell me about his brother Billy, who was doing a lifer, and how Billy was in, and friendly, with IRA prisoners in England. Often Paul's cell would be packed with guys and we would wait until we could talk alone together. I would never speak about my Republican stuff, but all of us would natter generally about our backgrounds, how we got caught, what we would do next time not to get caught.

'We had some good nights in that jail, partying, drinking whisky and other booze that was smuggled in by our visitors. It was a new prison and the screws hadn't got all the dodges covered yet. But some of them didn't really care anyway; all they wanted was a quiet life. Sometimes we'd be sitting in a cell scoffing cream cakes and smoking hash and screws would walk past and never say a word. Once a screw even helped me back to my cell after I got legless on smuggled whisky.

'Paul introduced me to a lot of other guys. One of his closest friends was Gerry Rae, who'd been convicted of robbery. Another guy I saw from time to time was Gerald McQuade, who would sadly make the headlines a few years later.

'It wasn't easy for Paul and me to meet up because we were in different halls. But then I beat up one of the medical staff, attacking him with a fire extinguisher. I beat fuck out of this guy, wellied him while he was trying to hide under a table. One of my hands had been broken years earlier in a Gaelic football accident. It kept on breaking and it broke in Shotts, and I said I needed to go to hospital to have it fixed, but this screw refused. I warned him that unless something was done I'd end up breaking somebody's nose, and when nothing happened I attacked him.

'They dragged me off to segregation, where I spent the remaining eight or nine months of the sentence. Paul would send down every now and again asking if everything was all right and wanting to know if there was anything he could do and if I wanted him to get anything down to me. Whatever I asked for, he organised: biscuits, a bit of tobacco, maybe reading material, but never drugs. Then he found he was being released and sent down an address with a number for me to contact him when I got out. Paul used to organise a place for Sally to stay when she came over, would get her picked up, brought to the jail, dropped back again to the airport or wherever. He was very thoughtful.

'After visits from Sally, I'd always find my cell in segregation had been wrecked and Loyalists in there had pissed all over my bedding. I suppose that was the contribution of these gallant boys to the war in Northern Ireland.

'Each day one of the prison governors would check on all the prisoners in segregation. I used to make a point of being up and ready to see him, I'd be shaved and stood up, and he would walk in and say the same thing every time: "Good morning my little terrorist friend." I used to reply, "I'm not the terrorist, you're the fucking terrorist."

'Once it was around midday when he showed up and I decided I wasn't going to stand up for him. He came into the cell and the screw said, "Stand up for the governor." I said, "I won't, I'm sitting here eating my meal." The screw again said, "Stand up for the governor," and I told him no. At that, the governor came over and leaned over my shoulder and I turned and looked at him and said, "You're putting me off my fucking dinner." It was a battle of wills between him and me for the final eight months of my sentence, all of it in segregation.

'The official rule was that after 30 days in solitary there had to be a review of your case. When my spell ended, a governor came to see me and said they'd done a review and I was being kept in for a further 30 days. The same thing happened at the end of that 30, but by then they had reached the maximum time their authority allowed them to keep me in solitary confinement. But the governor didn't want me back in mainstream and so the Home Office was brought into it. They didn't want me returning to mainstream either and so I remained out of circulation for the remainder of the sentence.

'When the day of my release finally came, there was a big problem because technically the minute I stepped outside the jail I'd be in breach of my banning order again. They scratched their heads over what to do and decided to release me in my cell, then take me straight to a police car and drive me to Glasgow airport and put me on a flight back to Belfast, where I was met by the RUC in Belfast City airport.

'They took me into a room and I spent ten minutes listening to the usual crap: "You're home. Is there any point in telling you not to get involved?" I didn't even reply. They knew what my answer would be and simply released me. When I reached home, I said to Sally, "That was the longest football match in history!"

'My Republican comrades visited me at Spamount Street to give me some money to help me get back on my feet. They told me, "Take your time deciding what you want to do. Think about whether you want to carry on. There's no rush and no pressure on you. Everybody will understand if you feel you're not up to continuing running the unit. When you want to report back, just turn up; if you don't then just don't show. Nobody is going to think badly of you, you've already done as much as anyone could expect."

'But even before they had arrived, I'd known what my plans were. I'd come to a decision long ago in prison and knew I would always return to my unit. Being arrested and locked up for two years for basically wanting to watch a football match had hardened my resolve and determination to fight for what I believed. I took a six-week break and then returned to active service. A couple of years later, for a reason I never knew, I was told the banning order had been lifted.

'After I'd left prison I had received phone calls from Paul. He came over to Belfast for a short break with some of his family. Our conversations were very general; nothing important or of any significance was ever discussed, because we knew the chances were that somebody was listening in. But he always emphasised, "If you ever get the chance to come back over to Scotland, make sure you look me up." I promised I would, and it was a promise I told myself I would keep.'

13

IPLO

WITHIN THE RANKS OF THE INLA there had long been growing disquiet and dissent. There were numerous reasons why cracks in the organisation were widening into chasms. The betrayal of so many colleagues by supergrass Harry Kirkpatrick had left those who escaped his venom wondering if they might still be next to hear the RUC and British Army Land Rovers rumbling up to their doors. Kirkpatrick had succeeded in doing what the police, soldiers and Loyalists had failed to achieve, which was to effectively pull the carpet out from under the INLA and the IRSP.

It wasn't just Kirkpatrick's treachery that now caused so much dispute and feuding. The bombing of the Droppin Well Inn had been a massive kick in the face to the British Army, but at the same time it had taken the lives of those young Irish people on who both Republican and Loyalist organisations would depend to carry on the fight in the future.

As a propaganda exercise, the deaths of those civilians had turned the incident into a near disaster, because among the killed and mutilated were Catholics. Patricia Cooke was a young Catholic who had been horribly injured in the blast and died ten days later in hospital. And Catholic paramilitaries were not there to destroy Catholics or antagonise those very communities on who they depended. The bombing caused murmurings among the INLA rank and file as to whether by attacking civilians the organisation was heading in the right direction.

The police had determined those responsible for the outrage would not escape, no matter long it took to track them down. The finger of suspicion pointed at Dominic McGlinchey, who denied planting the bomb but admitted involvement in the planning. That brought increased heat not just on McGlinchey but on everyone associated with him. It took nearly four years, but at least some of the bombers were caught. Anna Moore, aged 40, and her sister Helena Semple, 29, both from the Bogside, Londonderry, along with Semple's partner Eamon Moore, 25, and Patrick Shotter, 40, the boyfriend of Anna Moore's daughter Jacqueline Ann Moore, aged 19, were all jailed for life. Jacqueline was jailed for ten years for manslaughter when it was agreed she had been forced into taking part. While Anna was serving her 17 life sentences, she not only severed her links with the INLA but went on to marry an Ulster Defence Association member who had been jailed for murder. The marriage did not last, but like her, others were becoming disillusioned. Some believed a much harder line was required, a more violent approach.

While Manny was in jail, the arguing and infighting had come to a head and a core of the INLA, including Gerard Steenson, Manny's good friend Jimmy Brown and Martin 'Rook' O'Prey, had broken away and set up the Irish People's Liberation Organisation. At Brown's behest, a political wing, the Republican Socialist Collective, was also formed. That set off a furious explosion of murders, with INLA and IPLO supporters threatening to wipe out the other.

Among the victims was Doctor Death, Gerard Steenson. He had argued the INLA was an ineffective paramilitary group that instead of concentrating on attacking those wearing the uniforms of the RUC and the British Army had fallen into the trap of sectarian violence. And he warned that too many of its leaders had become involved in criminality for their own benefit, an allegation that would come to be levelled at the IPLO.

Steenson had been on a drinking spree one night and was spotted by his former comrades as he and a friend drove through Ballymurphy. Their car was raked by gunfire and both later died in hospital.

Manny knew he would have to decide whether to remain with the INLA or join the IPLO. His own beliefs mirrored those of the latter.

'I never saw romance or glory in what I was doing. I was never one of those who hung flags from my windows or shouted from the rooftops for others to follow me charging the British Army or the Loyalist barricades. I was in it simply because I wanted to live in a united Ireland free from British rule.

'I knew there were people in it for their own selves, for what they could get out of it, and after a while you could spot them. And there were some who gloried in being called "terrorists", but I wasn't a terrorist and I didn't regard what I did as terrorism. We saw it as our country being illegally invaded by the British Army backed up by Loyalist organisations and the RUC and we wanted to put an end to that.

'At the start I was in it to do as much damage as I could to anybody who stood in our way, but after a while, when I'd read the history of our country and seen how there were Presbyterians and Protestants who had suffered fighting for a united Ireland, it changed my views and made me realise they had as much right to be in Ireland we did.

'The infighting was partly about a mistrust of the INLA leadership, partly because we didn't believe it was being run in the right way and partly because people were looking on us with suspicion. They thought we were involved in the drugs trade, which wasn't the case. We wondered if the leadership was sufficiently committed to getting the troops out, and the RUC disbanded. There were lots of meetings at the highest level within the INLA, although as a foot soldier, albeit a unit commander, I wasn't involved. I was one of the troops out on the streets, although units like mine were being kept informed of what was happening.

'Not long after I rejoined my unit, I talked the situation over with Sean [Caldwell] and some of the others. He and I had joined the INLA on the very same day; we'd been involved in a lot of operations together; we shared information, we shared guns, we shared a lot. Now when we were asked to join the IPLO we agreed to do so. Our units went together, but while it was to a group with a different name, as far as we were concerned we were still following the rules of the INLA. The main difference was that those in the IPLO were violent, ultra violent; there were no rules, anything and everything went. Frankly, they were the worst of the worst, and I'd joined. The IRA wasn't happy about the break-up of the INLA. They'd been a sort of Big Brother to us.

'And while the IPLO had a political wing, to be honest everybody in that was in the military wing also. Like so many aspects of those in organisations in Northern Ireland during the Troubles, one day you'd put on a pair of trainers and jeans and you were called a terrorist, and the next if you put on a suit and tie you were a politician.

'In the IPLO we went about things differently to the INLA. Now if a Catholic was shot dead, there were times we would go to the extreme of threatening Protestant people by telling them through coded calls to newspapers or the Samaritans, "If this happens again we are going to kill ten of you." Sometimes for organisations such as the IRA and the INLA to exist, you need the support of the people. If you don't have their encouragement, you can't function. You need them to provide you with safe houses, hide your guns, you need the people to support you, and at this time the UDA was involved in shooting Catholics just because they were Catholics. We felt there had been times when Catholics had asked for help and the INLA hadn't been really interested. But the IPLO Volunteers were different. Our only rule was: "If you shoot us, then we'll shoot you."'

Manny and Sally were long-time friends of the Kane family who lived in Upper Meadow Street, which ran parallel and next to Spamount Street in New Lodge. Bridget Kane had lost her husband Eddie when McGurk's bar was bombed. He was just 29 when he died and she'd been heartbroken.

'Bridget was a lovely lady with a natural terror of losing more of her family. Her son Eddie had joined the INLA and was in my active service unit when we transferred to the IPLO. Now his brother Billy, who was just two when his dad had been murdered, was pestering me to become a paramilitary. He said he wanted revenge for his da and wanted to kill Protestants. Once he said that, I thought back to my old days in Long Kesh where I'd said the same thing and had been told, "That's not what we want." So I had to say to Billy, "That's not what we want, Billy, we don't want people like you." And his mother had begged me, "Manny, don't let Billy do this." Billy was a good kid, a great kid, full of life. When Sally and me were first married he would sometimes come and stay with us.'

Manny was at home having a meal in January 1988 when there was a knock at the door.

'The British soldiers knew I was one of the unit commanders in the area. When the cheeky buggers were introducing a new patrol to New Lodge, showing them the ropes, they'd rap at the door and if I didn't answer it I'd be called out and standing there would be two soldiers, the guy just about to complete his tour of duty and his replacement, who would be told, "This is Manny McDonnell. Take a good look at him, because he's the commander of the fucking local INLA," and I'd shut the door on them.'

'That day in 1988 Sally went to answer the knock. A soldier was standing there. "I've got a message for your man," he told her. "Well, what is it?" she asked, and he said, "Tell him his mate's dead."

' "Who?"

' "Billy Kane" was the reply, and the soldier marched off.

'When Sally gave me that message it was unbelievable, devastating. It was even more dreadful when we found out what had happened. It had been the middle of the day. Billy's front door was wide open and the killers, there were three of them against an unarmed youngster, just walked in. He was lying on a settee in the living room with a pair of earphones on listening to music, and when they saw him shot him dead. He didn't have had a chance, because the earphones meant he could not have heard them.'

As the gunmen were leaving, one had asked, 'Did you shoot him right?' and at that more shots were fired into the teenager's body. Then the trio ran off.

Distraught Bridget and local people confirmed Billy had no connection to any paramilitary or political organisations. It was widely believed that the real target had been Eddie. And there were others who were convinced that the RUC had colluded with the murderers. It was a view backed up by Bridget, who said a British Army patrol had warned her, days earlier, 'Billy will be pushing up daisies in a fortnight.'

'Afterwards I couldn't face Bridget, because I thought that if I had stopped Eddie from joining an active service unit, then the gunmen wouldn't have come looking for him and shot Billy instead. We'd decided we were going to do something about this in the long term, not the short term, because the cops knew that we were ready to spring into action and we were being watched. We tried our best to find out exactly who had done the shooting and it went back to Adair's mob, his UDA "C" Company.

'Adair liked to put himself about as a hard man, but the fact was that he was regarded as a daftie, a joke. He adopted the nickname "Mad Dog", but that was the tag given to Dominic McGlinchey one day by a leading English politician. Adair was actually known in Belfast as "Deputy Dog" or the "Mad Pussy". Maybe that was connected to one of his mates being gay.'

In fact, the police got to the killers first and two men would later be jailed for life for the murder of Billy Kane.

The death of their friend hit the McDonnells hard. But just four days after Billy's murder, one of Manny's relatives, Anthony McKiernan, aged 44, disappeared. His body was discovered in West Belfast the following day. He was a veteran IRA Volunteer and the Provisionals released a statement claiming he was killed because he was an informer on the payroll of the RUC.

It would later transpire that shortly before he was executed, Anthony had been due to meet with the then head of IRA security Freddie Scappaticci, since exposed as a British double agent known by the codename Stakeknife. Some reports have pointed out that a number of murders of 'informants' were of men who may have been suspected by Stakeknife of knowing he worked for the British authorities. Anthony's family have strenuously denied he was an informer and want his name cleared.

Throughout the Troubles, wholly pointless murders like those of innocent youngsters such as Billy Kane often led to the bloodiest acts of revenge. And when an organisation such as the IPLO, which thrived on violence, was asked to take action on behalf of a Catholic community, the result could be devastating.

The murder of student Gerard O'Hara caused a furious outcry and demands for action. Gerard, known as 'Soggy' to his pals, earned pocket money delivering newspapers, never knowing he would make headlines himself. He was at home one Sunday teatime watching television when three masked gunmen smashed through the window, burst in and confronted the teenager. His mum, Bridie, pleaded, 'He's only a wee boy, don't shoot him, shoot me,' but her appeals were ignored and bullets blasted the life from the boy.

Next day, the then Northern Ireland Secretary of State Patrick Mayhew said, 'I did not know Gerard O'Hara. But I am going to remember his name. For in the threat of the supreme act of hate that shot down Gerard O'Hara in his 19th year had called forth from his mother the enormous act of love that offered her life for his. Let the scarlet wickedness of his murder never fade from memory in Northern Ireland.'

They were fine words, but in the Catholic community around Gerard's home in North Queen Street, most were convinced the British Army and RUC had colluded with his murderers, a view strengthened when the UFF admitted responsibility, claiming Gerard was in the IRA, something denied by his family and even by others in the security services.

'Too many Catholic people were being shot; something needed to be done. The community felt it was supporting us; now it wanted our help. So we sat down to plan an operation. The target was to be a club called the Orange Cross, a haunt of paramilitaries right in the middle of a Loyalist area in Shankhill Road. We didn't want to be indiscriminate. Somebody suggested, "Just bust the doors in, go in and shoot everybody," but that was rejected because there would also be innocent people in that club drinking.

'We were after skinhead types, the sort of thugs who followed the Mad Pussy. The plan was to go into the club, separate the skinheads, those who we thought would be connected to paramilitaries, from the others and take them out. We knew there would be UDA people in there. It would be a risky operation, because it required getting inside the club first, which wasn't easy, because they usually had surveillance cameras watching anyone approaching, and steel doors protected the entrance. But we got together a good team and the Volunteers walked up some stairs, produced a sub-machine and did their best to separate the ordinary drinkers from the paramilitaries before opening fire. But to be honest, by the time the unit returned home, although it knew people had been shot it wasn't very sure who they were: innocent Catholics, innocent Protestants or UDA members.'

The shooting resulted in one fatality, the victim being 36-year-old Stephen McCrea, a Protestant Red Hand Commando who had been jailed in 1972 for killing a Catholic teenager. He had served 16 years of a life sentence. McCrea had been caught at the time after being dragged down by a police dog as he ran away, and he was alleged to have said he murdered the youngster for being 'a Fenian bastard'.

'Word spread fast. Cops and the Army were everywhere. Then the IRA got to hear about it and weren't very happy. We explained to them that they had been sitting back watching Catholic people getting slaughtered without being prepared to do anything. But my own view was that an operation like this was a distraction, bringing us off the true path, which was to take out soldiers and the RUC.'

The Orange Cross incident was the final straw for the British government. It added the IPLO to the list of proscribed organisations. The Parliamentary Under-Secretary of State at the Northern Ireland Office Lord Skelmersdale said in 1990, 'The Irish People's Liberation Organisation is perhaps one of the less well-known terrorist organisations outside Northern Ireland. Unlike other terrorist organisations, its activities have been confined solely to Northern Ireland and, compared with the Provisional IRA, for example, it is comparatively small and has accounted for only a relatively small portion of terrorist attacks. But it is no less deadly or ruthless for that and it has been responsible for some of the most cruel and callous incidents since 1987, when it came into being as an offshoot of the Irish National Liberation Army, itself a proscribed organisation.

'It was also responsible for a particularly nasty shooting attack in the bar in the Craven Street Orange Cross Social Club in Belfast when customers were sprayed with bullets and one man died. It is abundantly clear that any organisation which has such a total disregard for human life can have no place in a civilised society.'

Although the search for Adair continued, Republican organisations in general gave him little or no credence and even Loyalists regarded him as a liability. He boasted of how he moved about freely in Catholic areas of Belfast, mystifying opposition groups as to how he was able to do so without being recognised. Pussy Cat himself provided the answer.

'He released a video of himself at one of his birthday parties being presented with a cake. There was a tiny figure on top of the cake that was obviously meant to represent him and the figure was wearing a Celtic top. A guy in a Celtic shirt wouldn't rate a second glance in a Republican area, where most people were Hoops supporters. It was the perfect disguise, so we couldn't understand why anybody would be so dopey as to give away something like that.'

14

COCAINE BONANZA

MANNY WAS AT HOME with his family in Spamount Street when he became aware of a commotion outside. He heard the sounds of an ambulance, police sirens and the heavy trundle of British Army Land Rovers. It was never a good idea to open the door without first checking what lay outside in case a diversion had been deliberately created to lure him into an ambush. But after a quick scan he found himself outside talking with neighbours who recounted a horror story.

Further along the street Gary Campbell, a dad of one, had been watching television when two gunmen smashed their way in, shot him in the chest and fled. Gary was a Catholic with no connection to paramilitaries. His partner and their toddler child were in the house at the time but unharmed. The UVF claimed it executed the quiet, likeable young man because he was a member of the IRA, an allegation vehemently denied by his family. He was almost certainly killed by mistake. Someone else with the same surname had lived in the house until a few weeks previously and neighbours told of this man being regularly hassled by police and the British Army. Gary's was a pointless killing, achieving nothing, but it was yet another reminder to Manny of the ever-present danger he and his loved ones faced.

As the years had rolled on he had increasingly asked himself whether the mounting death toll in Northern Ireland and elsewhere could be justified. Sometimes he wondered if the singers had sung their songs to a captive audience but then forgotten most of the words.

Manny was still an active and loyal Volunteer in the IPLO. Unlike many others, though, those who became his enemies did so not because of the church they attended but the uniform they donned each day. Like his fellow Volunteers, he was forever searching out targets and gathering intelligence. Republican organisations did not normally collaborate in the planning of operations and it was not unknown, although rare, for separate groups to find themselves engaged on operations in the same location, although with different targets. Through that intelligence, the IPLO investigated the practicality of an attack on the British Army that would have caused carnage on an immense and terrifying scale. Later the IPLO would learn the IRA had stumbled onto the same idea, although the latter would never know it had already been discussed at senior level by the former.

'We were always interested in the arrangements for the troops. We found out the SAS had doubled the length of their tours to 12 months so they could get a better chance to familiarise themselves with areas and individuals. But ordinary troops spent three months in an area before moving on. Sometimes Volunteers would give the impression of being friendly and would chat to soldiers to find out where they came from, when they were going home to England and how. We learned they went by boat to Liverpool and the boat was in Belfast Docks. Somebody asked, "I wonder if we can blow the fucking boat up once they're on it, or ambush them on the way to the docks?"

'So, okay, it might have sounded pie in the sky, but a successful operation of this scale would have had a catastrophic effect on soldiers' morale and so we spent a long time examining whether it was possible to bomb the boat. We were surprised to find security around the vessel wasn't nearly so tight as we'd expected.

The drawback was that in an attack there would be many civilian casualties. There were those in our ranks who argued, "Yes, that's true, but this is a fucking war," but in the end it was the thought of civilians, women and children among them, being killed that stopped us going ahead. A little while later we discovered the IRA had hit on the same idea, but, maybe just as we had, they were put off by the certainty of so many innocents dying.'

In Scotland, another boat was the subject of an investigation, but this time by customs investigators. The *Dimar-B* was ploughing through heavy seas towards the northern coastline of Scotland. Off South America an aircraft had dropped 16 bales of drugs into the sea. They had been collected and stowed on the rusting cargo vessel. Two men on board were the targets for the hunters. They were sure Chris Howarth and Noel Hawkins were up to no good and were somewhere in the world on board a ship. But the pair had eluded close surveillance. Then radar tracked the vessel to the north of Scotland.

Unknown to the customs team, the precious *Dimar-B* cargo would be brought ashore and hidden in Clashnessie Bay, 30 miles north of Ullapool. The investigators knew only that it had been landed somewhere because Howarth and Hawkins were spotted back at their Ullapool homes. Some days later the cargo was found in the back of a van heading south on the A9 when it was stopped near Newtonmore. Officers believed they had uncovered a huge haul of hashish. It was only when forensic experts examined the find that it was announced the outcome of Operation Klondyke was the uncovering of half a tonne of Colombian cocaine worth £100 million.

The drugs bust made headlines that raised eyebrows throughout Britain and even abroad. The vast fortune amassed ten years earlier by Alexander Sinclair had encouraged a spate of drug smugglers to go into business. But when the sheer scale of the *Dimar-B* cocaine haul was made known it signalled the start of drug smuggling as the most prolific and most lucrative crime.

It was true that the smugglers, when caught, were given heavy sentences, Howarth being sent down for 25 years and Hawkins 15. But while the customs team had displayed undoubted skill and doggedness, the discovery of the van containing the immense cache was largely down to luck. It might easily have taken its load to its destination in England. Major criminals saw that and reckoned the rewards outweighed the risks. In any case, there were enough crooks around willing to chance a long spell behind bars in exchange for a hefty boost to their bank balances.

In Glasgow, Thomas McGraw and his associates, including some who had done well from the proceeds of the deeds of the Barlanark Team, now saw the means by which they could get really rich. And luck had favoured McGraw as a result of a downturn in the fortunes of his great rival, Godfather Thompson. Thompson's plan had been that when he became too old to run his empire, the reins would be handed to his eldest son, also Arthur but to others, in private anyway, 'Fat Arty' or the 'Mars Bar Kid' because of his liking for the chocolate bars.

At one time the older Thompson had introduced Ferris onto his payroll as an enforcer, a glorified debt collector, hoping his son would learn from the bright, brave, wily Ferris. Then Arty had jumped on the drug-dealing bandwagon, but instead of relatively mild hashish, something to which police were prone to turn a blind eye, began dealing heroin, where the returns were vastly higher. And Arty had been nicked. His dad had asked McGraw to be a witness for his son. McGraw refused and the result was an 11-year sentence for Arty.

The old man was no pushover, but without his son, a skilled armourer, he was vulnerable, even more so after a bitter split with Ferris, who sided for a time with McGraw. The underworld bookmakers reckoned that with Thompson slipping, there were just two candidates for the new ruler of the roost, McGraw and Ferris, although each was adamant they did not want the Godfather's crown. When he was in his heyday, little went on in

Glasgow without Thompson giving it the nod. But with his menace waning because of the absence of his son, the road was clear for McGraw and Ferris to move in.

McGraw and his wife Margaret had invested his share of the proceeds of the Barlanark Team into a highly successful bar, the Caravel. Its regulars included young men dabbling in small-scale drug smuggling in cars. McGraw noted how the *Dimar-B* team had almost got away with bringing in a boatload of cocaine. In his mind, the kernel of an idea was forming. If you were going to smuggle, then smuggle big. But how?

Drugs were also on the minds of an increasing number involved in the Northern Ireland paramilitaries. The IRA had always declared drug dealing would not be tolerated. Known dealers found themselves warned and then punished, often severely, if they continued to offend. The INLA had declared itself opposed to drug dealing, but with the formation of the IPLO came suspicions among Catholic communities that in Belfast its members were involved in the drugs trade, an accusation strongly denied. At the end of the day, the IPLO was able to boast that no Volunteer was ever convicted of a drugs offence. But it was torn by infighting and feuding, and the scale of its violence was being seen as a problem to other organisations, especially the IRA and PIRA, who were beginning to grow weary from years of fighting and were wondering if a meaningful dialogue with the British government might achieve a just settlement.

Manny listened carefully to what was going on about him. The first, faint signs of disillusionment were starting to appear among his thoughts. At the same time, a friendship with Paul Ferris was developing.

'I couldn't visit Paul in Glasgow because of the banning order. From time to time he would telephone and we made sure our conversations were very general to things like, "How are you doing? How are the family?" Nothing specific was ever mentioned because we could never be sure that what we said wasn't being taped by Special Branch. He'd say, "If you ever get the chance to come to Glasgow make sure you look me up. You'll find me at the Cottage Bar in the east end. Any taxi driver knows it, and when you get there just ask for me."

'Then suddenly, out of the blue, I received a letter saying the British government had lifted my banning order, which meant I could go anywhere I wanted in Britain. I decided to celebrate by seeing a Celtic match and travelled to Glasgow with three friends. When we arrived, I told them I wanted to look Paul up and we caught a cab to the Cottage Bar.

'Four of us walked in, and when I asked for Paul Ferris the fucking bar just went silent. Four fucking Irish guys suddenly appearing from nowhere looking for him. I thought I'd made a mistake and said to one of the guys with me, "I wonder if we're going to walk out of here?" The guy I'd asked said, "What do you want Paul for?" and I explained I'd been in the nick with him, had gone back over to Ireland and he'd asked me to pay him a visit if I came over. This guy turned out to be one of Paul's very best and most trusted friends, Bobby Glover.

'Bobby told us to sit down, got us each a drink, said, "Hang on there," and disappeared. I assumed he was making a phone call. He came back and said, "Paul will be with you in about 15 minutes," and sure enough, a quarter of an hour later, Paul arrived with a pleasant young man who he introduced as Joe Hanlon. We had a long chat, met a few other guys, and then all of us parted friends with one another, promising to keep in contact. That was the real start of my relationship with Paul. From then on I'd come to Glasgow occasionally and get to know a few people who were curious about the IPLO.'

After one of these visits, Manny began receiving frequent information from a high-profile Glasgow underworld figure.

'I'd get letters telling me about a strong UDA cell in Glasgow, who was in it, where they lived, what they did. There were maps showing their addresses and meeting places, and sometimes even photographs purporting to be of named UDA supporters. I passed this information on to IPLO staff but do not know what became of it. The IPLO did not have a cell in Scotland, but information of this calibre would have been as manna from heaven to the IRA. It was extremely detailed and clearly came from somebody who had intimate inside information about the UDA.'

15

BUNGLED BANK JOB

SOMETIMES MANNY WOULD FLY to Glasgow rather than take the longer ferry route, but despite the lifting of the banning order, police, alerted by seeing his name on the Belfast flight passenger list, were always waiting to meet him at the airport, taking him aside and wanting to know the reason for his visit, where he was staying and who he would be meeting. His answer was always the same: that he had come to watch a football match. But he was always on the lookout for tails. Mostly he took the chance to meet up with Paul Ferris, and gradually the circle of his acquaintances in Glasgow increased. Friends almost always accompanied him on these trips.

'I didn't want Paul to talk too much about the criminal side of things, because the people I was with were staunch Republicans and wouldn't have been happy if they thought I was getting involved with a crook or was into crime. So when we were all together, we were limited in what we could discuss.

'Back home in Belfast, the organisations to which I had belonged, the IRA, the INLA and the IPLO, as well as the other Republican groups, took a stance in public that they would punish anyone found to be involved in what they saw as antisocial behaviour such as drug dealing, stealing or child abuse. But of course they did not have any jurisdiction in Scotland, and Paul wanted me to work for him. So when we were on our own I told him I would consider anything, and I had a couple of friends who felt the same and who I could call on. Paul and me had the same policy: we would never ask anyone else to do anything we wouldn't do ourselves. Make no mistake, Paul had plenty of balls.'

There was work in Glasgow for men with the sort of experience garnered during the Northern Ireland conflict. And there were plenty in gangland eager to recruit anybody skilled in using weapons. But, just as with lots of paramilitary operations in Northern Ireland, things did not always go to plan.

One exploit that concerned a carefully drawn-up plot to rob a bank in the Anniesland area of Glasgow would have had any comedy writer purring with delight. The raid was to be carried out by three armed Irishmen who travelled over from Belfast. The plan was simple. The trio, armed with two shotguns and a sledgehammer for smashing the anti-bandit screen protecting the tellers, would arrive in a van, park close to the bank, run out, their heads covered by masks and balaclavas, storm inside and force staff to hand over piles of banknotes. Clutching their haul, they would then make their getaway in a car earlier parked outside the bank before transferring to another car driven by a fourth man. He would take the gang to a safe house for the cash shareout.

On paper it sounded a cracking plan. To make sure the getaway would be smooth, the night before the hit the car in which they would make their initial escape was driven to Anniesland and parked outside the bank. It was the following morning that things went wrong. The robbers drove up in their van but couldn't find a parking space near the bank. They drove around a few times, but the nearest space was at least 60 yards off and they reasoned that three hooded men carrying shotguns and a sledgehammer running along busy streets headed towards a bank were bound to attract attention. Eventually the raid was abandoned.

Frustrated, the three went back to Belfast. A few weeks later they received a call bringing them to Glasgow for another robbery on a security van. This time the raid went well, even though the haul was not as big as had been hoped. The robbers had a heart-stopping moment when they were introduced to their getaway driver and discovered he was an old-age pensioner. Paul Ferris was one of the names in the frame when police investigated bank robberies, but suspecting him was as far as it went. He was never charged and the robberies remained a mystery.

Irish accents were heard during an attempt to kidnap a Glasgow school janitor caught up in a gangland feud. Three men flew over from Northern Ireland and were handed boiler suits and masks. They pounced in the early morning as the janitor was arriving to open up his school. Manny was later told by a friend who often picked up Glasgow underworld gossip that the wannabe kidnappers had explained to their paymaster, 'He escaped by the skin of his teeth. As soon as he saw us, he was over the back fence of the school and off like a whippet. There was no way we could catch him.'

Manny enjoyed his outings to Glasgow. 'It was like visiting a holiday camp, compared with Belfast. Guys in Glasgow didn't know the meaning of pressure. At home we were forever looking over our shoulders, changing routines, forever having to be on the lookout, and once I joined the IPLO, the INLA joined the list of those who were a threat. It was really, really violent, but in Glasgow, if you had hassle with somebody then the only one you needed to worry about was him. It wasn't as if 10,000 of his mates were coming after you.

'I was being offered little contracts quite regularly and getting well compensated but was really careful how it was spent. Like the other Volunteers I lived off my giro cheque, but now I was disappearing for four or five days at a time and then maybe even taking a holiday abroad. I could tell others in the IPLO were beginning to wonder where the fuck I'd gone, because I was meant to report in at least once every day. What was worrying me was that they might have started thinking I was getting paid by the police, because guys were being shot dead for coming under less suspicion than that. It was a real juggling act, trying to take advantage of the work in Glasgow and trying to hide that for the first time in my life I had money.

'I was very close pals with Paul by this time. But one day he said something that puzzled me: "Manny, you listen with your eyes." I asked what he meant and he went on, "Well, when somebody's talking to you, you seem to be listening with your eyes." I still didn't know what he was talking about and he said, "Exactly what I'm saying, you listen with your eyes." I didn't know what to make of this, so I asked, "How can you listen with your eyes? Don't you listen with your ears?" At that, he fell about in fits of laughter. Later I wondered if he was saying that because of my background in Ireland I missed nothing.

'Sometimes during conversations at the Cottage Bar I heard the names of Tam McGraw and Arthur Thompson mentioned, but at that time they meant nothing to me. Lots of people came into the pub, where Bobby and Joe were very well liked, and among them was James Mullen, 'Mudsie'. One day Paul had to go off and asked James to look after me. James took me to the Caravel, where later on I met Tam for the first time. I liked him right away; he had a great sense of humour and just about the first thing he was to me was, "So, you're the Irish bastard?" and we both starting laughing. He was really interested in what was going on in Ireland and I had the impression he wanted to get something going there.

'At that first meeting he made it plain he didn't much like Paul. He said, "I don't get on with the wee man. We have our differences, but I don't want to go into them because I don't really know you," and I told him, "That's fair enough." We chatted for a couple of hours over a few drinks. I gave Tam my telephone number and address and said if he was ever in Belfast he was to call on Sally and me and if we could ever do anything for him we would do it.

At that meeting he asked, "Could you get me a couple of guns?" When I wanted to know what they were for, he would only say, "I'm having problems with somebody." Then he asked, "If I needed something doing, would you and your people be willing to do it for me?" I told him, "Yes, we would."

'As it had done in conversations with Paul, Arthur Thompson's name cropped up. It was obvious Tam didn't much like him either, and I thought back to my teenage days coming out of Long Kesh and being pissed off with the IRA old-timers. It seemed to me the situation with Thompson, Paul and Tam was a similar scenario. He was old school and they were younger bucks. There was a power struggle going on there, but I'd seen all that before.'

As his taxi drove him back into the city centre to be reunited with his friends, Manny looked at the quiet streets with children happily playing in safety. No bombs here, he thought, no need to run away if a stranger parked a car and left it. He wondered if the mums of those children knew what it was like to be living in constant dread of hearing an explosion and rushing to see if sons and daughters were alive. From the start of the Troubles, when little Carol Ann McCool and her sister Bernadette had been blown up, children, babies even, had borne a terrible burden of suffering. Age was no protection from the bombers and snipers.

Tracey Munn was two and Colin Nicholl just a few months old when they were blasted into heaven by an IRA bomb planted outside a furnishing company; Angela Gallagher was just one year old and in her pram when an IRA sniper's bullet intended for a British Army patrol took her tiny life; baby Alan Jack was just five months when an IRA bomber failed to give an adequate warning about a bomb left in Strabane, and the infant died as glass and debris showered his pram while his frantic mum tried desperately to push her son to safety. And so it went on.

By the time the worst of the Troubles ended, more than 270 youngsters aged 17 and under had been killed.

© PA IMAGES

As a boy, Manny became used to scenes like this, in which terrified crowds fled from yet another bomb blast as smoke belched over New Lodge Road in Belfast.

Crowds at a Requiem Mass for Father Hugh Mullan, who was killed while trying to help an injured man during a riot. He was only one of the 1,700 people who died during the Troubles in the area of Belfast known as Murder Triangle, where Manny lived.

Playgrounds for youngsters like Manny were bombed and burned-out transport depots like this.

© MIRRORPIX

Armed police and troops intervene in a tense stand-off between warring Republican and Nationalist communities in a Belfast housing scheme in 1972.

Masked and heavily armed paramilitaries from Manny's INLA brigade pose and show off their automatic weapons at the funeral of a fellow Volunteer.

Manny's close friend
and Volunteer colleague
Sean Caldwell (right) with
Manny's son Ciaran (left).

Manny (left) was devastated when his
best friend Billy Kane (right) was shot
dead. Here, the two share a joke. Not
long after the picture was taken, Billy
was murdered.

A youthful Tam McGraw ran a lucrative team of safecrackers in Glasgow at the time Manny was becoming an active Republican paramilitary in Belfast.

Arthur 'The Godfather' Thompson (right), seen here with his brother Robert (left), ruled Glasgow's underworld until his death from a heart attack.

During visits to Glasgow, Manny (right) became close to Tam McGraw (left) and Tam's brother-in-law John 'Snads' Adams (middle).

Manny became friends with Paul Ferris (left) in Shotts prison. Here, Paul relaxes with long-time pal Bobby Glover (right).

Manny met Bobby Glover (right) and Joe Hanlon (left) at the Cottage Bar during a trip to Glasgow. Both were later murdered and their bodies dumped outside the bar.

Hannah Martin acted as a courier, helping to smuggle hundreds of thousands of pounds into Spain to buy hashish. Manny threatened her boyfriend Graeme Mason after discovering him drunk.

The bringing into Scotland of more than £100 million of cocaine on the rusting *Dimar-B* encouraged gangs and paramilitary organisations to begin drug smuggling on a huge scale.

Sun-kissed Tenerife was the favourite holiday location of Tam McGraw, who bought an apartment on the island. It was during a holiday there that he came up with the idea of raising the floors of the holiday coaches to give youngsters a better view – and to create more room for smuggled hashish.

Scottish detectives investigating links between McGraw and Manny spotted the Irishman at Rocky's Pub in Benidorm but gave themselves away by wearing distinctive luminous yellow coats.

Handsome Gordon Ross was one of the men in the dock along with Manny accused of hashish smuggling He was acquitted but was later murdered.

Manny worried about Billy McPhee's wild antics in Spain. Billy also made enemies in Glasgow, and this dramatic photograph shows him grim and upset at the funeral of Gordon Ross after being warned his life was in danger. He was murdered shortly afterwards.

A pensive Manny McDonnell, who still lights candles in memory of youngsters Johnathan Ball and Tim Parry, victims of a 1993 IRA bombing in Warrington.

Manny wasn't alone when he thought about the dead children and wondered if he and the others were walking the right path.

'By this time I was beginning to get a wee bit disillusioned with the Republican cause. Innocent people were getting killed. Kids were getting killed. The result was that I was not only taking a close look at it but beginning to look at myself too.'

He had walked close to death for so long that he had become almost immune to sorrow when yet another companion was lost. And it was becoming increasingly dangerous to continue in the IPLO, especially as gossip that some among the leadership were using their reputations to cash in on drug deals was more rife than ever. It was said that in collusion with the UVF, the IPLO hierarchy had been setting up a major drug deal with a leading gang of English smugglers. There was talk of Loyalists in the west of Scotland becoming involved. Drugs and Republicans should not mix, that was a golden rule. Further killing was almost inevitable.

On Friday, 16 August 1991 Manny's friend Martin 'Rook' O'Prey, prominent among the IPLO commanders, was cuddling his seven-year-old daughter on the settee in the living room of his Belfast home under a British Army observation post when one of his trusted allies quietly unlocked the back door and made a telephone call to a waiting UVF unit. Moments later two gunmen slipped in and began recklessly blasting O'Prey from point-blank range, ignoring the presence of the child. Rook died with up to 20 bullets in his head and body, while although the youngster was hit, her injuries were not severe. At the dead man's requiem Mass, Father Matt Wallace wondered why the shooting was not seen from the Army post but, at the same time, pleaded for no retaliatory acts. Manny did not know it, but O'Prey's murder was the first in a series that would have a bearing on his future.

The following night, in Glasgow, Arty Thompson, allowed out for a weekend as his prison spell neared an end, was nearing the family home, having been into the city centre for a curry. A car, stolen earlier and belonging to a police officer, drew up in the street with three men inside. One climbed out clutching a gun, walked up to Arty and shot him three times, the third penetrating his backside and spinning into his vital organs. As the killers fled, Arty staggered to the door and his family drove him to hospital, where he died a few minutes after midnight on 18 August. Old Thompson had no doubts about who had shot his son. In Ireland, it was Republicans against Loyalists. In Glasgow, the shooting started a conflict that was about to become no less vicious. It was the Godfather against Manny's friend Paul Ferris.

Arty's funeral was set for 18 September. He would be buried with other family members in the cemetery behind his parents' home. The following day, the 19th, Manny was at home in Spamount Street when Sally looked up from her newspaper. 'What was the name of Paul's pal in Glasgow?' she asked.

'Bobby, Bobby Glover,' he told her, adding, 'Why?'

'Because it's here in the paper that Bobby Glover and his friend Joe Hanlon have been murdered. Didn't you know them?'

Manny took the newspaper from his wife. The article told how the bodies of the two men had been found in a car left outside the Cottage Bar.

'The Cottage Bar, that's where I met them with Paul,' he said. 'They were a couple of nice guys.' He had become used to having close friends in Belfast killed, but not in Glasgow.

On the night before the discovery of their bodies, Bobby had received a call from a one-time friend William Lobban, who asked to meet up with him. Not long before, Bobby and Ferris had been arrested and questioned about the murder of Arty. While Ferris remained in custody, Bobby had been bailed, but his car was still being held by the police. Bobby rang Joe asking for a lift and his friend obliged. When they met up with Lobban, they were joined by another man, Lobban's uncle William 'Billy' Manson. Manson was a friend of the Godfather. Minutes later, Bobby and Joe were dead. A businessman friend of Thompson arranged for the bodies to be temporarily laid in a yard for the Godfather to inspect, before they were thrown into a blue Ford motor that was driven to the Cottage Bar and abandoned. The significance of the Cottage Bar was that it was regarded as a headquarters, a favourite meeting place, for Ferris and his friends. Lobban fled to London, while Manson began counting bundles of cash.

Unable to contact Ferris, who was in jail, Manny rang Tam McGraw. 'What's happening? Do you need help?' he asked.

The reply was firm. 'Don't come near Glasgow, Manny, whatever you do. It's fucking hot over here.'

Ferris was eventually charged with murdering Arty but after a lengthy trial was found not guilty. Manny waited several weeks after the killings before coming back to Glasgow to watch Celtic, but he took the opportunity to call at the Caravel. It was by now obvious to him that what friendship had existed between Ferris and McGraw was doomed.

'In a way, it was just how things developed in Northern Ireland: men who had been friends would gradually turn against one another and that ill will would turn to murder. At the start when I was friendly with Paul and Tam, they seemed affable enough with each other, but then I could see a rift developing and widening all the time. It was a situation where I didn't have to make a decision which of the two to side with. They were both my friends and I could go with whichever one I wanted at any time. But I saw things were going to get ugly and they had started criticising each other to me. There was going to be a power struggle, and to me there would only ever be one winner, and that was Tam.'

McGraw had already had a taste of what life could be like across the water in Northern Ireland. A few years earlier, somebody had tossed a fragmentation grenade into the Caravel. At first some of the customers played football with the mystery object, not realising what it was before somebody tumbled to it being a grenade. Even so, one of the customers still showed enough nerve to pick it up and lob it into the cemetery next door, where a bomb-disposal team detonated it. Manny heard the story from McGraw.

'If somebody walked into a bar in Belfast hell-bent on causing mayhem, they wouldn't have forgotten to pull out the firing pin,' he told him. 'You're just playing at fighting with each other here, to you it's like a game, but where I'm from it's real, people are getting maimed and killed.'

As if to demonstrate the truth of his words, in October that year an IPLO unit was ordered to execute UDA member Harry Ward. According to one account, the team had been after a Loyalist paramilitary tagged 'Bunter'. But Manny is in a better position to give the more accurate version, which is that Ward, a 42-year-old Protestant, was the specific target.

'The team was planning to kill him one night and sat outside the Diamond Jubilee bar on Lower Shankhill Road waiting for Ward to come out, but they were beginning to get noticed. One of the guys eventually said, "Oh, fuck this, I'm going in to get him," and another member of the unit went with him while others waited outside. The two who went in didn't know what Harry Ward looked like and so decided to simply yell out his name. This was in the middle of a hard Loyalist area and the first IPLO guy opened the door, went in and shouted, "Harry Ward here?" Somebody asked, "No, but who are you?" The gunman said, "It doesn't fucking matter who I am, I'm asking if Harry Ward's here," but the customer said, "Well I'm asking who the fuck you are." At that, our guy said, "Well, this is who I fucking am," and shot him dead. It had been Harry Ward after all.'

16

PIZZA MAN

THE FEAR THAT THE CLOUD OF DEATH constantly hanging over the province might one day shroud his family, a close comrade or himself was never far away from Manny. His trips to Glasgow, now that the heat over the deaths of Arty, Joe and Bobby had cooled, were a welcome relief from the stresses of New Lodge. He knew his arrivals in Glasgow were monitored by both Special Branch officers in Scotland and the local police, who could not be certain if the various factions supporting all the dead felt their thirst for revenge had been satisfied.

Joe Hanlon had relatives in Ireland. Arthur Thompson had connections with major players in England who were cementing links with groups such as the IPLO and UVF over drug deals. Thompson himself had supplied guns to Loyalist factions. There was no shortage of guns and gunmen for hire.

Manny, while unaware of the twists and turns in the plots that had left three men dead and Paul Ferris awaiting a murder trial, was nevertheless never surprised when he was singled out from among those arriving from Belfast at Glasgow airport or Stranraer and asked what he wanted in Scotland. His answer was always the same. 'I'm here for the football, to watch Celtic,' he would say. He suspected he was rarely believed.

One trip ended prematurely.

'I had travelled over for a football match and to spend a few days looking around. Whenever I arrived in Glasgow I'd call on Tam and James Mullen. I was very friendly with James. I was at his home, where we were having a few beers and watching the Sky news channel about two in the morning when I suddenly sat up as I heard an item about a shooting in Belfast.

'Normally that wasn't such hot news, but I was interested to know where the incident had taken place. Then the announcer mentioned the name of the street and said it was where gunmen had tried to kill a man. Suddenly on the screen came shots of the scene and I said to James, "James, what the fuck is going on? That's Sean's house and that's his street." A reporter talked about a man having been attacked and shot and being critically ill in intensive care in hospital. "That's not Sean's car," I said. "But it's definitely his house. What the fuck's happened? I have to get back right away." So we drove to Stranraer and I waited around to get the first ferry back home. I went straight to New Lodge, then visited Sean and was able to piece together the story of what had gone on.

'Because Sean lived so close to the Loyalists, he was extra security conscious and that included changing his cars very regularly. Some of the paramilitaries kept lists of cars and car numbers, so if they were targeting somebody they would know what make and colour of motor to look for and the registration number. The reason I didn't recognise the car shown on television was because he had only just bought it while I'd been over in Glasgow. Because it was so new, there was no way anybody could know it was his. No way, that is, unless you were the police.

'Sean had only just got the car and was driving home when he was stopped by the police. They had recognised him but not the motor. "See you've got a new car, Sean?" they said. "This yours or you looking after it for one of your mates?" Sean tried to be non-committal. It didn't pay to tell the police anything.

'Loyalists knew Sean was IPLO and ran a unit. They were always on the lookout for chances to take out senior Republicans and must have had Sean on their radar for some time, because the plan they came up with was – and I hate to say this – well planned, well organised, well executed, carried out to near perfection, so good we would have been proud of it ourselves. But it could only have been possible if they knew which car was his. And there was no way they could have done that had somebody not had a word in their ear and said, "Sean has a different car. Here are the details . . ." And that somebody was the police.

'The plan was simple: to lure Sean out of his house when his defences might be down and shoot him. That would never be easy because he had security devices, cameras and so on, everywhere. That night, as usual, Sean parked his car outside his home. During darkness somebody sneaked up and poured paint over the bonnet. Next morning the damage was spotted by a neighbour. This guy was a Protestant who had actually survived being shot a few years earlier, but he was a good neighbour to Sean and his family. He called on Sean to warn him somebody had messed up the motor.

'Sean's street led to a junction with a busy road, and by the junction was a bus stop. Later on we found out that standing at the bus stop, trying to look inconspicuous, as though he was waiting for a bus, was a guy holding a walkie-talkie. As soon as he saw Sean appear from his house with his son to look at the damage to his car and start cleaning it off, this guy radioed to a two-man UVF hit squad waiting in a car parked out of sight a couple of streets away and told them, "That's him out on the street now. He's having a look at the motor. Time to move."

'The gunman was lying down on the back seat so he wouldn't be noticed. All anyone would see was a car approaching with just a driver inside. And that's all Sean remembered seeing as the car drove up to him. It came right alongside, and the gunman sat up and shot the fuck out of Sean. The driver wanted to get the hell out of it, but people living close by who looked out said they saw the man in the back actually put a gun to the head of the driver and at that the car started to reverse back to where Sean was lying. The gunman had wanted to make absolutely certain Sean was dead.

'Sean saw the car reversing. He managed to drag his head behind one of the wheels to give himself some protection but took another couple of bullets in the body before the unit disappeared. Sean was whisked off to hospital with six bullets in him but thankfully recovered.'

The Red Hand Commandos claimed they were behind the shooting. Formed in 1972 in Shankhill, one of the founders of the paramilitary organisation was John McKeague, a notorious paedophile who was under investigation for abusing boys when he was shot dead by two INLA gunmen in 1982. The RHC was popular in west Belfast and County Down and was linked to the UVF, the two groups sharing weapons and, from time to time, personnel. It said the attack on Sean was in retaliation for the shooting dead two days earlier of a member of the Royal Irish Regiment, a killing claimed by the IRA.

There had been many witnesses to the hit on Sean, but police who investigated had to admit nobody could recognise the gunman or his driver, although some people were able to describe the car and give part, if not all, of the registration number. That was enough for detectives to trace it. And the hitman had made a crucial mistake. When the car was discovered by the RUC, so were his keys. He was traced, arrested and charged with attempting to murder Sean but beat the accusation by claiming he had dropped the keys when he had been given a lift in the same motor two weeks earlier. His explanation was accepted, the charge was dropped and he was released.

But the IPLO was not prepared to let the matter rest there. It was given the name John Harbinson as the gunman, a father of four who worked as a taxi driver and sometimes delivered takeaway meals, including pizzas. One of Harbinson's associates was Mark Haddock, a senior UVF figure; another was Gary Haggarty, a UVF brigadier.

'The IPLO decided there was no way it was not going to do this guy,' recalls Manny. 'We had his name, his address, and he was going to be killed. But the hierarchy said it would take its time. When you joined a Republican organisation, one of the first lessons you learned was that of patience. Being patient meant you gave yourself time to gather all the intelligence you needed to plan a really good operation. And there was a really strong feeling against the crew who shot Sean, because he was well liked. It might take a week, it might take a year, but the gunman would always be found.

'Harbinson lived in a totally Protestant area of Belfast. He would never go out of that area, even to do pizza deliveries. If an order came in for a pizza and it meant going outside the safety of his Loyalist community, he would refuse to deliver it. So it was decided the only way to get this cunt was to go into his area, and that was dangerous, really dangerous. But the people who shot Sean had lured him out of his house and it was reckoned that the time Harbinson would be most vulnerable would be when he was making a delivery.

'So a plan was thought up that would get him taking a pizza to a house in a Loyalist area where the IPLO would be waiting. The intelligence people found the pizzeria he delivered for and then the active service unit took over.

'It picked a house, rapped at the door, pulled guns out, took the family hostage and then rang in an order for a pizza. The address was right in the middle of Loyalist territory; the unit was surrounded by thousands of RHC, UDA and UVF members.

'"What kind of pizza do you want?"

'They thought of the first pizza to come into their heads: "A Margherita."

'"Deep dish, thin crust?"

'"Thin crust."

'"What's your address?" The unit gave the address of the hostage family. "Phone number?" They supplied that too.

'"How long will it be?"

'"Not long, 15 minutes."

'"Okay."

'So they waited, and a quarter of an hour later saw a car pull up and the driver emerge carrying a pizza. It was him all right. One member of the unit was standing behind the front door, his arm extended holding the gun so that as soon as another member opened it he'd shoot the fucker. There was a rap at the door, it was opened, the gunman pulled the trigger and nothing happened. He was raging, shouting, "Fuck it, fucking useless gun," and tried again, but the same thing happened. Harbinson twigged what had happened and took to his heels, screaming blue murder and running down the street like the racehorse Shergar, knowing his life depended on getting away, which it did. Unfortunately he made it.'

Next day, Manny and other IPLO Volunteers were arrested and questioned about an attempt to ambush and murder a pizza delivery man.

'We were in the cells at Castlereagh and a copper was walking up and down the corridor shouting, "Who wants pizza, you want to order your pizza?" We said nothing, not even to stick in an order.'

All were eventually released without charge.

But the story would not end there. In May 1997, Harbinson was dragged into a car in the early hours and driven to the Mount Vernon estate in Belfast, where he was handcuffed to railings and beaten to death with iron bars. Special Branch officers were given the names of his killers – one of them a delivery driver for a Chinese takeaway – and told they had gone into hiding at Ballyhalbert, in County Down, but did not pass these on to investigating officers, who were led to believe the murder was a domestic incident.

And that was how it remained for the next ten years. A glove and one of the metal bars used in the attack disappeared from a police station, while the handcuffs and Harbinson's clothing were strangely destroyed within weeks, thus making sure detailed forensic checks could not be carried out. An official report concluded, 'Special Branch colluded with the murderers of Mr Harbinson.'

17

COPPER'S WARDROBE

JOHN MCKEAGUE'S PROMINENCE as a Red Hand Commando guaranteed him always being in danger. But irrespective of their religion, beasts faced extinction from any community. McKeague's liking for little boys put him doubly at risk, and it came as no surprise when he was killed. Manny remembers another paedophile, though, who probably thought he had escaped rough justice until Lady Luck decided his time had come.

'An IPLO unit tracked a UDR man, or so we thought, to a house in the Antrim Road. We were going to wipe him from the face of the earth. One of the Volunteers would do the shooting, and to make sure of a kill he was given a machine gun instead of the usual short-barrel revolver. "Make sure you put, ten, fifteen, twenty rounds into him," was the instruction. As soon as the door was opened, he'd whack the target. So off the boys went, rapped the door, the guy opens it and they machine-gun him all over his house. Stone dead.

'The IPLO delayed claiming responsibility for shooting a UDR guy, which was just as well, because it turned out he wasn't that but a paedophile out on parole from a long jail sentence. When the unit discovered that, it phoned newspapers saying the beast had been tracked for more than a year, that he was a known paedophile and our operation had been a complete success.'

Despite many arguing killings such as these could be justified, Manny could not put from his mind his concerns over the course of the war for freedom and fairness. Now another hurdle appeared on his road through the tragedy that was the Troubles. This incident plays a crucial part in his story, but, like so many in Northern Ireland, the family of the gunman involved have striven to remove the effects of his deeds from the course of their own lives in their struggle to return to normality. While others in the province will know his identity, for the sake of his family, and at their request, he will be called Charles in this account.

'This is a story that has followed me throughout the last 20-odd years of my life, and no matter how hard I try to push it to the back of my memory, it still emerges regularly. It is one I wish I could forget, but it had a profound effect on my thinking. A lot of the brutality wasn't necessary and the consequences very often terrible. Kill a man and that killing leads to many others. What then if there had been no reason to kill that first man? Does that mean all the others died for nothing?

'Another of my friends, who was the commander of an INLA active service unit, had spent a lot of time searching for a well-known and active UVF member. He was eventually tracked down and his movements monitored, with the result that two Volunteers were sent out on a motorbike to kill him.

'They found him in his car driving along the Crumlin Road, but when they drew alongside discovered there were two children in the back seat. There was just no way they could now go ahead with the hit. Even if they had killed the guy without harming the children, the car would certainly have crashed with them still in it. All they could do was return to base, hand in their weapon and wait for another time. And that came three months later when my mate told me they had now discovered the target ran a video shop in the Ballysillan area of Belfast and had a fairly regular routine when he worked in it. A watch on the shop confirmed all of this. It was a case of selecting the right man for the job.

'While he was in the INLA, my friend had recruited the members of his own unit, and it was one of them, Charles, who would do the job. They had all moved to the IPLO with him. I knew there were concerns about this guy. Another Volunteer had confided to me that he thought Charles was an absolute psychotic madman. Nevertheless, Charles was still given the assignment. So, everything went ahead: the shooting was carried out and Charles returned to the safe house. He told my friend, the commander, that he had got the target, that the guy was dead and that he could phone the newspapers and claim responsibility.

'So newspapers were given the recognised IPLO code word and told the organisation had carried out the execution because the shop was used by the UVF and the action was in retaliation for the continued shooting of innocent nationalists. Only it wasn't the right guy. It turned out that the UVF member had taken the night off and a 17-year-old kid who had no connection with politics or any paramilitary organisation was standing in for him.'

Gradually, a picture emerged of the tragedy. The victim was Andrew Johnson, aged 17, whose full-time job was in a jewellery shop, but to augment his earnings he worked part-time in the video store. His mother had pleaded with him not to work there, as there had been an earlier attempt on the life of the owner. He was also a community worker for the Elim Pentecostal Church and in love with his girlfriend, Julie Ann Carvill, aged 16. Julie Ann later said, 'We'd been going out for 18 months and were about to become engaged to be married.'

Around eight o'clock at night, the masked gunman had walked in and shot Andrew several times without realising a woman assistant was kneeling behind the counter. She escaped harm, but Andrew was pronounced dead at the scene. At an inquest, the coroner said, 'It would appear the IPLO would have been satisfied with the murder of anyone working in the shop. It was just Andrew's bad luck that person was him.'

Manny said, 'So a completely innocent Christian teenager had been killed, and we only found this out through news bulletins. By then it was too late, we'd claimed responsibility. Right away I knew Charles had signed his own death warrant, because the UVF were not going to be happy and would retaliate.

'What really sickened me was that when I went to see Charles, he was actually laughing. He was at the safe house, and when I wanted to know what had gone wrong he turned around and said, "It was a mistake, that's all, a mistake." I said, "Look, the kid was seventeen years old. I understand the guy you went in to look for was in his 40s, had a beard, wore glasses and was fat. You had everything you needed not to make a mistake. But you kill a boy of seventeen, seven-fucking-teen."

'Charles again turned around and said, "Well, he won't see 18, will he?" Then he went on eating a plate of sausages and beans. It was absolutely fucking disgusting. Later on he admitted that when he walked into the shop he realised the UVF guy wasn't there but saw the kid behind the counter and just decided to kill him instead.

'I called my friend in and said, "That fucker has got to go. He's going to turn on you. That is the worst case of sectarianism I have ever come across, and for him to sit there and laugh and boast is sickening. Either get rid of him now or you are going to regret it. He's going to kill you if you get in his way. The guy is a complete fruitcake."

'I went home that night to Sally and the family asking myself what this was all about. A fucking war? I was devastated. Where had we gone? What were we doing? Was this what it was all about? "This isn't freeing Ireland," I told myself over and over. "This isn't bringing us one inch closer to getting the troops off the streets. It's taking us backwards and I don't want to be part of that. I don't want to be part of the killing of kids."

'Two and a half months later, Charles met me one day and said, "Something really strange has happened. Martin O'Prey appeared to me in a dream and said, 'There's a place here in hell waiting for you.' What do you think that means?" I told him, "Just what he said." Two days later, Charles was shot dead.'

In his case, the killers made no mistake. Three gunmen drove up in a hijacked taxi, found him in the kitchen of the Ligoniel Community Association and, tipped off he would be wearing a bulletproof vest, shot him in the head. Then they pointed their weapons at close range at his chest and six bullets penetrated the vest. A UVF communiqué described the dead man as a senior IPLO commander and said he had been executed for killing Andrew. Police had warned Charles' family that not only he but they too were on a Loyalist death list. Even then, the loathing of what he had done was not ended.

'The police knew he had killed that boy because by this time we had been infiltrated by agents working for the RUC and Special Branch. His funeral was a nightmare. He lived in a part of Belfast that was completely surrounded by Loyalist areas. There was only one way in and one way out: one way for the hearse to drive in and the same way for it to come out carrying his body. To make things even more difficult, he was to be given a paramilitary funeral with the tricolour, his beret and gloves pinned to his coffin.

'His family demanded protection from the RUC, and on the morning of the funeral the police warned us that Protestants were gathering in their hundreds. They were determined to rip that coffin from the hearse, take the body out of the coffin and string it up on a lamp post. There was nothing for it but to try to go through them, and off we started. We ran into a crowd of around 500 people and at that the RUC just abandoned us. The crowd tried to snatch the coffin and to be honest I couldn't blame them after what he had done. It set me off again wondering what this was all about. A kid, dying like that: unnecessary. It was so brutal, and I found I was wrestling with myself, wondering, "What the fuck am I doing here? Where am I going? I'm getting fucking dragged down lower and lower." We did get him buried though.'

A few days after the funeral, Manny was contacted by another unit commander who Manny had introduced to McGraw during a visit to Glasgow to watch a Celtic match. This man had a remarkable piece of information he wanted to relate.

'A housebreaker normally operating in Belfast had decided to try his luck further north of the city. He had a careful look around and eventually picked on a likely target, a house that was in darkness and looked unoccupied. So he broke in and started going through the rooms.

'In one of the bedrooms he saw a wardrobe, opened the doors and discovered a policeman's uniform hanging up. He went through the pockets looking for a wallet, felt something solid and pulled out a gun. He made a second check, felt another lump and pulled out a piece of blow.

'When he got back to Belfast, he wanted rid of the gun and gave it to the IPLO but kept the blow. He'd been careless and left his fingerprints all over the place and so the police soon picked him up. They weren't much interested in anything he might have taken, except for the gun, which they demanded he return right away. He was so frightened he admitted giving it to the IPLO and the cops started putting pressure on everybody they knew in the organisation. The IPLO had been intending to use it on some of its own people who were suspected of being informers. Then the blame would have been put on the police.

'Everybody knew about a shoot-to-kill policy anyway, when paramilitaries were indiscriminately bumped off by the British Army, Special Branch and the RUC. The cops said they didn't care how the gun was returned or even if it had been used, they just wanted it back.

'Things got so hot it was decided to send the gun over to Tam and ask him to get rid of it. We didn't ask what he might do with it. He was told we were sending a weapon over to him, given the background to it and told there was no way it was being returned to the cops. He agreed we could send it to him. We wrapped it up in lead so it wouldn't show up in any scanners, addressed it to a fictitious person and posted it to a taxi office near the Caravel. It seemed a simple and safe plan. But there were times when you wondered whether Tam's mind was on what he was being told. Because a few days later we took a phone call from Glasgow to say the Army bomb-disposal people had blown up our parcel.

'I phoned Tam and asked what had happened. The idea had been for him to go to the taxi office and tell them there was a parcel on the way in the name of such and such and when it arrived they had to telephone him and he would come up to collect it. That's what should have happened. But not with Tam. He forgot to tell the guy at the office, with the result that when the parcel arrived with a Belfast postmark, he opened it up, saw lead wrapping, threw it out of the door into the street, telephoned the cops, who in turn phoned the bomb squad, who arrived hotfoot and blew it up.

'They wrapped up the pieces and rang the RUC asking if they'd lost a gun. The outcome was that the cops eventually came back to us and said, "We've got our gun. But what was it doing in Glasgow?" We told them, "Maybe somebody reckoned the cabbies talked too much."'

18

KILLING THE GODFATHER

MANNY WAS PERFORMING DANGEROUS juggling acts. In Glasgow, he was associated with McGraw and Ferris as their relationship deteriorated, a rarity, as it was widely believed friendship with one automatically meant enmity with the other; in Belfast, those like him with the IPLO were under threat from both without and within.

The trial of Ferris at the historic High Court in the centre of Glasgow for the murder of Arty and a string of other alleged offences, including an attempt to kill the Godfather, was sensational from the first of its 54 days to the last. But the appearance of the Godfather himself as a witness was astonishing. Just as the golden rule in Northern Ireland was not to assist the police, so it was in Glasgow. Yet Thompson entered the witness box and swore to tell the truth, and when asked if he knew the identity of his son's murderer looked long and hard towards the dock and said everyone knew the answer to that.

Afterwards, Thompson's associates defended his decision to collaborate with the prosecution. He wanted justice for the death of his son. The customary routine would have been for him to arrange the type of contract killing that had accounted for Hanlon and Glover. But if anything had happened to Ferris, the finger of guilt would have pointed at no one but himself. The fact remained, though, that by helping the Crown, Thompson had now put himself at risk. Many, mostly among the younger element in the underworld, the Young Teams, vowed to punish him for that act.

While Ferris was on trial, McGraw had been busy. The days of the Barlanark Team had come to an end. Sophisticated alarm systems and the installation of safes that were neither easily opened nor carried off had made safe-cracking too risky. And too many of the gang were by now too well known to the police. Special Branch officers were also on the lookout for links between the Glasgow underworld and Irish paramilitaries. The security services knew about the Godfather and his guns, but they were anxious to prevent support of any sort from Scottish gangland sympathisers reaching terrorists and helping escalate or prolong the Troubles.

McGraw knew he needed to be careful. An incident in the past had brought him considerable heat and he wanted to be free from the sort of intense surveillance the security services could put into place, surveillance that would make it impossible to kick-start a scam with the potential to make him and others very rich indeed. He and a couple of his crew had been surprised and arrested as they were about to burgle a post office near Cumbernauld.

During routine questioning, Special Branch detectives intervened and said they were investigating robberies of high-value postal orders issued in Scotland that were then turning up in Northern Ireland and being cashed in by known UDA sympathisers. The money was probably used to buy guns and explosives. McGraw was a prime suspect because it was known the Barlanark Team specialised in hits on post offices.

McGraw denied being involved or knowing who was responsible. The first was true but not the second. Another Glasgow team was carrying out crude smash-and-grabs, concentrating on sub post offices. He tipped off two men behind the robberies that the heavy mob were on to them and warned them to take down their scores elsewhere. He heard nothing more about stolen postal orders.

He and his wife Margaret, 'Mags' to her friends, were frequent visitors to Tenerife, off north-west Africa, which boasted year-round sunshine. They had fallen in love with the island after being persuaded to join friends on a holiday there and had bought their own apartment in the Torviscas area of Playa de las Americas.

McGraw had never moved away from his east end of Glasgow base, and the couple were able to afford a smart home in a good area, thanks to the success of the Barlanark raiders but also, to a much greater extent, because of the popularity of the Caravel, run by Margaret.

The McGraws had done well, much better than most of those with whom they had grown up. Lots of their friends from the past struggled; few of them could afford to holiday in Tenerife. And one day as he sat in one of the numerous Scots-run bars on the island, he had an idea. It was one he needed to work on.

In the meantime, while Ferris waited for the jury to declare him an innocent man, McGraw was widening his circle of friends. Trevor Lawson and Gordon Ross were often in the Caravel: they and the McGraws had known Billy McPhee since he was a youngster working for Margaret when she ran an ice-cream van. (Ice-cream vans driving around Glasgow housing schemes acted as mobile shops also offering a huge range of small items from crisps to cigarettes. During the early 1980s disputes over routes led to violence dubbed the Ice Cream Wars, culminating in 1984 in the deaths of six members of the same family after their flat was set ablaze. Margaret and the majority of van owners were not involved.) As the reputation of the Caravel as an interesting bar spread, others had become regulars. Ross and McPhee would sometimes disappear for a week or two to drive over to Spain, and it was whispered in the city underworld that they had gone there to pick up hashish, which they would hide in the boot of their car or under seats, and sell in Glasgow. Then Ross went missing for a year and a half, and when he finally reappeared it was to admit he had copped a jail sentence for hash smuggling. Much later, McGraw would recount to Manny and a handful of others the conversation he had with Ross on his return.

'How much do you make on one of these trips?' McGraw had asked.

'If we're lucky, a few grand,' was the reply.

'And what if you're not lucky?'

'Couple of hundred after expenses.'

McGraw thought for a moment. 'Gordon, you're bringing this stuff in a wee VW Golf. The customs see two guys in an old banger driving back from Spain with not even a tan. They're bound to get suspicious. You need others with you for cover.'

'We tried that,' Ross told him. 'And we got pulled. The more people in the motor, the less room for the gear.'

'That's if you use a car,' said McGraw.

'Well, it'll look fucking daft if we turn up in shorts and sombreros in a fucking lorry.'

'Aye, right, but have you thought of a minibus?'

'A minibus? Where would we get the money to buy a minibus?'

'Nobody said anything about buying. Why not hire one?'

Afterwards, as Ross repeated the conversation to McPhee, he wondered, 'Why the fuck didn't I think of that?' But he failed to ask himself why, if it was such a good idea, McGraw hadn't tried it for himself. In fact, as McGraw eventually related to Manny, he simply wanted someone he could trust to test out an idea he had been mulling over for a long time. Ross's minibus was, in a sense, the sprat that would catch the mackerel. If the scheme worked, and McGraw was certain it would, his own version would need a lot of investment.

Manny knew nothing of this conversation at the time. He was happy for his friend when Ferris was acquitted, and despite the ever-growing bitterness between Ferris and McGraw, he had no reason to fall out with either. When he travelled to Glasgow to watch a match, most of his fellow passengers were booked into the city's Thistle Hotel, while Ferris would reserve him a room in the slightly more upmarket Ingram Hotel in Ingram Street, in the city centre. Most of the meetings between the two men were held there, although occasionally Manny would stay with friends, usually of McGraw.

One day a well-known player in the Glasgow underworld rang an IPLO unit commander with an offer he was sure the organisation would not refuse. He explained he had been offered a sub-machine gun. The original idea had been for the weapon to be given to the police, thereby putting the police in the gangster's debt. But it was well known that some underworld players, Paul Ferris for one, had bitter reason to know the police could not be trusted, especially when it came to promises of deals. Others had learned from his experience and so it was felt the gun would be better off well away from Glasgow and with the IPLO.

The commander was at first wary, but after Manny confirmed he knew the Glaswegian as a man who could be relied on to keep his word, the offer was gratefully accepted. The gangster and the commander spoke on for a few minutes more, arranging a rendezvous.

'I'll check your guy into the Ingram Hotel, Manny knows it,' said the gangster. 'But you'll need to be careful. If the cops suss your guy at Stranraer, he'll be followed.'

'Don't worry,' he was told. 'I'm sending somebody they won't know. He doesn't even have a police record.'

The man in Belfast made another call to arrange a meeting with an IPLO supporter who had helped out before. This man had a unique advantage when it came to smuggling weapons or drugs – a hollow artificial leg.

'Can you go over to Glasgow on the next supporters' bus and do a favour?'

'Anything,' came the response.

'Okay, you'll be booked into the Ingram Hotel in Ingram Street. Somebody will meet up with you and hand you a sub-machine gun. Can you bung it down your leg?'

'Sure, no problem,' said the one-legged sympathiser. 'What kind of gun?'

'It's an Ingram.'

The courier looked blankly for a moment. 'This isn't a wind-up is it? Let me get this fucking right. I have to go to Ingram Street, to the Ingram Hotel, and pick up an Ingram gun?'

'Right.'

'Don't tell me the guy I'm meeting with will call himself Ingram?'

'Right again.'

The handover went off like clockwork.

Another swap that did not go so smoothly concerned an attempt to give a bullet to Arthur Thompson: several bullets, in fact. The Godfather had created many enemies, on both sides of the Irish Sea: by giving evidence against Ferris; the murder of Joe Hanlon, crudely shot simply because he happened to be the Good Samaritan who offered a lift to his friend Bobby Glover, had created much ill will in Ireland; and Thompson's involvement with the UDA and his link to the security services had all combined to make him a marked man.

Underworld players in Glasgow decided it was time to send Thompson to sleep with the fishes. They made contact with Republicans and offered guns and drugs in exchange for his execution. It has always been believed the contract was offered to the IRA; in fact, it was the IPLO, desperate for weapons and money, that was consulted.

The initial contact was Manny, who was asked whether he could arrange a meeting with Dominic 'Mad Dog' McGlinchey. The Glasgow group believed he was the ideal man to perform the hit on the Godfather. They had read his name and of his ruthless reputation in newspapers but were unaware that McGlinchey was not an IPLO member, having opted to remain with the INLA. Further, he was in Portlaoise prison in the Republic serving a ten-year stretch for firearms offences and was therefore unavailable. McGlinchey was, however, told of the interest in him. He was nearing the end of his sentence and remembered talk of a big bounty to kill a man who had supplied weapons to the enemy.

An IPLO unit had been in Glasgow on a weapons-buying expedition at the time of Arty's murder. Because of increased police activity resulting from that shooting, the unit was pulled out in case it might be hinted that paramilitaries had in any way been involved. With the ending of the Ferris trial, it was now felt safe to return.

Manny said, 'We knew the IRA would not want to be involved in what was seen as a gangland feud in Glasgow. But we needed weapons and cash and it all seemed to be a very straightforward job. People were being targeted and whacked nearly every day in Northern Ireland. The only difference here was that we'd need to use Volunteers who were not known to the Scottish police. That ruled me out. My role had been just to arrange the initial contact. I was told later what happened.

'The Glasgow crowd had some peculiar ideas about how to kill Thompson, such as taking his wife hostage and forcing him to give himself up to us in exchange; putting poison into his milk bottles; and bombing his local bar, the Provanmill Inn. Our team had proposed putting a bomb under his car until it was pointed out that someone had done this nearly 30 years earlier and the only victim had been an innocent woman, his mother-in-law, who had been killed. We didn't want non-combatants to suffer and so it was decided just to shoot him, knock on his door, and when he answered, blast him.

'A detailed file on Thompson's movements and even plans of his house were given to the IPLO by people in Glasgow. Two Volunteers came over to do the contract and were briefed, but before anything could happen the internal fighting back in Belfast became so bad that they were recalled and the matter had to be left there. Thompson was a very lucky man. He would have been an easy target.'

The feuding within the IPLO was causing heightened concern within other Republican paramilitary ranks. And as the rumours of leaders cashing in on lucrative drug deals became more widespread, there was pressure for action. Manny, meanwhile, realised the killing was moving even closer to home. On 18 August 1992, his good friend Jimmy Brown was assassinated.

'The IRA had asked a leading politician to simply state, as a goodwill gesture, that the north of Ireland no longer had any strategic or economic value to the British government. When he did, I sat back and thought, "Politics does work." We hadn't been able to bomb that guy into surrendering, but we had negotiated him to the peace table.

'There was a debate within the IPLO between those who thought that maybe negotiation was the way and who wanted to give talking a chance, while others took the view that if you could bomb the British into negotiating by carrying on, attacking them in their own back yards, hitting places like London, Manchester, Birmingham and so on, then that was the way forward. So it started off another power struggle and I knew that from the highest to the lowest levels of the IPLO nobody was safe. Jimmy was just one of a number to die. He was a really good pal.'

Brown had been trying to bring the internal fighting to an end. He was driving when he spotted another Volunteer with whom he wanted to speak. He pulled alongside the man and called to him. But his colleague thought he was about to be shot and pulled out a handgun and shot Jimmy several times in the head. Afterwards, Brown's faction and that supporting his killer each accused the other of refusing to stop drug dealing. Nobody has ever been accused of murdering Brown, but the executioner is widely thought to have been Huck, the man who lost his fingers in a premature bomb explosion. Huck later died from illness.

'Jimmy was more a negotiator than a military man and he was never afraid to speak his mind. He was the one appearing on television wearing a suit and tie rather than standing on the street corner with a balaclava covering his face and holding a gun. The IPLO was always being accused of involvement in drug dealing, but the truth is that I never had any connection with drugs in Ireland.'

Nine days after Brown's killing, a member of the guard of honour at his funeral, Hugh McKibben, was shot dead. Two weeks later, Michael Macklin, suspected of driving the car for McKibben's killers, was murdered. The feud was building to a crescendo. In between these deaths came another unrelated to the feud but that would become one of the most controversial issues of the entire Troubles.

Manny was at home in Spamount Street on 4 September when Peter McBride, a teenager who lived in the same street, was stopped near his home and searched by a British Army patrol. Finding him unarmed, he was allowed to continue on his way. He ran off but seconds later was shot in the back by two Scots Guards. The soldiers said they thought Peter, a father of two aged 18, was about to throw a bomb in a coffee jar. The tragedy sparked off a furious row in which Republicans insisted McBride had been murdered. Witnesses claimed they had heard one of the troops tell the other, 'Shoot the bastard.' The soldiers were later convicted of murder and jailed.

19

WIPEOUT

HALLOWEEN, OR ALL HALLOWS EVE, on 31 October, is an ancient festival that some say is a throwback to ancient celebrations like the Festival of the Dead or the Samhain, a Gaelic festival marking the beginning of the dark half of the year. It is a time for children to carve lanterns from pumpkins, for fun such as trick or treating, apple bobbing, fireworks, partying, telling horror stories and playing pranks on unsuspecting victims. In Belfast, Halloween 1992 produced its share of scares, but these were not tricks.

The IRA, the Provisionals and the INLA may have held different philosophies, but all were united in one belief: that the time had come for the IPLO to be taught a lesson. Accusations persisted, then proliferated, that the organisation was riddled with drug dealers, thieves and rapists. Since its inception, the war against INLA alone had resulted in a dozen deaths. Lately, IPLO members were even turning their guns on each other. Manny's Belfast faction had split in two. Now with the major Republican organisations beginning to weary of the war and looking for a route to peace, or at least a ceasefire, they saw the presence of the ultra-violent IPLO as a major stumbling block to progress.

Under cover of the Halloween celebrations, with the sound of fireworks masking the noise of gunshots, at least 60 PIRA Volunteers attacked members of the IPLO brigades in Belfast in what would become known as the 'Night of the Long Knives'. It began just after teatime, when the streets were thronged with children. Two gunmen walked into Sean Martin's Gaelic Athletic Club, ordered everyone to lie on the floor and singled out father of four Sammy Ward, leader of the breakaway IPLO group in the city. As the head of the organisation's official brigade watched, Ward was hit in the head and body by ten bullets.

Elsewhere in Belfast, IPLO fanatics were hunted down in pubs, clubs or their homes, and kneecapped and threatened. Those who were not shot were ordered to leave the organisation on pain of death. Manny was one of the lucky ones. He had been arrested by the RUC, who were investigating a shooting, and was being held at Castlereagh for questioning. By doing so, the police almost certainly saved him from serious injury.

'When it was over, there were around 25 of our people in hospital. Sean [Caldwell] was ordered to go to a social club with a priest. He knew there was nothing for it but to go, and the moment he walked in the door a hood was put over his head and he was warned, "Tomorrow morning we want you and your fucking cronies to tell newspapers you no longer exist." He was allowed to leave unharmed.

'Why did they do this to us? At the end of the day they simply got fed up, but the truth was that we would do things they would not. We were ten times more brutal. Yes, we knew we had drug dealers in our ranks, and we were trying to weed them out. We'd shot a few of them, but the trouble was we had attracted the Dirty Dozen type, people wanting to kill just for the kick of seeing others die violently, and this was an element we did not want.

'Where we had stepped over the line was the Orange Cross operation, where guys were told to go in and just shoot everybody. Admittedly that hadn't happened, but the possibility remained that it could have resulted in a real bloodbath and then that would have led to revenge killings and a real escalation of the Troubles. For years the IRA and Provos had tolerated us, but they knew that if they started a feud with the IPLO with the aim of wiping us out then that could cause them real problems. There had been threats from them, but we'd simply said straight to their faces, "Okay, you have the manpower and the firepower to wipe us out, but while you're doing that we'll be taking a few of you with us." They knew we had the capabilities to take out some of their leading members, and would have done so. And they knew we'd been looking at Gerry Adams and Martin McGuinness.'

Adams, the one-time near neighbour of Manny, had been working hard behind the scenes to negotiate a ceasefire; McGuinness, former second in command of the IRA in Derry, had also become prominent in discussions aimed at a peace deal. The loss of either man would be a massive blow to IRA hopes of ending the Troubles.

'The Provos had a superb organisation, of which any army would have been proud. They knew they could have crushed us, but at the same time were aware that while we lay dying our guns would still be firing and that they would be blamed for starting off the shooting. Surprise was their best weapon. They practically took us apart, from top to bottom, went through us like a dose of salts and told us to disband or die.'

The attacks were concentrated on IPLO members in Belfast. Groups outside the city in Newry and Armagh were not affected, as they were considered free from criminal infection. Technically these units could have carried on, but without the insurance of the Belfast brigades for protection and the supply of hardware they would have quickly been swept away. In any case, within three days the IPLO said it was dissolving.

As soon as he was released from Castlereagh, Manny did not hang about Spamount Street. He made for the home of friends in the coastal village of Balbriggan in the Republic, around 25 miles north of Dublin. Balbriggan had seen its share of violence. In 1920, Black and Tans had rampaged through the village, bayoneting to death two men, and smashing and looting dozens of houses, four bars and even a factory making 'balbriggans', the long johns that would later be made famous in John Wayne movies.

From time to time Manny sneaked back to rejoin his family, doing so discreetly and ensuring only his closest friends, Sean among them, knew he was back. But his days as a Volunteer were numbered. And he acknowledged that the time of the gun and of the bomb had passed. Not everybody saw it that way, of course.

Someone else's days were numbered too. Arthur Thompson had seen one of his daughters die prematurely young from natural causes and his eldest son murdered; his loyal wife Rita had been jailed for beating up a woman neighbour during a feud; his mother-in-law had been blown up; and he had survived three attempts on his life. But there was no escape from the Grim Reaper, and in March 1993 the Godfather died in his bed from a heart attack. He was 62. Hundreds from all over Britain attended his funeral, the question on the lips of most being who would now sit on the throne from which he had presided over the Glasgow underworld. There were only two candidates, and the Irishman Manny McDonnell was friends with both.

Paul Ferris had been keeping a low profile since his lengthy trial. Some newspapers claimed he was in hiding, others that he was on the run from Thompson's associates. Neither was the case. He was not a man to run from trouble.

Throughout these dramas, Thomas McGraw had been busy. He confided to trusted friends that calls for an end to the violence in Northern Ireland were growing, and when the ceasefire came, men like Manny who had been at the sharp end would look around for work. He reckoned he could use someone of the Irishman's experience. His closest confidants knew that before the disbanding of the IPLO, McGraw had sent one of his friends to Belfast to investigate just how true were the versions of life back in Spamount Street that Manny had given him during his visits to Glasgow. McGraw had wondered if it really was so terrifying as Manny made it out to be.

An associate of the Krays had said that as much violence was committed in Glasgow in a fortnight as had been done by the twins and their great London gang rivals the Richardsons in their whole careers on the streets of the capital. Yet according to Manny, Glasgow was tame compared with Belfast.

'Tam and his friend were always pestering me about wanting to see how we operated and what weapons we had. Sean had been in Glasgow from time to time and his band had done gigs at the Caravel. He also tried impressing on Tam what it was like to live and fight through the Troubles, but we had the impression Tam thought we were exaggerating. So we said to his friend, "Okay, fly over and we'll show you the way we work."

'So he arranged a visit. We took him to a safe house, where the very first thing we did as soon as he walked in the door was to hood him. He was shaking with terror. We took him to a flat, and when we removed the hood, all the guys from my unit were there in full battledress, all of us with our weapons, everything that we needed for a war. I said, "Well, this is it. This is how we go to work each day." He was overwhelmed, couldn't believe it. I knew he would be telling Tam about everything he saw.'

And he was right. McGraw would have a use for the Irishman, but first he wanted to hear how Ross had fared with the suggestion that he hire a minibus and use it to smuggle drugs. It had gone well, he was told, to a degree. A few friends had gone on the trip, but they had complained of feeling tired during the long drive to the south of Spain and back, and Ross did not have the resources to buy large amounts of hash. While he had made a respectable profit on the venture, it had been hard work and hardly worth the risk. When McGraw had asked whether getting hold of hash was a problem, Ross for once had a positive answer. 'Absolutely not, we're okay on that score,' he said and went on to explain why.

During a visit to Malaga with a friend, Chick Glackin, the two men had met up with and become mates with a Mancunian who we are calling Todd. Like Ross, Todd had a passion for pretty women. He had been in the south of Spain for a while and had got to know a Moroccan, Mohammed, and discovered he was a link between farmers in the Rif range to the north of the country who grew vast acreages of the cannabis variety of hemp plants. The resulting sickly brown resin, hashish, was driven by lorry to the coast and whisked over the Strait of Gibraltar to the Costa del Sol in high-speed motor boats. Occasionally Spanish gunboats would appear, but usually the smugglers simply sped off into the night. Todd, according to Ross, could get his hands on enough hash to fill every pipe in Scotland ten times over.

'The problem, Tam, was the time people had to sit in the wee bus. Everybody was complaining. That same crowd wouldn't go again and I don't know where we'd get replacements. Maybe stick a notice up at the next Celtic game offering the Hoops supporters free trips to Spain,' Ross joked. But McGraw wasn't laughing. An astonishing idea was forming.

He was not alone in having plenty to think about. Just before noon on Saturday, 20 March 1993, a caller rang the Samaritans, gave the recognised IRA codeword and warned that a bomb had been placed near a branch of Boots in Liverpool. Police immediately acted and, although they found nothing, began clearing the area as a precaution.

While officers were wondering if this was yet another hoax, half an hour later a massive explosion rocked the town of Warrington, 15 miles away. A bomb went off in one of several cast-iron litter bins placed around the town centre. This bin was outside a Boots store and a branch of a McDonald's restaurant packed with youngsters enjoying their weekend off school, mostly with their parents and siblings, including babies. As the windows of both properties smashed into thousands of razor-sharp glass shards that showered down on the heads and faces of screaming children, panic-stricken shoppers outside scurried for safety, many trying to take refuge in the nearby Argos store. As they did so, a second bin directly outside Argos burst into fragments and yet more glass and debris rained down, slashing faces and tiny bodies; glass dust blew into innocent eyes, blinding them and leaving victims whimpering in agony.

There had barely been one minute between the bombs detonating, and afterwards experts would reason that the choice of cast-iron bins was deliberately calculated to wreak even greater havoc and human destruction because the metal would have the effect of blowing a wave of shrapnel against anyone in the vicinity.

Amid the blood and suffering, teams of police and paramedics found the blood-soaked body of Johnathan Ball, aged just three. He had been with a babysitter while his mum, Marie, was at home, and astonishingly the babysitter was uninjured.

There was more tragedy to come. Among more than 50 others who were injured, most of them children, lay Tim Parry, aged 12, who had been shopping for a pair of football shorts and was right beside one of the bins when it was blasted into smithereens. Tim took the full force of the explosion on his head, and although surgeons tried all they knew to save him, he was only kept alive by a life-support machine. Five days later, after talking to specialists, his parents agreed it should be turned off.

The deaths of the children caused revulsion, an emotion not helped by an IRA statement that admitted Volunteers planted the bombs and added, 'Responsibility for the tragic and deeply regrettable death and injuries caused in Warrington yesterday lies squarely at the door of those in the British authorities who deliberately failed to act on precise and adequate warnings.' The organisation said two 'precise' warnings about the bombs were made to the Samaritans and the police. It was an accusation strongly disputed by the police, who hit back: 'If the IRA think they can pass on their responsibility for this terrible act by issuing such a nonsensical statement, they have sadly underestimated the understanding of the British public.'

It was not only the British public that was affected by the murders of Johnathan and Tim. In Dublin, thousands joined protest parades, many sending flowers to Warrington to be laid on the coffins of the little victims; the government of the Republic announced it would in future make the extradition of terrorist suspects easier; and the pop band the Cranberries released a song, 'Zombie', in protest at the deaths. It went on to be a huge hit.

Manny, like every Irishman and -woman, had been deeply hurt by the death of every child as newspapers regularly recorded the toll of misery, showing photographs of tiny coffins carried by distraught parents. And like many, he wondered whether the human heart had a limit as to the amount of grief it was able to handle. If this was the case, then with the tragedy in Warrington he had reached his.

'When the two kids were killed it made a lot of people look at themselves. I thought of it in this way: "I passionately believe in what I've been fighting for all these years, I want what I know justice owes us, but not at any price." To this day, people in Warrington won't know this, but a lot of Catholic mothers in Belfast were disgusted, sickened that Johnathan and Tim had died. It made Republicans sit down and look at each other, and to be quite honest, the deaths of those boys had a huge impact on a lot of people. It certainly did on me. Now we were being looked on as child killers. Hearing about the boys ripped my heart out, especially knowing they died because of our fight.

'It was after Warrington that I decided I'd had enough. As a Volunteer I could withdraw my services at any time, but I had to go to see senior commanders to tell them of my decision. It was accepted, but I was told, "Secrets stay secrets." But they knew I would never let them down.'

Manny was 35. He had fought with passion and sincerity from boyhood. He had sacrificed any faint glimmer of hope of a career other than that of a paramilitary; had suffered beatings, threats and imprisonment and yet retained the loyalty and love of his family. Now one minute of madness in a town in another country had destroyed an enthusiasm that had driven him through everything. He knew he would never lose his belief in the cause for which he had fought, but it was time to move on. He could hardly write down his particular skills on a curriculum vitae. And almost every day more and more men from all sides were joining the ranks of those wondering what they would do when peace finally came. He did not know it then, but a Godfather lay just around the corner.

Still, he could not withdraw totally from an emotional involvement in what was going on around him. Regularly, incidents with a bearing on the past cropped up. Five weeks, almost to the hour, after death had visited Warrington, an IRA cell drove a stolen Ford tipper truck packed with a giant one-tonne fertiliser bomb that had been smuggled from Northern Ireland into England via the Stranraer ferry route into Bishopsgate in the heart of London. A series of warnings was telephoned to police from a coin box in County Armagh, and as the Bishopsgate area was being evacuated the lorry blew up, injuring 44 people, some seriously, and killing *News of the World* photographer Ed Henty, who had ignored instructions to leave the area. The damage was immense, forcing insurers to cough up £350 million. The bomb had been aimed at hitting the British economy.

It would later emerge that while this was happening, an MI5 surveillance team had been in the centre of London watching an old pal of Manny from his days in Cricklewood, IRA fanatic Gerard Mackin. Mackin headed an active service unit that was suspected of planting bombs throughout the capital. At the moment the lorry went up, Mackin and his unseen watchers were just 200 yards from the scene. There was never any evidence that he had been involved in the Bishopsgate bomb, but his days of freedom were numbered. In October 1994, he was jailed for 25 years at London's Old Bailey for planting bombs.

Two days earlier, another of Manny's old acquaintances, Gerald McQuade, who he had met in prison, had been arrested after have-a-go hero David Dunn was gunned down during an armed bank raid at Bonnyrigg, near Edinburgh. McQuade was later sent down for 18 years.

Much closer to home, Manny would never lose his sense of guilt over the killing of Billy Kane. And now, he knew, decisions were being taken about Billy's brother Eddie, named after the father lost in the McGurk's bar blast. Manny had known Eddie since he was a child. He was sure Eddie was in no danger but that was not a view shared by his friend's mother. She had already lost a husband and son and constantly feared for Eddie. The young man was suspected of being too talkative. What happened to him, and others, was the subject of an Amnesty International report on victims of paramilitary punishments that made chilling reading: 'In December 1992 John Collett was shot in the legs in his house; both legs were amputated and he later died from his injuries. On New Year's Day in 1993 Christopher Donnelly, aged 22, was shot in both legs by the IRA in front of his mother. One of his legs was subsequently amputated and he was ordered to leave Northern Ireland upon release from hospital. Micky Sherlock, aged 20, also had a leg amputated after being "kneecapped" in August 1992. He was told to leave but the "expulsion order" was lifted after the amputation. They were shot for alleged "anti-social" behaviour. Tommy Smith and Phil McCullough were shot in the legs for alleged "joy-riding" (driving around in a stolen car); Phil McCullough developed gangrene. Damien McCartan, aged 21, was shot three times in the legs in March 1993 after refusing to allow his car to be used by IRA men in an attack. The IRA issued a statement that he had been shot as "punishment" for endangering the lives of "IRA Volunteers" and risking the capture of "war materials".'

When it came to the turn of 27-year-old Eddie, the punishment was savage, to say the least. He was shot in both knees and both elbows. He would be permanently maimed, have to limp through the rest of his life and be unable to use one arm. While he was in hospital, he received an IRA message ordering him out of Northern Ireland immediately, even though his treatment was incomplete. It would be many years before Manny saw Eddie again.

20

ON THE BUSES

GORDON ROSS HAD PLANTED in the mind of Tam McGraw the first seeds of an idea that would grow into a field of gold, that of offering something for free. Night after night in the Caravel, McGraw had wondered how to get over the problem of filling the hired minibus with people willing enough to put up with the discomfort of a lengthy journey.

His friend Manny came over, and McGraw suspected it was to see Ferris. He liked the Irishman but wished he and Ferris were not so close. His unease at the relationship meant he was careful just how much he told the Republican. During these trips to Glasgow, Manny made a point of calling at the Caravel to see McGraw and of looking up McGraw's friend James Mullen.

It was one of these trips that provided McGraw with a solution to his problems. During a mundane conversation he had asked whether Manny had flown. 'No,' he was told, 'I came over on one of the supporters' buses. It's a good way to travel because it's cheap and you can chat away and take your mind off sitting cramped up in a bus.'

The conversation turned, as it often did, to the Troubles. Manny talked about his decision to withdraw as a Volunteer.

'It's time to think of the family, Tam,' he said. 'Sally and the kids have stood by me for years. They haven't grumbled at all the sacrifices, probably because just about everybody in New Lodge is in the same boat of not having a job and having to make do with the giro. But I'd love to be able to have enough dosh to give them regular good holidays and not have to worry about whether I can afford to take the family for a night out. I've made a few quid over here doing turns, but I have to be so careful. If we suddenly started throwing money about there'd be questions asked as to where I was getting it from. But I'd just love to take the kids somewhere special, Disneyland or somewhere like that. There's been a lot of stuff on the telly about opening a Disneyland near Paris.'

McGraw would later tell a friend, 'I was trying to help Gordon and started thinking over what Manny had been saying. It hit me there was a way not just of getting enough punters to fill the minibuses but what to do about the long journey. I thought if football supporters were offered cheap trips to games in Spain, there'd be no shortage of takers. When I discussed this with some other people they took it a stage further, saying gear could be picked up there, stuck into extra suitcases and brought back that way. But then we worried what would happen if they got rowdy, caused problems and the police came into it. If they were young, though, it would be easier to control them. It was Manny's mention of Disneyland in Paris that gave me the idea of taking them there instead of all the way into Spain.'

Taking a party to Disneyland was the easy part. But how to get the hash there from Spain? Ross answered that one, one night in the Caravel: 'I'll take a car down to the Costa del Sol, pick up the gear and drive it to Disneyland and we'll load it into the bus there.'

'Who's your man in Spain?'

And Ross told McGraw about Todd. 'How much can you get in the car?' he was asked.

'About 60 kilos,' was the reply.

In their heads, the two men worked out what that would mean. A kilo bought in Spain for around £700 would sell in Glasgow for up to £2,300, giving a potential profit of £96,000. There were expenses, of course: the hire of the minibus, the cost of a car, fuel, ferry, hotel bills, but the sums still added up to a huge profit. 'Fucking hell,' said McGraw.

Much, much later, police would say Tam McGraw was at the centre of a multimillion-pound smuggling plot. But a jury would decide there was not enough proof to back up this claim. One explanation of his interest was that he was simply passing on suggestions to others, Ross in particular, and what they did with the information was a matter for them. McGraw maintained he did not benefit from drug smuggling. Similarly, Manny became for a time not just a central police target but also the main target. And while he and others worked for McGraw and others suspected of drug smuggling, and was aware of rumours that his work was a part of the smuggling operation, he always maintained he was never directly involved and had no knowledge of whether smuggling took place.

A few days later, Gordon Ross and his friend met up again, and this time the pal had an even more profitable proposal: 'Look, Gordon, what if you don't take anybody? Drive the bus over empty?'

Ross look baffled. 'How are you going to explain driving an empty minibus to Disneyland and back?'

'Simple, on the way out just say you're on your way to bring back a party of kids from Disneyland, get the gear, take out the seat cushions and stick the gear in there and then on the way back say you've left a party near Paris and are coming back in a week to fetch them. You're not footing the bill for anybody this way.'

Despite his misgivings, Ross agreed to go ahead. But there remained the question of finding around £40,000 to pay for the bus expenses and buying the hash. It was a lot of money, more than they could come up with, and so others in Glasgow, men running companies with high cash turnovers, were discreetly asked if they wanted to dip into their back pockets and take a share. These included a leading Glasgow businessman from the transport sector who insisted on knowing every detail and who was told that if it was found he had breathed a word of the scheme to anyone, 'You will get a visit from a friend of ours from Belfast. You just don't want this guy calling on you.' The businessman nodded. He had heard whispers of a Republican who turned up at the Caravel or in the company of Paul Ferris, sometimes with a group of others from over the Irish Sea.

In mid-1993, the empty hired bus was driven to Paris, where it met Ross, who had motored from Torremolinos. On the way back, the two bus drivers were conscious of the smell of their cargo and worried about it being detected during customs checks. But at both Calais and Dover, officers merely looked through the windows at empty seats and waved them on. Once on the motorways to Glasgow, despite the chilly early morning air, they opened all the windows, but before returning the bus to the hire garage the seats had to be scrubbed and sprayed with antiseptic. Their explanation for the unusually fragrant smell was, 'Some of the kids got food poisoning and were sick. We've cleaned it thoroughly.' The problem of the smell would remain until the operation was well established, when a unique solution would be found.

Ross refused to try the empty-bus trick a second time.

'There's every chance that the same customs guys will be on duty and maybe start wondering if there's something fishy going on,' he said. 'We've got to put bums on the seats.'

With his companion and one of the drivers, he mulled over where to find passengers, and the driver came up with an answer.

'I know a guy who helps run a football club for youngsters,' he said. 'Let's offer them free holidays to Disneyland and maybe try and fix them up with some games over there with other kids.'

'It's going to look too dodgy if you give trips like this away for free,' he was told. 'Maybe you should charge them a few quid each time.'

There remained one outstanding detail. Inevitably someone, most likely a parent, was going to want to know what lay behind the almost free holidays, who was paying for them and why. By now others who had had invested in the initial run were becoming part of the planning team. McGraw began hearing things when these men were boozed up and he thought there were too many with loose tongues in the know, a development with which he would not have been happy had he been running the operation.

But the combined thoughts of them all gave birth to a mysterious millionaire property entrepreneur named Colin O'Sullivan, who was said to have originally come from Glasgow but who now wanted to spend some of his wealth helping the deprived of the city. Manny happened to be making a visit to the Caravel with his friend Sean when the idea was mooted.

'We'll say he's in Ireland and never comes over here,' said the bus driver after hearing the two from Belfast sharing a joke.

Manny looked forward with increasing enthusiasm to his visits to Scotland, because in Glasgow he could relax, knowing the stranger who followed him into a bar was not going to be a Loyalist about to pull out a gun and shoot him, or a member of the RUC set to whisk him back to Castlereagh. The police both in Glasgow and Belfast were aware of his frequent trips and that he met up with the city's two highest-profile gangsters. He always knew when he was being followed by the police, but as time passed and the visits seemed no more than a football follower watching his side or meeting with old friends, interest in him began to wane.

Loyalists had been quick to avenge the deaths of the Warrington children at the hands of the IRA. On the day Tim Parry's parents agreed to doctors turning off his life-support systems, four Catholic workmen were shot dead by Ulster Freedom Fighters as they arrived in a van to start work renovating houses on a County Derry estate. Damian Walsh, just 17, was murdered by the same organisation, shot in the back as he swept the floor at a coal depot in West Belfast where he worked as part of a youth training scheme. In Damian's case there were suspicions of collusion between the British Army, the RUC and his killers.

In mid-1993, the cheap trips for young footballers got under way when 16 hopefuls, aged 14 and 15 from the Highbury Boys Club, a side run as a nursery for the English club Arsenal, were taken on a short holiday to Camp Davy Crockett, part of the Disney complex near Paris. The youngsters were asked only to make token payments of £30 to part cover the cost of diesel fuel. The men in charge of the trip, on the other hand, had already collected a thick wad of cash. Some of this left in a car a few days before the coach departed to be taken to southern Spain, where it would purchase another 60 kilos of hash – equivalent to the weight of a medium-size adult – while the remainder was left with the bus crew to cover expenses and the cost of the stay at the camp.

This time the hashish was well wrapped in damp cloths and bin-liner bags and packed inside suitcases, stowed in the boot. Even so, the drivers remained anxious that its smell would attract attention, particularly from the sniffer dogs occasionally brought on board during customs checks.

While the youngsters relaxed at Camp Davy Crockett, on the final night of their stay the bus disappeared for a couple of hours. When it returned, it was 60 kilos heavier, while the occupants of the car it had met, having handed over their load, continued on their way to Glasgow. It had all been so easy. There were more trips that year as the cut-price holidays to Camp Davy Crockett continued.

By now, more of McGraw's friends were in on the act. It was ironic that he was forever lambasting others for careless talk, because while he could be discreet, he had a habit of wanting others to know just how successful he could be. He was also known, but not to his face, as 'Tam add-a-bit' through an at times irritating habit of exaggeration. He overheard stories of huge amounts of hash being smuggled from Spain, but when he repeated these to men he thought he could trust and who he thought might be interested, the figures involved grew ever higher. Even now, there were too many in the know.

When the hash arrived back in Glasgow, it had to be collected and paid for. The buyers were hardly likely to implicate themselves, but already there were some wondering where the seemingly endless supplies were coming from. Trevor Lawson, who McGraw had once rescued from a stabbing at the Caravel, was now among the investors, and so was Billy McPhee along with Ross and others who had been close to him over the years. John Healy, a relative of McGraw and a shrewd investor, had been in almost from the outset. He had introduced Graeme Mason, known as 'Del Boy' because of his remarkable similarity to the television wide boy portrayed by David Jason in the *Only Fools and Horses* series.

The bigger the pool of those involved, the less there was for each at the end of each trip when it came time to share out, usually at a comfortable Glasgow hotel. The Marriott became a favourite venue of the smugglers. And then another joined in – Greed. As the grumbling over the decreasing size of the envelopes containing the shares grew, the smugglers decided to liberally enlarge the operation. That meant hiring a bigger coach, taking more boys and, as a consequence, being able to bring back more hashish, thereby giving the profits a hike. It was to be something of an experiment, a test run, but before it could get under way the entire operation was put on hold.

Suspicion continued to abound over what happened in the minutes before and after the killings of Joe Hanlon and Bobby Glover. The identities of the shootist and his paymaster were soon being whispered throughout the city. But who took the still-warm bodies to their temporary morgue and then on to the Cottage Bar? The name of a fringe figure in the underworld, Paul Hamilton, had been mentioned, and he did little or nothing to dispute any involvement. He had been questioned by murder-squad detectives but released without charge.

But it was a dangerous situation, because the dead men had lots of friends, and in November 1993 Hamilton was found shot dead, slumped over the wheel of his Daimler car. His widow, Georgina, later claimed he had been murdered after receiving a telephone call from Paul Ferris asking for a meeting to hand over money owed to Hamilton. The killing sparked fears of a turf war, and major players such as Ferris and McGraw were put under additional police surveillance. That was especially awkward for the latter, who was slap bang in the middle of having his advice sought over one of Scotland's biggest-ever drug-smuggling rackets. It meant that for several weeks the bus runs were put on hold.

By the beginning of 1994, however, the gang felt the heat was lukewarm enough to get back to work. And so 32 young players went off to Camp Davy Crockett for three nights. It meant extra work for the car and its journey between Paris and southern Spain. This time it carried nearly 100 kilos, and the only real problem for the smugglers was finding room to stow all the suitcases. Financially the trip was a success, although limited by the capacity of the car making the delivery from Spain and the room available on the hired bus, a 36-seater.

It was time to take the operation a stage further. Hiring buses just added to the cost of each run. The smugglers decided to put the racket on a real business footing by setting up a bogus travel company with its own vehicle. And so BMH Travel was formed with an address in Scotland Street, Glasgow, which happened to neighbour the stables housing Strathclyde Police horses. However, acquiring a bus was not so straightforward. Tongues would wag if McGraw or Healy were to be seen buying a luxury travel coach. Graeme Mason, on the other hand, was a little-known figure and it was he who was deputed to be the buyer. Scores of coaches were looked at before Mason, calling himself John Balmer, turned up at an auction in Glasgow at the start of February and successfully bid £12,000 for a white 24-seater Mercedes bus that had formerly belonged to a defunct travel firm.

Another £8,000 was laid out on fitting new seating and a toilet and making the coach comfortable enough for overseas trips. It made a successful run to France with a party of youngsters, but its next trip was a disaster when two cars transporting the hash from Spain to meet up with the bus were stopped by French customs officers, searched and the drugs discovered. Three men and a woman, all from Glasgow, were arrested and hash with a street value of £260,000 seized. The men were given long prison sentences, but the woman skipped France and fled home after being bailed and was told to stay in a hostel to await her trial.

It was a disaster for everyone and a financial catastrophe for the syndicate back in Glasgow, who lost more than £85,000. The weakness in the scheme was having to use cars to transport the drugs from Spain to France. The answer, it was decided, was to take the coach all the way to the source. Furthermore, some of the youngsters were becoming cheesed off with trips to Disneyland. Cheap holidays in the sunny south of Spain sounded a much more attractive proposition.

The first trip to Spain in the white coach left on 12 May 1994 and 17 youngsters spent eight nights in the Las Palomas Hotel in Torremolinos courtesy of Colin O'Sullivan. Among their luggage on the return journey were nearly 300 kilos of hashish worth, on the streets of Scotland, nearly three-quarters of a million pounds. There was only one snag. The coach was just not up to such long runs. It barely made it back to Glasgow. But who cared when money poured in? It was time to think big, very big. If an old coach could carry 300 kilos, why not a bigger, newer one that could carry double, or treble that amount?

The smuggling gang came to McGraw and sought his views. If he knew he was being asked about carrying illicit drugs, then by now he had determined the subject was never to be discussed anywhere where anyone might be overheard. And rather than thinking out aloud, he took his thoughts with him when he flew to his Tenerife apartment for a winter break. He loved the balmy nights when he could wander through the bars, often meeting up with old friends from Glasgow, some of them on the island to stay out of the way of police back home. One day, while having his favourite steak and chips, he saw a coach party of children passing the restaurant and noticed the kiddies standing so they could see through the windows. He thought, 'If the floor was a bit higher . . .' and an astonishing brainwave came to him. Back in Glasgow he mentioned it to a friend.

In June, the mysterious Mr Balmer, representing BMH Travel of Glasgow, was in Carlisle, where he paid £52,000 for another Mercedes, a much newer vehicle. It was sent off to a specialist body shop where the owner was instructed to raise the level of the floor. It was an unusual request but explained by, 'We're concentrating on taking parties of children and want them to be able to see out of the windows without standing up. If they're on their feet and the bus has to stop suddenly, the kids could get hurt.' The work cost £20,000 and meant a sizeable gap beneath the floor, large enough for a substantial number of suitcases or boxes to be stowed.

As for the first Mercedes coach, the order was given to one member of the gang to have it scrapped just in case any traces of hash remained in it. The instruction was never followed. In fact, the vehicle was sold to a local bus company in Ireland, where it plied country roads, the passengers sometimes sniffing and remarking on the peculiarly sickly odour coming from the rear. It was evidence in motion.

21

PARADISE

TWO FRIENDSHIPS WERE DEVELOPING, both of which would have a dramatic effect on Manny. He stayed in contact with his old comrades in arms but was disappearing more and more to Glasgow, sometimes accompanied by Sean and others involved in the Troubles. McGraw seemed intrigued by the situation across the water and fascinated by descriptions of operations carried out by the IPLO active service unit Manny had led. The Irishman, on the other hand, was not impressed by what he saw of and learned about Glasgow.

'The gangland scene was totally different to what we were used to. To us, the Troubles were as far removed from the Glasgow underworld as night is to day. People in Glasgow believed they were gangsters, but they'd been watching too many movies, they were cardboard characters, and we thought we were in the middle of amateurs. We were willing to work for the highest bidders and knew that because of our experiences and background in Ireland we would have had no fears carrying out assignments the Glaswegians were reluctant to take on. Tam realised that and knew that should he ever need reliable help in the future, he could turn to us. But, for now, he put that thought to the back of his mind.

'One day, out of the blue, I got home and there was Tam sitting chatting to Sally. It was a complete shock to see him in the living room. He said he'd just wanted to get away from Glasgow for a time, had driven down to Stranraer and jumped on the ferry. And once in Belfast he headed for my house. He said he wanted to see around Belfast and so I got hold of some of my old unit and we showed him around; they let him see some of their equipment, weapons and ammunition, told him how we operated and how we evaded capture during operations. I still had lots of good friends in the Republican movement but had taken a big step back after the disbanding of the IPLO, because there were still people wanting to kill guys who used to be in the organisation. There had never been any problems with my easing out; guys respected my decision and my reasons. As a father, I still felt sickened about the Warrington bombs.

'As we were looking around Belfast, Tam came across an antiques shop and had a wander around inside. He got his eye on what looked like a Second World War German helmet and a German officer's sword; at least, that's what the labels said they were. The guy behind the counter said he was German and could vouch for the helmet being genuine and the sword being very rare. Tam always had a good bundle of cash on him and handed over a big wad, hundreds of pounds. He was really happy with his buys.

'He said he was always looking for potential investments. And he wanted somewhere he could run to now and again and chill out. A place where nobody knew him and nobody was interested in him. A hideaway where the police or newspapers weren't watching him. I said I knew just the spot and drove him to Donegal. Donegal is a lovely town, a very strong IRA area, although we had supporters and safe houses there as well. For Volunteers like me, it had had the huge advantage of being in the Republic, which meant that once we crossed the border into Ireland we could relax. It was also very quiet and a favourite with the Americans. I knew it well.

'It was a great place for a policeman wanting a quiet life to be based, because the Republicans never caused any bother and the only lawbreaking was a spot of riding a bike without lights or a bit of illegal fishing now and again. I showed him other places in the area, like Ballyshannon, but right away Tam fell in love with Donegal. We walked around and everybody was friendly and polite. He was a nobody, just another visitor.

'I took him into the Paradise Bar and he loved that too. He started chatting to people in the bar and it was obvious they took a liking to him. When he left he was very thoughtful, but I didn't ask what was on his mind.

'Once he was home he must have asked somebody to take a close look at what he'd bought in the shop, because I got a phone call from him. He was raging. "That German fucker sold me a pile of shite," he said. "The fucking sword's worth about 20 quid. Can you go and see the fucker and tell him I want my money back or there'll be a crew coming over from Glasgow to sort him." I told him to send the sword back over and I'd look after this for him. When it was delivered, I took Sean along to the shop. The owner wasn't having any of it until we showed him the sword, explained who we were and told him, "Either you take it back or we'll ram this through you." He coughed up the money right away.'

Manny was becoming closer and closer to McGraw and his circle of friends, turning up in Glasgow every couple of months or so.

'I was still friendly with Paul Ferris and split my time in Glasgow between seeing him and Tam, looking around at what was happening, working out if anything was going to happen. I tried keeping my ear to the ground and my eyes open. I sensed that, with Tam, there was something major going on but couldn't work out what it was. And I wasn't going to risk losing his friendship by asking. I reasoned that when and if he wanted me to know, he'd tell me.

'He and Paul each knew I was seeing the other and the pair of them were like old women. "I don't like him, he doesn't like me, he doesn't like so and so." They were always bitching on about one another, who was friends with who, and how one wasn't going to speak to somebody because he'd talked to a friend of one of them. It was crazy. I liked both of them: simple as that.'

Just as there were rivalries in Glasgow, so the war in Belfast continued to be waged on his doorstep. It was impossible to be completely divorced from it. Dominic McGlinchey, the one-time cell mate of Manny's friend John, had been released from prison in the Republic bemoaning the fact that he had missed out on a potentially lucrative contract to shoot the Glasgow Godfather. McGlinchey was still the dominant figure in Manny's former group, the INLA, but in February 1994 he was shot dead by two gunmen as he made a call from a Drogheda coin box.

Then that June came an astonishing incident when, as office workers bustled about Shankhill Road seeking a bite and buying messages during their lunch hour, three members of the UVF, David Hamilton, Colin 'Crazy' Craig and Trevor King, were standing on a street corner discussing the meeting they had just left at which it had been decided to kill a fourth man, suspected of being an informer.

Former INLA Volunteer colleagues of Manny were returning from a mission in Shankhill to kill a UVF member, which had been aborted when the target failed to show up at a regular location, possibly benefiting from a tip-off by an informer. Disgruntled and frustrated, the members of the INLA unit could hardly believe their eyes when they saw the rival group, clearly unaware of the danger in which they suddenly found themselves.

The INLA unit leader, Gino Gallagher, ordered his driver to pull up, and despite it being lunchtime and busy with pedestrians, he leapt from the car and walked up to the trio before pulling out a handgun. He shouted out 'yo, yo' to attract their attention and, as they turned to face him, shot and killed all three. Manny knew Gallagher to be as fearless as he was ruthless.

'It was a miracle to find three UVF guys out in the open so close together. After that, Gino was known as "Yo Yo".'

A year later, when the new, more expensive bus was running well-established regular and highly profitable trips to the south of Spain, Tam and Mags McGraw took up an invitation to be guests at the wedding of a close relative of Manny. They were about to discover just how close the Troubles could come to those thinking they were safe and at a distance.

The couple were spotted by police at Glasgow airport boarding a flight to Belfast. Movements of high-profile criminals such as McGraw always set police telephone lines buzzing. Why Belfast? Colleagues in Northern Ireland were alerted and asked to make discreet inquiries about the McGraws, who were followed to the popular and busy Europa Hotel in the city centre, where a member of staff confided to an inquiring Irish detective that they were attending a wedding. At that the police lost interest, but the visit was noted all the same.

Manny was waiting to greet them and joined them for a drink.

'I knew a guy who worked at the hotel. He was on the point of finishing his shift, so I asked if he'd like to come over and sit with us. He told a very funny story about how he'd been a Republican Volunteer at one stage and his unit was constantly being given the job of bombing the Europa. The hotel was a favourite with journalists and a bomb always guaranteed publicity. He said he'd gone in with one bomb, put it on the counter in reception and warned that it would go off in a quarter of an hour. At that, the receptionist picked it up and threw the bomb into the street outside.

'So, my friend went back a week later carrying another bomb, walked up to the same guy on reception, squirted superglue on the counter, planted the bomb on top and told him, "Try moving that you fucker." I think the bomb went off but don't know how much damage was caused. The Europa was bombed about 70 times. Some time later my pal got a letter telling him to report to the labour exchange. They said they had a job for him and handed him a card with the details. The job was at the Europa Hotel. He was asked if he knew where it was. "Oh yes, I know it very well," he'd said.'

Following the wedding, the McGraws and Manny paid another visit to Donegal. The Paradise Bar was closed when they arrived. They found the exterior drab and, peering inside through the windows, saw the interior was no better. Mags was not impressed with the pub nor the town, finding it dull. The real purpose of the trip was for McGraw to pay a call on the Allied Irish Bank to open an account. He left a deposit with the promise that there would, over the coming months, be more deposits, some of which would be substantial. Occasionally, he would send money to Manny in Belfast and ask him to drive down to Donegal with it. Some would be banked with the Allied Irish; some would be handed over to a Glaswegian friend of McGraw.

Word was spreading on the streets of Glasgow about the chummy relationship between McGraw and the Belfast Republican who showed up occasionally. It was not welcomed in all quarters.

'One night I phoned Paul from Belfast. Paul had told me he was going to do Tam, but by this time I was really matey with Tam, and because I'd run an active service unit, with the experience and capability we all still had, Paul wasn't a problem to us. When he told me what he was planning, he asked what I thought. I told Paul I didn't like it and that Tam had made friends in Belfast, and if anything happened to Tam, I and others would take it personally.

'Paul asked, "Is that a threat?" I said, "Let me put it like this, Paul, if anything happens to Tam, we are going to retaliate." I didn't want to fall out with Paul, because he had been a good friend over many years. Paul never forgot that conversation. Years later he reminded me about it one day and asked, "Do you remember the conversation we had about Tam?" I said, "I remember it well, Paul." He said, "You know what you said, don't you?" and I replied, "I know exactly what I said. What are you getting at?" He said, "Nothing, I'm just reminding you."'

During a visit to Glasgow after he had introduced McGraw to Donegal, Manny had his first firm suspicions as to what it was his new friends might be involved in and why McGraw seemed to have so much money. But because he could not be and never would be absolutely certain, he bit his tongue and said nothing.

'I knew he was bursting to let me in on a secret, because at times Tam just couldn't stay quiet. He was starting to drop heavy hints. For instance, when I met up with him and his friends I'd hear comments such as, "There won't be any shortage of blow in Glasgow for a couple of weeks," and "They'll be smoking fucking spliffs a fucking yard long." So I was sure now what it was they were into, although I had no idea, then, of either the scale or how it was being done. And I wasn't sure whether Tam was part of the gang or just acting as a sort of adviser to them.'

Then Manny found himself even infuriatingly closer to discovering all when one of the close friends he had made in Glasgow asked him if he had any money to invest. 'Invest in what?' Manny had asked.

'Oh, just a little thing that some of us are making a few quid from,' was the answer.

Manny had done work in Glasgow and had been paid, but that had gone mainly on a couple of holidays abroad. 'Wish I had money, but I've only got the giro every week,' he lied cheerfully.

'Well, don't worry, I'll lend you 5,000 quid; you can invest it and pay me out of your profit.'

Until he knew exactly what the investment would be in, Manny was reluctant to take on a debt he might have trouble repaying to a friend. 'Let me think about it,' he said.

It was the second friendship, though, that would threaten to prove almost as devastating to Manny, and to others, as had been his involvement with Republican paramilitaries. Around the time Eddie Kane was facing his tormentors, Hannah Martin was wandering around the Thornliebank area of Glasgow looking for candidates willing to become customers of Kays catalogue.

Likeable Hannah had a strange and sad background. Her sister had died in a road tragedy, and when Hannah, a distant relative of Arthur 'The Godfather' Thompson, was just 16 she had been raped after a night out in Glasgow that included a visit to the famous Barrowland Ballroom. The attack was around the time three women had been murdered after attending dances at the Barrowland. These killings were blamed on a scripture-quoting stranger who would be known as 'Bible John'. Hannah's attacker bore a remarkable resemblance to police photofits of the killer. She found herself pregnant, but after giving birth to a baby girl was forced, by her harsh father, to have the child adopted by a couple who showered love on the infant and who would help her grow into a beautiful and successful businesswoman.

As she grew older, Hannah's world slowly sank into a loveless, dull existence. She struggled for money and the warmth of a man in her bed, and to supplement her wages in a local factory became a Kays representative.

One wet and windy night Hannah found herself in Clova Street, Thornliebank. Her knock was answered by Graeme Mason, who told her he did not want to buy anything but invited her in for a hot drink and the use of a dry towel. As they chatted she found him pleasant enough. He told her he sold salvaged goods, curtains, bedding and the like, and made a decent living. When she finished her drink and said she needed to look for more customers, he suggested she return before heading home, and this she did. He took her to two local bars and introduced her to the fit, well-muscled owner of both, who said his name was John Healy. Hannah was instantly smitten, but it was to Mason's home and bed she went that night. They became lovers.

Over the coming weeks, after bouts of sex, Hannah would find herself listening to an astonishing story. That first night he had hinted at being part of 'something big', but as time wore on he let slip more and more details, painting a picture of himself as the big-time boss of a huge smuggling operation bringing hashish to the streets and houses of Scotland from the Rif Mountains in Morocco. Mason left her with the impression that he was the genius who masterminded the business.

Throughout their relationship, Hannah gave her body to Mason but her heart lay with Healy, her junior by ten years and, as far as she knew, happily married. Still, Mason was kind and when he suggested they take a holiday in Spain for which he would pay, she was instantly agreeable. 'Where are we going?' she asked and he told her, 'Malaga.'

'You sure you can afford this?' she queried.

'Oh yes, no problem, I'll be checking up on one or two things and taking a message over to give to somebody. The holiday is on expenses and I get a wee bit of spending money as well.'

'It's nothing dodgy is it?' she asked, and he promised, 'Oh no. Don't worry yourself.'

The 'message' was a bag containing £150,000 in banknotes. Just before the couple set off to catch their holiday flight, John Healy arrived, handed over the money in a carrier bag, wished them a good trip and disappeared. Hannah knew instantly they'd be in trouble if they were caught with so much cash but made no effort to talk Mason out of carrying it. Her reason was simply that it was clear this was a favour for Healy, and if he wanted it she'd risk all for him. She carefully hid the bundles of notes in their clothing, packing some in her brassieres, others in her vanity bag, yet more in a nightdress. She still did not know why the money was needed, and while her curiosity persisted she was sufficiently savvy not to jeopardise her fortnight in the sun by asking too many questions.

22

LIGHTING CANDLES

THE OUTLAY ON THE SECOND COACH topped £70,000, but that was peanuts compared with the potential return. No one knew just how much hash could now be stowed in the space beneath the floor, accessible via a series of panels down the centre opened by a lever close to the driver's seat.

After the panels were closed, dirt was rubbed into the seams to give the impression these were sealed. There remained the problem of smell. The passengers were young and keen, with a good sense of smell. They were bound to notice the sickly pong of hashish. Then someone came up with a brainwave after watching a butcher wrap up sausages in polythene that kept them airtight but also removed any aroma. Two second-hand machines were bought and delivered to the team in Spain who prepared the drugs after each consignment had been bought from Mohammed or his assistant Mustapha.

Despite being tightly wrapped and packed into cardboard boxes, which were then sealed, the fear was the hash might still be detected by sniffer dogs, regularly taken on board coaches at the various customs checkpoints, at the crossing from Spain into France, Calais and then Dover. That was solved by one of the driving team arranging food fights as the coach approached these areas, encouraging the young passengers to throw crisps, sandwiches, cakes and sweets at one another, leaving the floor covered in a sweet and salty gunge that fooled the nose of every dog ever used to check for contraband.

To make even more believable the cover story that Colin O'Sullivan wanted to encourage the development of young footballers, an approach was made to the Scottish Football Association, and the result was contact with sister associations in Europe and the setting-up for the teenage passengers of matches and tournaments in Spain and France.

Beneath those feet that the young owners hoped would one day grace Hampden Park or the other great soccer stadiums of the world stage, it was possible to hide 710 kilos, nearly three-quarters of a tonne of hashish. While the cost would be around half a million pounds, it would sell for a potential £1,633,000, giving the smugglers a vast profit, still well over one million pounds even after the cost of buying the raw material, transporting it, paying for accommodation for the holidaymakers, bus crew and everybody else involved and handing out wages to the 'employees' of the travel company

Of course, not every journey brought back a full load to Scotland. Sometimes it was not possible for the Moroccans to supply such an amount, either through difficulties in getting it from the mountains or because of increased coastal security. There were times when the Glasgow market was unable to absorb the full cargo and part of the load would then be sold to eager buyers elsewhere, in Manchester and London in particular. When Mohammed and his gang could not come up with a full load, space under the floor of the Mercedes would literally be sold to other drug outfits. The rule was 'hash only', but nobody checked on what was stowed behind the panels once they were opened.

Being asked to come up with half a million pounds, especially on a regular basis, would have given any banking official headaches, but it was never a problem for the smugglers. The initial load had been paid for by some of the gang, mostly putting in small units of around £5,000 each, but principally by a handful of other enthusiasts who dug deep into their cash.

Three leading and successful Glasgow businesses are, to this day, in existence on their present till-jingling scales solely due to their owners taking up options to gamble on that initial cargo and some subsequent loads. Each took an enormous risk, putting up between £60,000 and £95,000 each. Everyone who took a chance and handed over cash had the amounts trebled within three weeks. Some of the load was given on trust by Mohammed, who expected and received £1,000 a kilo once the consignment had been distributed.

Of the many issues that needed to be resolved, two required especially careful handling. The first was getting the money to Spain and the second was what to do with the enormous profits. Taking half a million pounds on buses likely to be searched at any time and carrying among the passengers some who were, to put it gently, on occasion not entirely honest was too risky, as regular thefts of souvenirs from Disneyland Paris confirmed. The solution was to recruit teams of couriers, ordinary families or couples who, in exchange for a healthy pot of spending money and a free holiday, smuggled over, hidden in their luggage, bags of cash varying between £150,000 and £180,000. This accounted for the carrier bag handed by John Healy to Graeme Mason and Hannah Martin. The couriers always travelled separately from the bus parties and, with the exception of Mason and eventually Hannah, were generally not aware of their link to the coaches.

Even more difficult was the problem of what to do with the money once it was shared out in Glasgow or handed as wages to bus crews and the collectors and packers in Spain. Police and customs investigators were continually on the lookout for criminals trying to legitimise money made illegally. Money laundering, as it was known, turning dirty cash into clean, dishonestly made into legitimate earnings, tested to the extreme imaginations ranging from those of market-stall fiddlers to high-powered financiers. Putting it in a bank invited awkward questions and trouble. Bank managers were legally required to report large cash deposits. On the other hand, some banks were not subject to the same swingeing restrictions. Banks, for example, with bases outside the United Kingdom.

The first trip in the larger coach was to Torremolinos, the popular resort to the south of Malaga, where a party was booked into the giant Hotel Sol Principe. The young passengers played in a junior soccer tournament, returning to Glasgow two weeks later. A series of other trips followed to different Torremolinos hotels and the smugglers grew richer. In the meantime, Tam McGraw made a visit to Belfast and Manny drove him to Donegal, where he deposited money in the Allied Irish Bank.

Sometimes Manny desperately wished he could distance himself completely from the Troubles. There seemed no escape from the continuing murders and bombings or from the memory of that terrible day in Warrington. Each March, on the anniversary of the deaths of Tim and Johnathan, he went to church to light a candle and say a prayer for their memory. Talk of peace became ever more prevalent, yet on 30 January 1996, as Yo Yo Gallagher, the INLA's chief of staff, queued in the Falls Road dole office, another waiting customer, fellow INLA Volunteer and drug dealer Kevin McAlorum, walked up behind him and shot him dead. It would be claimed the assassin was paid £10,000 by another senior INLA figure, Hugh Torney, to carry out the killing. Later in the year, Torney was murdered.

The Troubles seemed a million miles from Donegal, but the sleepy town was about to be invaded by wild Glaswegians. A day after Yo Yo died, the Paradise Bar was sold for £135,000. Tam McGraw's name would never appear as the owner, but he put up the money. Where had that come from? Manny, for one, was not asking, although as time went on others would. The new ownership celebrated with a charity football match in which a number of showbusiness celebrities took part, followed by a raucous night when music blared loudly and copious amounts of drink flowed. It was the start of occasional visits by parties from Glasgow, but one threatened to cause real trouble, as Manny remembers.

'Donegal's law force amounted to the equivalent of two cops on bicycles, and then suddenly this mob from Glasgow descended. They arrived driving convertible cars and wearing Versace suits and seemed hell-bent on shagging anything that moved. It was just like a scene from *Goodfellas*, overdressed and over-rich characters and the women with them not knowing how to behave themselves.

'One guy started looking for drugs. It was a town where, certainly then, there weren't any drugs. If you wanted drugs, you brought your own with you. But he went up to the barman and asked, "Where can I get a bit of gear from?" The barman hadn't a clue what he was on about and leaned forward, as if he was having difficulty understanding what the guy was saying, and asked what he was talking about. "Well, a bit of the thing, you know," said this idiot from Glasgow, tapping his nose, and I realised he was looking for cocaine. '

"I don't know what you're talking about mate," he was told. "I don't know what gear is."

' "Coke, I mean coke." At that, the barman went ballistic; he was screaming to everybody in the place, "This guy's looking for fucking drugs." I thought some of the locals were going to lynch the character who had asked about them. The rest of us had to apologise.

'These people came over, splashed money around as if it was water and couldn't see they were doing what a gangster or a paramilitary should never do, which was to draw attention to themselves. I knew Tam wasn't happy about what he saw and heard. "They're fucking clowns, Manny," he told me, and I agreed.'

There were other parties celebrating the success of the bus venture and the venues included Celtic Park with showbusiness celebrities, among them stars of the various television soaps joining in, totally ignorant of the source of the money footing the substantial bills. On odd occasions the television personalities would show up at the Paradise Bar. One morning Manny arrived there to discover Bill Tarmey, the actor who played Jack Duckworth in *Coronation Street*, serving behind the bar and pulling pints.

It wasn't just the antics of some of those linked to the bus runs that worried the smugglers, and again they consulted McGraw. When it began he had advocated running a tight ship, but now too many cooks were spoiling the broth, and one particular toerag was creating waves, as Manny would shortly discover.

'One day in April, I was at home when the telephone rang, and it was a friend from Glasgow. I asked how he was, but he said, "Listen, Manny, I can't really talk. There's a problem and Trevor and Gordon are on their way over to see you. Can you meet them at the airport and take them to the Lansdowne Court Hotel. Tam will be following in a couple of hours. He wants to talk to you about a business proposition. He'll get a taxi to your house and see you there. It's really important." I said, "Okay," and went off to the airport.

'As the guys were coming out of the arrivals area, I noticed a number of coppers who seemed to be with them giving me the eye. I was used to being stopped and asked where I was going when I flew to Glasgow, and was stopped at the Glasgow end and asked the same thing. But this was different. I wasn't going anywhere apart from back home.

'After meeting the guys we set off to the hotel, and on the way I said, "Did you see all the fucking cops? What did they want from you?" Gordon said, "Look, Manny, we were stopped by Special Branch, who wanted to know where we were going and why we were in Belfast."

'"You didn't tell them, did you?" I asked.

'Gordon said, "They would have turned us back if we said nothing, so we just told them we were meeting you and gave your name and address."

' "Fuck sake, Gordon, they're going to want to know what you're doing meeting up with me."

' "Sorry, couldn't be helped, we had to tell them something."

'I wasn't happy, but the damage was done. I knew what the score would be. The cops would be on the phone to the people in Glasgow giving them the names of Trevor and Gordon and wanting to know what they wanted with me. The police there would straight away know their connection to Tam, and they'd know Tam was on a flight to Belfast as well. If they'd just said they were coming over to go fishing, anything, and given the address of the hotel, the cops would have been no wiser, because Tam wasn't with them. Now the cops were bound to put two and two together, start wondering what the connection was between Tam and a paramilitary, and probably come to the wrong conclusion. But I kept all that to myself. In any case, at that stage I didn't know why Tam wanted to see me.

'After leaving them at the hotel, I had some business of my own to do. By the time that was finished and I got back home, Tam was sitting there having a cuppa. I asked, "What's up?" and he said, "There's something I want to talk to you about, but when there's nobody around. How about giving me a lift to the guys?" I knew he meant Trevor and Gordon and so I took him into Belfast. I didn't mention what they'd told Special Branch; there seemed no point.

'We went for a drink in a quiet area of the Lansdowne Court and Tam said, "I'm going to tell you something and this is the only time I will ever say what I'm going to say. This is a one-off. I suppose you know something's going on, but you don't know what." I said, "You're right, and I haven't poked my nose in. I had the feeling you'd tell me at some time." He said, "You're involved already, but you don't know it. You've already been asked if you wanted to invest in something, haven't you?" I agreed and he said, "We wanted to keep all this from you because we know the Republicans come down really hard on drug dealing. We thought if you found out what was happening, you might get pissed off and want to do something about it."

'I said, "Look, Tam, what happens in Northern Ireland happens in Northern Ireland and what happens in Glasgow happens in Glasgow. Since those kids were killed in Warrington I've felt ashamed to call myself a Republican, even though the people I was with had nothing to do with it. This is all about drugs isn't it?"

'Tam said, "Not in the way you might think. Okay, gear is coming in, but it's only hash. You might get a shock when I tell you how big the thing these people are running is." While he spoke, I knew he was leading up to something, so I said, "You want my help? Tell me how."

For the next two hours, McGraw dominated the conversation. He spoke of a Glasgow-based gang – most of the members his friends – that was involved in an operation in Spain and earning fortunes.

'When he told me how much money was being made, my reaction was, "Fucking hell, man," but kept that to myself. Instead I asked why he was telling me this. I knew it couldn't have been to ask if I wanted to come in and be one of the gang.

'He said, "There's a wee job on offer for you, and if you're up for this I'll tell you what it is. It means going to Spain to oversee a couple of things. You can take somebody with you and you can pick him yourself. If you have any hassle over in Spain from anyone at all, phone me and I'll speak to them. Or you can sort it out, whatever way you want. Your wages will be ten grand each. You can go over in one day to do the job or you can stay there for two weeks with all expenses paid. How long you stay is up to you, but it involves nothing illegal. If you don't want to go for what's on offer, if you're not totally sure that it's right for you, then don't go for it and I'll accept your decision. But if you don't give me the nod, then I want you to promise never to talk about this ever again."

'I said, "Tell me what you want me to do."

'He told me, "Things are going on over in Spain that some of us are just not happy about. These people are my friends and I don't want to see them getting into trouble. I'm worried about security. They reckon it's a great operation, but a lot of things aren't right. I want you to go over there and see just how much you can pick up. My pals reckon that if you can find out what they're up to just by wandering about and listening, then the police could do the same."

'Without saying it concerned drugs, he talked about worries over how many people were now in the know, loose talk, guys cheating over expenses and an attitude of general carelessness. He said, "I've seen how you people operate, how careful you are about security, how you keep everything very tight and put the fear of God into anybody who steps out of line. Go out to Spain and have a look, tell me what you see, what you can learn about what's going on and see what can be tightened up. I can't go, because the cops would be straight on to me."

'I knew there was something behind all of this. "You're still not telling me everything Tam," I said. "If I'm going to give you advice on security then I need to know why you reckon something's wrong and what this is really all about." Then the real story behind his flying visit came out.

' "Somebody's been to see me, but I'm not going to mention his name because I can't risk anything happening to this twat. He's probably put something in writing and given it to his lawyer. This bastard told me he knew everything. Somebody's been talking out of turn. What's most worrying is that he reckons I'm involved."

'I asked what the nosey bastard wanted and Tam said, "He wanted in. I should have told him to go fuck himself, but I couldn't believe how much he knew. He's been offered a share."

'I was appalled and said, "Fuck it, Tam, that's blackmail. You whack blackmailers."

'He said, "Manny, the reason this has been done is that the people running this are desperate for the guy to keep his mouth shut and now he knows that so long as he does that then there'll be money in his pocket."

'I could see his reasoning but wondered how many other guys would have been so generous. If the guy had tried something like that in Belfast, he'd have ended up on a slab in the mortuary. Loose talk had encouraged one blackmailer to crawl out of the woodwork. Just how likely was it that more would get to know and come along with their hands outstretched? Tam was their target. That's why he wanted to know how much damage had already been done. He knew I'd do the job for him. The money was a big attraction, but he was my friend and needed help. For the third time in my life I had a job. I was a security consultant.'

23

DANIEL O'DONNELL

SPECIAL BRANCH DETECTIVES IN GLASGOW knew about the meeting in Belfast between McGraw and Manny, and according to rumour, they and their CID colleagues were 'going potty' at not being able to work out why the terrorist was meeting the crook. What was the connection? There was much head scratching, because an operation to investigate McGraw in depth had been running for more than a year and had given no hint that he was connected to, or interested in, the Irish People's Liberation Organisation. The inference was that police scrutiny left a lot to be desired.

McGraw was classed by the Strathclyde Police as a 'core criminal': in other words, a serious underworld player. A former police officer explains what this meant.

'Once it had been decided to have a close look at his activities, a series of routines were started. Intelligence logs were regularly received from sources such as beat cops who may have seen the target, in this case McGraw, travelling in an unfamiliar car or with a stranger.'

On their own these didn't mean much, but an examination of a few of these reports produced a pattern showing his movements and contacts. A copy of the itemised bills covering 1995 and 1996 for his home telephone was obtained without his knowledge and an expert was called in to work out if some numbers were called more frequently and if the calls coincided with known crimes. Background checks were then made on the people he had called, and these showed up numbers in Belfast. A similar investigation was made into calls made from his mobile telephone, with similar results.

Official permission was given to tap his telephone and those of known associates, including Gordon Ross and John Healy. Like all other targets, McGraw's name was entered into the Police National Computer, which meant that if, for instance, he flew from Glasgow to Belfast, his name would register at Glasgow, because lists of all passengers were given to the police in case any were known or suspected terrorists. Glasgow police would then alert the RUC to his presence. The RUC would be expected to keep an eye on him, but this was asking a lot of a police force already creaking at the seams because of the Troubles.

The former police officer said, 'Senior officers were convinced it was essential that the mystery over his association with Manny McDonnell was solved. They knew from contacts with the RUC that Manny had been actively involved with paramilitary organisations and so a formal inquiry to delve into their activities was set up and codenamed Operation Lightswitch. By coincidence, another investigation had started around this time into Paul Ferris. It was examining his links with other known criminals in Scotland and England and was named Operation Shillelagh. Part of that inquiry was to look into his connections to the Glasgow security company boss Bobby Dempster and major drugs player Rab Carruthers. Carruthers had just been jailed in Manchester for heroin dealing.'

McGraw was no fool. He knew how the police worked. Like any big-time criminal worth his salt he had contacts within the police, but most of his information concerning police activities came from traffic-warden pals who passed on snippets they overheard in police stations and, in particular, police-station canteens. It was astonishing how a cup of tea seemed to loosen a cop's tongue. He knew never to say anything important from the telephone at his home in Mount Vernon. That was basic stuff. A top-rated criminal never uttered anything vaguely incriminating that could be overheard, whether it was on a telephone, a bar, a restaurant or even outside on the streets.

McGraw also changed mobiles regularly, buying them for cash and topping up with vouchers so there was no trace of ownership. Important calls were made to and from coin boxes by prearrangement, but most of the organisation of the bus runs was done by personal contact. During one of the gang's regular party sessions at Glasgow's Marriott Hotel, a cover for meetings when further holidays were planned, police bugged some of their bedrooms, including a device hidden in a light switch, thus giving the operation its name. It produced nothing of value.

In Ireland, the RUC used its own contacts in Loyalist para-militaries to see what information might be gleaned about Manny and his growing interest in Glasgow. Once again it produced nothing of value. The police were still in the dark. The police were still in the dark even after turning on Operation Lightswitch.

Strathclyde Police did their work thoroughly and painstakingly. But the initiation of Operations Lightswitch and Shillelagh meant drawing heavily on already overstretched resources. Each was costly, eating into budgets, and there were pressures to come up with answers, particularly in the case of McGraw. Informants were drained of every scrap of information; the police even tried the old dodge of putting it about that McGraw was making a fortune but keeping old pals out of whatever wheeze he was running, hoping that age-old sin of envy would encourage those disgruntled at being out of the loop to grass. Information trickled in but none of it was really helpful. The involvement of so many in the bus runs – at least 50 people were by now in the know – inevitably led to indiscretions, nothing devastating but enough to hint that somehow McGraw was concerned with or knew about importing very big quantities of cannabis into Scotland. There was no proof of that, of course.

Police knew hash had become surprisingly easy to get hold of, and while many would happily have snitched on those supplying what they saw as evil cocaine, heroin and even ecstasy, blow was looked on as a very sociable pleasure, no more harmful – even less so, it could be argued – than tobacco or booze. Even getting wind of the fact McGraw was somehow connected to the blow trade wasn't particularly revealing and certainly hardly surprising. McGraw's associates, such as Gordon Ross, had convictions for smuggling the stuff in cars. What continued to baffle the boys in blue was how the drugs came into the country and, just as importantly, why the Irishman was involved.

The ill feeling between McGraw and Ferris had continued to grow, with each making claim and counter claim against the other. Manny still looked on both as his friends – he was one of the few in Glasgow or elsewhere who throughout remained supportive of each – and was disappointed at the extent of the mutual animosity. In Belfast, he had told Sean, 'The tragedy is that if the pair of them settled their differences and worked together, they'd be unstoppable.' But it was obvious that was not going to happen. One day, Ferris was visited by two senior Glasgow detectives who told him they had information that his life was in danger. In his book *The Ferris Conspiracy*, Ferris says one of the cops named the plotter as McGraw. That represented a highly unusual move by any policeman and Ferris suspected it was an attempt to lure him into a police trap by taking action against McGraw. Time would show the detectives had been telling the truth.

Mags McGraw had called it a day in her fight to continue running the Caravel. In its heyday it had been a real money-spinner, but a persistent barrage of frivolous complaints from the police had meant expensive and time-consuming court appear-ances by her in an effort to stay open. Now she finally lost patience and announced its closure. Three weeks later it was flattened by Trevor Lawson's firm, making room for a small estate of new houses. The sudden disappearance of the pub led to a bizarre claim that the action was to hide damning forensic evidence that would confirm it had been used as a temporary dumping ground for the bodies of Joe Hanlon and Bobby Glover after their murder five years earlier, a suggestion that caused particular amusement among those who knew where the corpses had really been temporarily housed.

While running a busy pub in Glasgow's east end, Mags had witnessed occasional violence. But nothing could have readied her for what she experienced when she and Tam, along with a party of friends, visited Manny and Sally in Belfast for a second wedding, in July 1996. Trouble had been building up for some days throughout Northern Ireland after the RUC initially refused to allow the Orange Order to march mainly through a Catholic area from Drumcree Church at Portadown to an Orange Lodge. When the Loyalists began objecting, Republicans came out to challenge their complaints. Riots kicked off and the McGraw party was flying right into the middle of them. The situation worsened when the RUC partly reversed its original ban.

The wedding guests were monitored at Glasgow airport waiting for a Belfast flight and word was passed to the RUC, but there was little chance of policemen in Belfast having time to keep an eye on a party from Glasgow even if the word was that they might link up with a one-time member of the IPLO.

When the McGraws landed they were met by Manny and driven off to a hotel. Next morning, Mags awoke to the sensation that she was in hell; television pictures were of cars and houses on fire, of rubber bullets flying, and of the sky black with the smoke from burning motors. Manny assured her all would be well, pointing out that in situations like these it was normal for those with motors on their last legs to torch them and claim the cost of replacements from the British government. Despite their fears, the party made its way safely and without trouble to the wedding, but the riots caused a number of casualties, including the death of former INLA member Dermot McShane, who was crushed under an armoured car in Derry.

During the wedding reception, Manny and McGraw found a quiet corner for a brief chat. The Irishman wondered when he would be given the green light to head out to Spain. McGraw told him, 'They want you to wait a wee while. A few things are already planned and they don't want to make any changes until they've gone ahead. Can you hang on till September?' Manny agreed and was told, 'When you are in Spain, there are one or two people we need you to look at.'

A few days after the wedding, Tam and Mags were on their travels again, this time to their apartment in Tenerife. They were clocked by police at Glasgow, but it was assumed that McGraw could hardly be up to much stuck five hours away in the Canaries. In fact, his whistle-stop round of the Torviscas bars would include calls on old associates from Glasgow.

McGraw's was a familiar face on the island, and from time to time he had come across the popular Irish singer Daniel O'Donnell, who had an apartment at the time in nearby Adeje. A couple of years earlier the two had shared a drink together and discovered a common love for Donegal – superstar Daniel was born near the town. The singer's millions were as loose change when compared with the fortune the holiday coaches were earning. O'Donnell probably wondered what the lively group of Scots ensconced in a corner of the Irish Fiddler bar were celebrating when he wandered in and was invited to join them. If he did, he was too polite to ask but simply sat down and enjoyed a beer before having his photograph taken with a slightly unsteady McGraw.

While the McGraws were on the island, the Mercedes made yet another long trip from Glasgow to Torremolinos, where the party booked into the 411-room Greigo Mar hotel. On its return, the group was given standard checks by customs officers after it drove from the cross-channel ferry at Dover, but there was no reason to suspect that this was anything other than a happy, if tired, group of youngsters on their way home to show off their tans and let their mums nurse their sunburn. Just over two weeks after it arrived back in Glasgow it was off again, taking advantage of youngsters being on holiday from school. This time the destination was the Sol Principe in Torremolinos, but after a few days the group moved back north to the Don Pancho hotel in Benidorm to take part in a soccer tournament arranged with the help of the SFA. Each of the runs was worth a fortune to the smugglers.

The first of these trips had coincided with yet another holiday for Hannah Martin with 'Del Boy' Mason. Hannah later confided to a friend that she complained to him about his drinking and was slowly becoming less enamoured of him, but it was difficult to think of abandoning the lure of regular holidays abroad. She thought he didn't act like a criminal big shot. Now John Healy, he was a different matter. It seemed to her that it was John who gave the orders.

A few days after the coach returned from Benidorm, Manny received a call asking him to come over to Glasgow the following week. 'Take the ferry, we'll pick you up at Stranraer,' McGraw told him, adding, 'Bring an overnight bag.' The two chatted on the long drive to Glasgow along the winding road. 'That Spanish job I asked you to do,' said McGraw. 'They'd like you to go ahead. Things are starting to get out of hand, but let's have a meal in town and I'll fill you in on what I've been told has been happening.' They booked into the Marriott Hotel and, despite his home being only a quarter of an hour away, McGraw checked into a room. When they went for a meal in the city centre, they were followed.

The next day, before he was taken back to Stranraer, Manny was handed an envelope. It contained flight tickets from Belfast to Malaga; a voucher showing he had been booked into the Sunset Beach Club Hotel at Benalmadena, just a short bus ride from

Torremolinos, for ten days; a return flight to Glasgow; and a thick pile of spending money. 'Get over there and just have a wander around, keep it low key, relax, have a few beers with the guys. Some of them know you're coming over, but they're not sure why, so they'll be asking what you're doing. And they don't know how much you've been told. People are bringing money over; have a look at one or two of them and let me know what you think of them. See if things can be tightened up, but take a look at everything. Don't say anything to anybody about what you think, keep that for me when you get back. I'd love to go over, but I know the cops are on the watch and would clock me. You'll be the eyes and ears of the guys operating this. They know I know and trust you, that's why they asked me if I'd get you to do this job for them.'

Manny flew into Malaga, took a taxi to his hotel and after checking in began his mission. He wandered around to get the feel for the area. The main holiday season was coming to an end, but the beaches were still a mass of white, red, brown, golden, bare, nubile, wobbling, shaking, gross human flesh. He'd been supplied with a list of names and hotels and hooked up for a time with Ross. He in turn introduced him to likeable Chick Glackin, who was there with members of his family. There were others from Glasgow, some of whom he recognised. They spotted him wandering around and wondered what he was doing. 'Tam asked if I fancied a wee break,' said Manny. 'He thought it would be good just to get away from Belfast. He and Mags got a shock when they were over in July and wondered how we managed to stick it out.'

Among themselves, the group wondered about his presence. Another bus was due and they suggested he might have been hanging around in the hope of getting some of his own gear on board. They knew about him, knew he could be a hard, frightening man and guessed he would be skilled with weapons and able to easily get his hands on them. Ross tried reassuring the others, telling them, 'He's a good guy and Tam trusts him. He's not into drugs, because if the Republicans find out you're doing deals even in the stuff we're running, they'll blow your kneecaps off and boot you out of Ireland. Just don't fuck him about.'

Todd had been there when Ross made his little speech. The Englishman didn't like a stranger suddenly turning up and seeming to know an awful lot. He'd have to watch this guy from Belfast. He'd been one of the main middlemen in the hash market for years, had made a fortune, was still making a fortune, and he wasn't going to let an Irishman in on the act. He'd have to speak to McGraw and the others about this, but that would mean a trip to Glasgow. He put the idea to the back of his mind for the time being.

Manny was appalled by what he found over the next few days. He'd been told one of the main players, Graeme Mason, was coming over with his girlfriend and some money, and he wanted to see how the cash was picked up. Manny came from a background where discretion was the byword and the need for thrift a fact of life. Here, he found gluttony and stupidity. He called on Mason at his hotel, but instead it was Hannah who met him in reception, apologising for her partner being too drunk to get out of bed. 'The money's already been picked up,' she said, and when asked if it had been counted by the collectors told him, 'Oh no, they never bother doing that.' Elsewhere he found the smugglers wallowing in drink, snorting cocaine openly and splashing far more money around than ordinary holidaymakers could afford.

He discovered one of them had been twice accused of rape. They were generally loud, boorish and totally indiscreet, bragging during their never-ending parties about the racket, attracting attention from other bemused holidaymakers and hotel workers. He knew that the Spanish police, having already investigated the allegations of sex attacks, would be keeping an eye on the individual concerned. The last thing anybody wanted was for undercover detectives to be sitting listening to the boasts and waiting for the inevitable careless word.

Manny himself had to act the part of a carefree holidaymaker. There was, he knew, the chance that the RUC might have alerted their counterparts on the Costa del Sol to his presence and had him watched in case he was looking for potential terrorist targets. Cops in Belfast would have known he was no longer in the ILPO but may well have assumed – wrongly – that he had rejoined the INLA.

He completed his mission within a few days but did not want to create suspicion by breaking his holiday earlier. No one was meant to know the real reason why he was there, and to suddenly vanish in the middle of the trip was bound to set tongues wagging. So he watched and listened, growing more astonished every hour by the degree of greed that had set in. Not content with their handsome returns from the bus runs, some of the group were running their own sidelines, even expanding into cocaine and heroin and, he suspected, sneaking their little but valuable caches among the boxes of hashish.

The whole thing needed to be brought under stricter control, he reasoned. But he saw Todd as the main problem. For a reason he never fully understood, he just didn't like the Englishman. So much about the two men didn't match. But the principal difference was that Manny's was a faithful marriage while Todd made no secret of having two 'wives' back home, one official, the other a long-time mistress.

Manny's task accomplished, he flew into Glasgow and rang McGraw. They met up in a nearby hotel. 'Tam, this whole thing is a mess. Your friends should be worrying,' he warned. 'The people over in Spain behave like kids wanting attention.' He went through in detail what he had found and, slightly to his surprise, saw his companion nodding.

'I know some of this, Manny,' said McGraw. 'I've heard about the drug taking and their wee crafty deals. And their expenses rip-offs. One of the bills had been £4,000, but when the guys had a closer look there was a "1" in front.'

It was Todd on who Manny spent most of the discussion. 'I know you like him, Tam, but he's a fucking liability. He thinks he owns this whole show.'

McGraw thought for a moment. 'Leave this to me. I'll pass it all on so they can think it through.' He handed over a bulky envelope. Inside was £10,000. 'That's what we agreed on, wasn't it?'

Manny took the money gratefully. But as they parted and he headed off to check in for his flight back to Belfast, he wondered how he was going to spend the windfall without his fellow Republicans asking awkward questions.

24

LATE-NIGHT HIT

THE ILL WILL TAM AND PAUL showed towards each other worsened into outright loathing and contempt. In Glasgow, such feelings sometimes led to one man killing or trying to kill the other. This was no different. A meeting between the two had ended in bitterness. Weeks after Ferris had been told by police of his life being in danger, the threat became fact, although it would be a long time before he discovered just how lucky he had been. The mystery was why police did not intervene.

The Operation Lightswitch team were monitoring McGraw as he met some of his closest associates at the Marriott Hotel. Ross was there, and so were Lawson and Manny, who had been asked to fly over from Belfast to discuss his findings in Spain. Plain-clothes cops tried mingling with the party, and during the evening the discussion turned, almost inevitably, to Ferris and allegations he had made that his one-time friend was a police informer. In the underworld, the greatest insult one player can heap on any other is to call him a grass. Just as it had the potential do to in Northern Ireland, it was akin to a death sentence.

One of the smugglers would later admit, 'With so much money at stake we just could not have Ferris having a pop at Tam and spoiling the whole thing. He didn't know what was going on, but his constant sniping was pissing people off. It all came to a bit of a head so we decided to go and do something about it, to kill him. We'd been tipped off where he might be. When we found him, we would phone somebody who would bring a gun.'

That Friday night as many city drinkers were about to leave bars for clubs to dance and maybe seek a partner for the coming hours, the four men walked into the darkness of the rear of the Marriott and climbed into Trevor Lawson's car, which drove onto the nearby motorway and headed north-east, while a hastily assembled series of unmarked police cars took it in turn to discreetly follow.

The watchers reasoned Lawson was probably taking the party to his home, a farm at Dunipace, near Stirling, but less than 20 minutes later he turned off the main road. The motor entered the one-time mining village of Croy and when it reached the favourite local bar, the Celtic Tavern, four necks craned to look inside. Just over 100 yards behind, a detective told a colleague, 'They're looking for Ferris or his car. I think he's sometimes in there.'

Seeing no trace of either, Lawson headed back towards Glasgow and this time drove to Rutherglen, at the south-east end of the city. 'Bet I know where they'll go,' said the same detective. 'Ferris has an office here.' The car stopped near the headquarters of a security firm linked to Ferris. All four men climbed out and peered around for signs of life but, finding none, went back to the Marriott.

By now it was past midnight, but a while later they were climbing into a taxi, which was followed to Thornliebank, where Graeme Mason and Hannah Martin shared his home. It stopped outside the Thornlie Arms and all four disappeared inside, where they were seen in earnest discussions with the owner, John Healy. They were there until the early hours before taking another cab back to their hotel.

The detectives had been instructed simply to watch the quartet and report on their movements: a decision some old hands would later find strange. A former intelligence collator said, 'It was well known there was bad blood between McGraw and Ferris. A team went looking for Ferris and among them was an Irish paramilitary. For all anyone knew, they went armed and with the intention of shooting Ferris if they found him. Clearly it was decided not to stop and search them because that would have alerted them to the fact they were under police surveillance. In other words, if necessary Ferris was to be sacrificed rather than blow a drugs operation.'

The next day as Manny was about to leave for his flight back to Belfast, McGraw took him to one side and told him, 'I'll be over to see you at the end of the month. I want to put another proposition to you.'

As November drew to a close, McGraw flew to Belfast for a lengthy meeting. Over beers and sandwiches, the Glaswegian said, 'They've talked over what you told us and agree something needs to be done. The hope is you'll go over to Spain on a regular basis and run the show, take over and operate it like you'd run a hit in Ireland.' Manny thought and told his friend, 'Tam, I'm still not sure I know everything about this. And Spain isn't Belfast.'

'I appreciate that, Manny,' said his friend, 'but I want you to operate thinking you are in Belfast.'

'So what is it you want me to do? It's obvious this is all about drugs, but I'm not going to start smuggling them. I might as well shoot myself, because that's what will happen if I'm caught and sent back to Belfast.'

'They know that. They just want you to keep an eye on things, check the couriers, and mostly stop the fiddling.'

'I can't do this efficiently on my own,' said Manny. 'I need a couple of guys to help me.' He gave the names of a former IPLO unit commander and an IRA Volunteer.

'Fucking hell,' said McGraw, 'Weren't you fuckers trying to kill each other a while back?'

'Yes, but that's in the past. I trust these people completely. Believe you me, they'll do a first-class job and will never let anybody down.'

'Your word is good enough,' McGraw said.

The Republican was used to surprises, but what followed left him briefly speechless. He had collected £10,000, paid in full, for his 'consultancy' work and assumed that was a one-off. Now he was told that each member of his three-man team would receive that same figure each time they were called on to work in Spain. When he was asked how often that would be, the man from Glasgow told him, 'Once a month, and you start next week, so get your skates on.'

The Scot went on to outline what would happen. 'You'll get a phone call in a few days and that's when you get out there and get everything ready. We have a friendly estate agent who we ring and ask what villas he has available and we book one from him for a fortnight. He hasn't a clue what's going on, he thinks we're just a group from Glasgow who like to come over regularly and look for a decent place to stay. That's where you'll stay. The people who look after the gear will stay with you.'

A week later, Manny waited near the telephone in a Republican club, and sure enough right on time the telephone jangled. He picked it up to hear a familiar voice asking, 'You got your team together?' When he confirmed they were ready to go, he was told to fly to Spain and start work. 'Your main job is to look after the money. We book the hotels for the couriers so we know where they are. All they need to do is ring with their room numbers once they've checked in and when you call me I'll pass that on to you and tell you how much each of them should have. Give the money to Todd, he'll buy gear from the Moroccans and it'll be delivered to the villa where your team will be staying and the others will look after it from there. You don't have to touch it or even see it.'

Manny was unhappy at the prospect of working with Todd, but the extravagance of the wage packet should, he thought, be enough to smooth over his dislike of the man.

When they reached Spain and started work, Manny's doubts about the efficiency of the operation were increased after his team called on Mason and Hannah. Mason, remembered Manny, had been drunk the previous time. Now Hannah opened the bedroom door to their knock, and they entered, saying nothing, and as they did so Manny immediately turned off the room light so they were in darkness. The less anyone saw of the trio the better, they reasoned. Inside Mason lay drunk on the bed, snoring loudly. Hearing voices, he woke with a start and began arguing when his visitors complained at his being drunk in charge of money.

They silenced him by threatening to throw him over the balcony, pointing out that it would be assumed that in his drunken state he had simply fallen. Hannah, angry and embarrassed, opened the door of a wardrobe and handed over a polythene bag. It was meant to hold £150,000. Much to Mason's annoyance, the three men announced they would count the contents there and then. The bag was around £200 short. Mason protested neither he nor Hannah had touched it. 'This better never happen again,' they were warned as the collectors left.

There was money missing from the bags handed over by the other couriers and Manny phoned Glasgow and told his contact, 'These people are nuts. They seem to think that if they nick a £20 note here and there from the bundles it won't be noticed. We need to make an example of somebody.' But he was persuaded that John Healy already had a difficult enough job finding carriers who could be trusted; if word leaked out that they might end up being kneecapped, it would not help with recruitment. Nevertheless, Hannah and Mason would soon drop out.

An east end of Glasgow family acted as couriers, hiding cash in their children's bags. The Irishmen counted £70,000 from a youngster's school rucksack, which had passed safely through an airport security check. They wondered if a stewardess had helped the boy, no more than seven or eight years old, stow this paper fortune in a locker over his head for the flight.

Very occasionally, a courier might try being high-handed with the Irishmen, complaining at their insistence on entering a bedroom, or demanding increased expenses for risking having baggage given a thorough search, even though the chances of this were minimal. They were already receiving a free holiday and generous spending money. The objections lasted only so long as it took their visitors to show the guns tucked into their coats. After that, nobody was ever heard to refuse to hand over the money.

Each trip used three or four couriers who, in addition to Mason and, as Manny confided to McGraw, 'that mad bird of his', came from a pool that included a married couple, two teenage girls, a family of five and two old-age pensioners, all from Glasgow. They looked nondescript and carried ordinary suitcases, nothing that would make them stick out from any others on their flights. On an odd occasion, some money would be brought over on the coach.

Once the money had been counted, Manny rang his contact in Glasgow to confirm its arrival. It was then taken on to Todd, who rechecked the bundles, generally adding the total to an average of just under £500,000, all of it in used sterling notes and a high percentage of these issued by Scottish banks. The Irish team insisted on being present during Todd's count, their presence irritating him and increasing his feeling that he was slowly being pushed out of the picture.

One of the three enforcers told another member of the smuggling team, 'Security is premium. Okay, we're stepping on a lot of toes, but to be honest we don't give two fucks who we upset so long as the job is done properly. People have been getting away with too much and if they don't like it that's their hard luck. We have guns and if necessary we'll use them. Keep whatever you hear being discussed to yourself because if we hear any different, that you've been letting your mouth go, then we're going to fucking shoot you. We'll shoot you here, we'll shoot you in the market, on the beach, in a bar, it doesn't matter where. We'll shoot you or anybody else who gets out of line.'

The couriers too found themselves subject to a new and brutal regime. They were told that in future money would always be counted in front of them. If there were discrepancies, they were told, 'We'll let you off this time, but if it happens again we'll fucking do you.' The message hit home. From then on they handed over the exact amounts Manny had been told they would be carrying.

Before the arrival of the men from Belfast, Todd had taken charge of the money and once he had counted it contacted one of the Moroccans, who occasionally sent along a dogsbody to check while the cash was counted yet again in front of him and the total confirmed. He would then meet up with Mohammed or Mustapha and place an order. It was felt this gave him too much leeway, that he could easily claim a higher price was being asked and then pocket the spin-off. It was decided that in future two of the Irishmen would attend these discussions while the third remained with the money.

The meetings usually took place in Ronnie Knight's, the Benalmadena pub run by Ronnie Knight, the east end of London robber who was on the run from British police following a £6 million security-van heist. Knight, a pal of the Kray twins, spent 11 years on the Costa del Sol – known to the Media as the Costa del Crime because of the number of villains holed up there – and during that time his marriage to Carry On actress Barbara 'Babs' Windsor ground to a halt. The size of the order normally depended on how much money had been smuggled over, and the following night the Moroccans would collect the payment at the same time as one of the smugglers was waiting at another villa in the Malaga area for a van bringing the hashish. A call, confirming its arrival, was the signal for the cash to be handed over.

The hash came in bags or boxes packed with bars of the resin, four to a kilo and each the size of a video cassette. It had first to be tested, which meant smoking it. Manny had never before used drugs; to do so in Northern Ireland could earn the death penalty from fellow Republicans. Now he was sometimes given a sample and asked what he thought of it. This developed into a habit he regretted. If the others considered it fresh and untainted, 16 bars at a time would go into the machine to be wrapped tightly in polythene. That produced a block roughly the size of a briefcase. It was hot, sweaty work and needed to be done immediately. The smugglers could not afford to have such a huge amount in storage for long, risking a sudden raid by Spanish police. The polythene parcels were then placed in cardboard boxes or suitcases.

The night before the coach was due to start its return journey to Glasgow, the parcels were loaded into a van that met up with the coach, usually in a car park well away from the hotel housing the passengers – the crew could not afford to have prying eyes asking awkward questions. The panel up the centre of the bus was opened up, the containers loaded in and the panel closed and sealed. If, on the other hand, there were doubts about the standards of the hash, the Moroccans would change it for a fresh supply without any argument.

After the bus left, the Irishmen waited two days before flying off, heading to different airports, usually Glasgow and Shannon, to further confuse any surveillance. They reasoned that the delay was worth it, believing that should anybody be monitoring the operation then the watchers would concentrate on them, hopefully allowing the bus to get to safety. In Glasgow, Manny was met by one of the gang, who handed over an envelope containing wages for all three in cash. It was always for the correct amount.

The hash was unloaded from the bus and distributed, dealers paying in cash. The investors were then given a rundown on the profit from each run and how much they were due. These explanations of the balance sheet took place at a variety of locations, including the Marriott, the Swallow on Paisley Road West, Glasgow, and sometimes at hotels in East Kilbride. The investors rarely, and in some cases never, met one another.

Running a racket on such a huge scale was expensive. The couriers received up to £5,000 a time; each of the coach drivers £15,000; a Glaswegian hired to act as a chauffeur to the teams out in Spain, including the Irishmen, £5,000; there was accommodation for the bus passengers and the couriers; villas to rent for the smuggling team; cars to rent; and sundry expenses claimed by the smugglers in Spain, which seemed to mount with every trip. And now Manny's team.

At a briefing in Glasgow, Manny again complained bitterly about Todd. 'He's got to go,' he said angrily. 'He can't keep his mouth shut and I just don't trust him. He thinks he's running this whole thing.'

This was a problem because McGraw liked Todd; the two had done business for four years and he was looked on as one of the gang. The members asked McGraw if he would try to soothe Manny over and he organised a meeting with the Irishman.

'Look, Manny, I know it's difficult, but can you leave things as they are for now? The guys know it's not perfect, but it's a pretty good operation and I was asked to bring you in because the others think you can make it run even more smoothly. Maybe Todd and you will be able to sort your differences.'

In fact, McGraw already knew of the friction. Todd had flown over to Glasgow after his very first meeting with Manny to complain. 'I just don't like that Irish cunt's attitude. It's too military style. He barks out orders as if the guys are troops in his unit. And he carries a fucking gun.'

'Look, Tam,' said Manny, 'in any sort of operation everybody must have a specific role; they do that job and don't poke their noses into whatever somebody else is doing. It should only be on a need-to-know basis. Here you have people sitting round gossiping like a bunch of old women. Even the couriers know more about what's going on than we do. They should just be getting here, handing over the money, enjoying a holiday and going home. It's a mess.'

'Okay, run it your way, but try not to step on too many toes. Anything else?' asked McGraw.

'Well, there is one thing,' said the Irishman. 'It takes ages to count that fucking money and you just need to make one mistake and you have to start all over. Any chance of getting one of those counters they use in the banks?'

'I'll pass that on,' said McGraw, and the two shook hands and parted. All the same, Manny headed back unhappily to Spamount Street. There was more chance of Gerry Adams organising a birthday party for Ian Paisley than there was of he and Todd getting along.

During his next trip to Spain, Manny was visited at his rented villa by a man who had travelled over on the bus. He handed over a box and inside was a counting machine.

He had another problem. After 25 years living off the contents of his weekly giro cheques, he found money coming out of his ears but was unable to spend it in case his former comrades began wondering where it was coming from, wondering whether it had been given to him by MI5 or the police. At the same time, there was no way he was going to give up the work. As the move to peace gathered pace, hundreds of men who had been active during the Troubles were finding themselves with nothing to do and with guns hidden in their rafters. He knew that if he hadn't taken up McGraw's offer, there were many others who would have.

25

MOVING EXPERIENCE

BY THE TIME HE AND HIS TWO FRIENDS next met up in Spain, Manny had made up his mind that one way or another Todd was going. An hour after arriving, they met the big man and Manny told him, 'You no longer make decisions. We're in charge from now on. Any decisions needed to be made will be made by us, not you. If I don't make them, these two guys here will.' Todd was visibly angered but conscious of being outnumbered, and Manny went on, 'I'm not here to be liked, I'm here to do a job.'

Still, Todd was not giving up without a fight. When the next consignment of hash arrived, he changed its destination and it was delivered to a lock-up garage 40 miles away. One of the waiting packers rang Manny. 'Ask the Moroccan where the gear is,' he said. Manny grabbed Mustapha. 'What the fuck's going on?' he demanded. 'The guys want to know there the stuff is.'

Mustapha told him, adding, 'Todd told us that's where it had to be dropped off.'

'Fuck Todd,' came the furious shout down the telephone line when Manny called the packer back. Manny's mood was not improved by the discovery that a quad bike had arrived. 'Who the fuck is this for?' he wanted to know and the driver told him, 'Trevor.'

Trying to calm down over a beer, Manny told his friends, 'The situation is ridiculous. These fuckers haven't a clue how to act. Tam told me Trevor's gone through 20 cars in four years and he gets them from the same dealer that half of the cops in Glasgow use. They've been throwing money about on holiday houses, caravans, motors galore, swilling champagne, you name it.'

His disquiet grew with the arrival from Glasgow of Billy McPhee, who joined in the general frenzy of fighting, drug taking and women chasing, at one time forcing Spanish police to intervene in a bar brawl when women complained they had been groped.

'These people are a fucking disgrace,' grumbled Manny. 'They'll get everybody locked up.'

The Irish trio mostly kept themselves to themselves, generally sitting in their rented villas in quiet residential areas of Benalmadena or Torremolinos and venturing out only to meet the couriers, check with other members of the gang that all was okay, and only occasionally dine out. An exception came one night when Manny wanted a break from counting money and he visited a number of bars, ostensibly to check on how his Glaswegian charges were behaving. He arrived back at the villa the worse for wear to discover some of the gang had joined them. 'I'm going out to shoot this cunt Todd and I want you to vote on it. Hands up who's for it?'

Every hand in the room went up, believing this was an example of odd Irish humour and wondering what the punchline would be. They soon found out when he produced a gun, telling one of the others, 'I hope you haven't been fucking about with this,' at which the gun went off, the bullet whining a millimetre from the driver's face and imploding a double-glazed veranda window. The noise of the exploding glass was deafening and panic erupted. When they looked through the smashed window they saw the damage was even worse than they had first thought. The bullet had continued through the window of the next-door villa. Luckily

It was empty, but the din was sure to have been heard and there was every likelihood somebody had called the police.

Grabbing clothes and £450,000 they were minding, they rang for taxis and checked into hotels. One of the group volunteered to stay behind to take out all the broken glass from the window frames, hoping that only a close inspection would show the frames were empty. That should give time to arrange for a glazier to repair the damage. A couple of days later, when nothing had been heard and no police had come calling, they returned, glad to find glass restored to the frames in both villas.

The near tragedy only worsened Manny's already shattered relationship with Todd and finally he decided enough was enough. His fellow Irishmen concurred that something needed to be done but could not agree on what. One of the group wanted him kneecapped, but another pointed out, 'If we run around Malaga shooting cunts' kneecaps off, the cops are going come down like a ton of bricks because they'll think the place is being taken over by terrorists.'

Manny told him, 'Leave it to me. I'll think of something.'

Two days later he awoke with his mind made up. 'Fuck it, let's just go ahead and shoot the cunt,' he announced. 'We'll go over to his apartment and if his wife's there we'll just leave it, but he's usually there by himself, and if he is I'll put one in his head.'

'Wait till you talk to Tam,' the others pleaded and eventually he agreed to hang fire.

Occasionally McGraw would ring Manny from a newly bought mobile that would be ditched after a few days. The chats were deliberately brief, both men being wary of police somehow managing to bug their calls. But during one, McGraw sensed the tension with Todd was reaching breaking point. The decision to carry out the shooting was put on hold simply because Manny knew of McGraw's friendship with Todd. But McGraw was increasingly worried about the possibility of a shooting, not only because of his long friendship with Todd, but also because the certain fallout from any subsequent police investigation was sure to lead to everyone he had been doing business with. At one stage he suggested he join the two in Malaga for peace talks. That was out of the question. The smugglers could not have police following him into their nest; when he mooted the idea to Manny he was told, 'We can't have you over here Tam. You will be a danger to yourself and to everybody else. You could lead the cops right to us.' The argument won the day.

Around the time Manny was thinking of making Todd's wife a widow, another relationship was coming to an end. For a long time Hannah Martin had suspected there was more to Mason's involvement than he admitted. She knew she was risking being arrested every time she carried money over to Spain for him and listened to his constant bedroom bragging that drugs were involved, but he had always refused to tell her the whole story of how it was being done, something she resented, believing it meant he did not trust her.

One day while she was alone, she answered the telephone at his home and a caller asked for 'Mr Balmer' and said it was in connection with his bus. Hannah pleaded ignorance but told Mason about the call when he arrived home. 'You had no right to answer my phone,' he told her, furious. 'Stay out of my business.' The incident started the rot in their relationship. The final straw came when he eventually admitted youngsters were being used as cover, sitting on top of a fortune in hashish while they and their parents believed they were benefiting from the kindness of Colin O'Sullivan. Hannah packed her bags and went back to her own home, but she was no angel herself, as time would show.

She was not alone in making a new start. In Glasgow, Operation Lightswitch had been run by Strathclyde Police drugs squad. The police were in no doubt, as a result of a tip here and there, that they were dealing with a very large-scale smuggling scam and that somewhere along the line Tam McGraw was involved. His name tended to be wrongly linked to any major crime going, drugs, robberies and especially murders. Taxi drivers, the best or worst gossips depending on which side of the fence you sat, told of overhearing back-seat conversations in which the words 'McGraw' and 'blow' were mentioned in the same context. Word of those conversations eked its way into police notebooks and then on through the various channels to the drugs squad.

At the start of 1997 the squad announced it had a new boss, Detective Superintendent Bob Lauder, who had spent most of his police career as a detective, including working in the Scottish Crime Squad, an elite unit dealing with major offences and investigating the top underworld players. Operation Lightswitch was one of a series of inquiries, but, along with Operation Shillelagh, it had special status. Each day, Lauder and his team were briefed on what officers listening to telephone conversations between the two principal suspects and their cohorts picked up. But nothing had been heard that could give a reason why McGraw and McDonnell should be colluding together.

Manny came up with a new and painless idea that would get rid of Todd. He knew from the occasional appearance of the drivers and their conversations that somehow buses were involved and that they were bringing over parties that included young people, but nobody had told him about false floors or what was stored underneath. He stayed away from the buses but noticed one gripe of the drivers was the length of the journey from Glasgow, a 500-mile, eight-hour drive to the Dover ferry terminal, followed by a two-hour crossing of the English Channel and then a further 19-hour drive to Torremolinos. The operation needed to be based in the south of Spain to be near the source of the hash. It was a long time to be at the wheel, even when the driving stints were shared, and a long time for youngsters to be cooped up on a coach, even one with television and a toilet.

One day in Malaga, Manny heard his name shouted and when he turned there was an old friend from New Lodge. The pair shook hands, and over a quiet drink and shared confidences he learned this man was now running drugs from Spain.

'That's a coincidence; where are you based?' Manny asked.

'Benidorm, near Alicante,' was the reply.

'How do you get the stuff up from the south?'

'No problem, the Moroccans don't mind running it up because they can drop it off on their way into France. The advantage of being in Benidorm is that the Spanish cops think most of the villains are in the south, so you don't get so much heat.'

'Could you take on another customer?'

'How much are you looking for, Manny?'

'Look, you better talk to the guys running the show. I'm only here keeping an eye on the money side,' said Manny. 'Other guys are running the whole thing. I've heard stories about a bus being used.'

'A bus?' You're kidding.'

'No, that's just what I hear. I can put you onto somebody who knows the crew behind it. You can trust him 100 per cent.'

It was left at that, and when Manny next saw McGraw he suggested a move to Benidorm might be a good idea. 'It's a good couple of hours less to drive,' he said. He sensed in his companion a reluctance to change a winning formula, but the Scot too was increasingly worried by the antics of most of those around him. Some were spending wildly; Ross, Lawson and Glackin had been stopped at Vancouver airport carrying £50,000 by the Canadian Mounties, who had contacted cops in Glasgow, who in turn were wondering how the trio had so much loose change. The explanation that it was for a holiday did not seem plausible.

By March, the smugglers had been appraised of the suggestion to transfer their Spanish base and agreed a change of location might well work, although McGraw continued to have reservations. McGraw, John Healy and Manny arranged to get together in the Chinatown Restaurant in New City Road, Glasgow, for an early evening meal. But tapping the McGraw telephone paid dividends when the listeners picked up the suggestion of a meeting there. And so the police knew of it. There was nothing to hint at anything illegal, but two female detectives were ordered to keep a watch on the restaurant. They spotted John Healy go in, and followed. The place was empty apart from John sitting on his own, yet for some bizarre reason the policewomen plonked down at the very next table. When John's two companions joined him, Manny saw the women and instantly warned, 'Cops. Keep it low.'

Later, one of the policewomen would claim she overheard the men discussing Benidorm, Nice as an escape route, Tenerife, the need for three drivers, a four-hour wait at an airport, and how people were monitored by customs officers. She would say she noted the conversation down on a table napkin – which, strangely, was lost. Manny's recollection was of telling his friends about his niece who had been stopped by customs officers; McGraw told of friends who had been forced to wait four hours on a flight back from Benidorm and how he would be off to Tenerife on holiday the following week. Manny's back was almost touching that of one of the women. It was true the word 'three' had been used, but not in the context of three drivers. These words had crept into a conversation about a suggestion by McGraw of taking a party by coach to Donegal and then on to Dublin and how three drivers could share stints at the wheel.

Manny never liked any rendezvous in public, preferring meetings in the privacy of a hotel room over coffee. Outside, he again warned his friends the police were on to them and that they would need to be ultra careful, pointing out that if undercover detectives got alongside others partying and gossiping from Scotland to Spain, they would be certain to pick up enough to move in. And there was another good reason to move north, of which McGraw and Healy were conscious. The many millions of pounds worth of Scottish banknotes flooding banks and change shops in southern Spain and Gibraltar were causing problems.

Although the final decision would not be his, McGraw wasn't enthusiastic about moving base. He could see the advantages but wanted to investigate for himself. He mulled over the situation while holidaying in Tenerife but came back to disturbing news. Two Glaswegians, Donald Mathieson and Robert Gillon, had been arrested at a Torremolinos villa with 470 kilos of hash. They had been spotted earlier at the resort with two women, one of who was Hannah Martin. The women disappeared back to Glasgow in a Land Rover. Suddenly and frighteningly, things were falling into place for the police. Detectives from Glasgow, wondering whether there might be a link to McGraw and McDonnell, flew over to see Mathieson and Gillon, who earned huge respect among the underworld fraternity by refusing offers of lighter sentences in exchange for giving information about others in the smuggling business. After a year in a grim Spanish jail, each was sentenced to three years.

Their arrests meant police in Spain and Scotland would be looking closely at the Costa del Sol and the criminals living there. Maybe Manny was right and it was time to pull out. While the suggestion was being mulled over, Todd rang McGraw to say he was returning to England for good. 'There's too much police activity here and I don't like some of the people I'm dealing with.' McGraw knew who he meant.

The smugglers trusted McGraw's judgement and, looking for reassurance that switching to Benidorm was wise, asked him to assess the man from New Lodge who was offering to be the new supplier, and the two agreed to meet in Belfast. That meant McGraw flying over from Glasgow, where he was picked up by the Operation Lightswitch team, and then he was clocked again teaming up with Manny when he landed in Northern Ireland. Who he was meeting there and why, though, remained a mystery to the police.

Back in Glasgow, McGraw reported favourably, but among the smugglers some were dubious at the wisdom of effectively putting the whole operation in the hands of two Irishmen, one of them a total stranger. 'Tam you'll need to go over to Benidorm and let us know what you think,' he was told. McGraw agreed. It was a huge mistake.

When he informed Manny about his intention to fly into Alicante, he was told, 'You're crazy. The cops have nothing to link anybody to Benidorm. But if you go there you'll be clocked and they'll come in like a swarm of bees wondering where you've hidden the honey.'

His words fell on deaf ears. 'The guys have asked me to go and I'm going, that's it,' McGraw said.

'Well at least try and think up some story as a cover,' said Manny.

It was an easy enough task for the police, with the help of their Spanish counterparts, to follow their targets to Benidorm, but in the packed resort they lost their quarry. They were sure of one thing, though. It seemed to them to be Manny who did most of the talking. Back in the offices of the Operation Lightswitch team in Strathclyde Police headquarters in the centre of Glasgow, the name of McDonnell was chalked up as the mastermind of a major drug-smuggling racket. But was it to line the pockets of Glasgow gangsters, or did it have the even more sinister motive of raising vast amounts of cash to buy arms to ensure a continuation of the war in Northern Ireland?

26

DEATH OF A BUTCHER

TAM HAD FRIENDS EVERYWHERE. One, John Malloy, was opening a nightclub in Glasgow with a long-time mate, Billy 'Bluey' McGrath, his nickname acquired through an addiction to Glasgow Rangers. The club was to be called Penelope's and there happened to be another of that name in Benidorm. John joined the little group with the aim of chatting to the manager there and picking up a few tips on running a nightclub. It was purely coincidental, he told Bluey, that the visit happened to be at the height of the summer season, when beaches would be crowded with semi-naked women.

McGraw made sure the story went about Glasgow that he was out in Alicante purely to keep his pal John company, to have a few days in the sunshine. The hope was that police would be taken in by it.

In the Benidorm club, a stranger bounded up to McGraw and hugged him. A face from the past, McGraw told his colleagues. He had known the stranger back home. The man had been on the run in Spain from Scottish police, living off the proceeds of a now defunct but once lucrative drug-smuggling operation. He was in his mid-50s but looked ten years younger and put his youthful appearance down to having fallen in love with one of the dancers. He pointed her out and introduced her. She was tall, leggy and heavily tanned.

Next day as Manny was strolling along the seafront, he saw her on the back of a motorcycle, her arms around her Scottish lover, the pair of them roaring along reminding him of Richard Gere and Debra Winger in a scene from the movie *An Officer and a Gentleman*. He thought how far such a carefree, happy scene was from the bombed and bloodied streets of New Lodge where the approach of a motorcycle signalled pedestrians to run for cover, fearing it carried a gunman looking for random victims.

While McGraw and the others generally seemed sympathetic to the plight of families like the McDonnells, there were some who resented the Irish simply for being Irish, as Manny discovered later that day when he met yet another exiled Scot who was an avid Rangers supporter. We'll call the new arrival 'Jock'. Manny remembers his first meeting with the new man.

'This guy had been doing some work for one of the Colombian cartels in the Benidorm area, but something must have gone wrong, because he'd been hiding from them in Tenerife, where he'd come across Tam and they'd stayed in touch. Tam wanted him to meet some of the gang and had asked him to fly over. We'd been drinking in a bar when he came in, obviously looking for Tam, who had a chat with him then brought him over. Tam gave him my name; I said hello and let them go on talking. I heard the guy say, "I'll work with anybody, as long as they're not Irish." Tam looked at me; I looked at this newcomer and said, "Well, I'm fucking Irish." He said, "Well, that's the way I feel," and I told him, "Well, if that's the way you feel you can fuck off."

'It was pretty tense, but Tam calmed things down and smoothed everything over. He was very good at that. The guy turned out to be a real gem. Later on, he told me, "Manny, when I said I didn't want to work with anybody Irish and you opened your mouth, I wished a fucking hole had opened up in the floor and swallowed me. It was the worst experience of my life, I think." He said the reason for his feeling that way was that an Irish gang had shot up a bar with which he was connected in Malaga and when he banned them they returned with a machine gun. I don't know how it ended, but I was glad he survived because he was a cracking character, the type you could trust with your life.'

Jock had a snippet of news that made the hairs stand up on the back of Manny's neck.

'I don't know why you're here,' he said, 'And it's none of my business. But watch what you're doing. There's a Spanish cop in town who loves getting himself on television, a Chief Inspector Ignacio Bulanyos. He nicked Donald [Mathieson] and Bob Gillon and maybe you're the reason why he's come up here.'

The news set alarm bells ringing. Manny decided that even if the others weren't, he would be ultra careful from now on.

He picked up a newspaper to pass the time and was astonished to see an item from Belfast telling of the murder a few days previously of 'Basher' Bates, a member of Lenny Murphy's Shankhill Butchers, from who Manny and Sally had so narrowly escaped all those years before. According to the newspaper, Bates was shot dead by the son of someone he himself had murdered 20 years ago. He knew Republicans would welcome Bates' death, but as for himself, he was out of the violence now and still troubled by what had happened in Warrington.

McGraw had assured his friends it made sense to move to Benidorm, and shortly after the six-day fact-finding trip the first bus filled with youngsters and their parents from the east end of Glasgow made the shorter journey to the Costa Blanca. The new supplier had agreed to charge the old rate of £700 a kilo, despite having a longer haul from the south. All appeared to be back on track, but developments elsewhere were heading the operation in a direction that would take it off the rails.

In the middle of July, yet another party, whooping at the prospect of starting off their long summer break under Spanish sun, set off from Glasgow, from where Manny flew to join up with his two colleagues, who had driven down to Shannon and caught a flight to Alicante from there. By now, Detective

Superintendent Lauder had taken charge of the McDonnell investigation. He and his team were convinced Manny was bossing a vast drug-smuggling enterprise and they were determined to catch him.

The police listening team had picked up a scrap of conversation while tapping the McGraws' landline. This had been an especially wearisome task, sitting hour after hour sweating under headphones listening to the sort of routine and innocent conversations all families and friends have. These meant absolutely nothing. The police were certain McGraw was aware of their intrusion; the telephone tapping, surveillance, constant stopping of him and Mags as they drove around, and even the installation of a camera in his street, which had bemused neighbours, was done as much to merely irritate the McGraws as to pick up information. It was a tactic police used frequently.

Then one day a single word gave the listening team a vital clue. Manny only found out about the telephone call to the McGraw home later, but it left him puzzling whether it had been a deliberate attempt to pass a hint to the police.

'I believe the guy who made this call was a grass. He was a pal of Tam who had been on the run and for some reason that I never found out had come down to Benidorm. It might have been that one of the others had told him things were being moved there and he'd decided to see if there was anything going for him. But while he was in Benidorm he phoned Tam on his house phone and told him he had seen the "bus".

'Tam didn't mention this right away, but a few weeks later, when he did, I flew over to Glasgow and asked him to meet me in the Swallow Hotel. I said, "Three things, Tam. Number one, why did he phone your house when the line was bugged, 100 per cent bugged, and he knows that but he still phones in? Number two, has he ever seen the bus before?" Tam said no and I said, "Well, how can he phone you up and say, 'I've seen the bus?' I haven't even seen the bus. How can he tell you he's seen the bus if he's never seen it? And do you know how many buses are in Benidorm? There's thousands of them. Why mention one bus? And, number three, why did he travel to Benidorm?" In Belfast, those three things would have been enough to have him taken away. To this day, I still believe he was the man who gave it all away.'

Not unnaturally, the police have never said what put them on to the smugglers. They have maintained they did not know about the existence of a bus until weeks later. But the fact is that due to the conversation they were made aware of it, and their own records suggest that following its mention, the intensity of their investigation was stepped up.

The call had been made from Benidorm, and it was to there that Detective Superintendent Lauder headed, taking with him Brian Ferguson, a likeable customs officer who had spent much of his younger life in South America and spoke fluent Spanish. The two met officers from the *policía* and told them what they knew, emphasising the fact that the man they believed to be the main player was a known Irish paramilitary.

It was mid-July. Surveillance in Glasgow had picked up McGraw heading into the city branch of the Allied Irish Bank and emerging with a green holdall. It appeared to be heavy. Manny had been negotiating to buy a flat in Barlanark, not far from the McGraws, and the watchers spotted the two men there, and with John Healy at McGraw's home. What they did not spot that same day was the Mercedes bus leaving Glasgow en route for Dover, Calais and Benidorm at the start of a two-week holiday.

Bob Lauder's ventures into the Spanish resort would earn him the tag, from some colleagues and smugglers alike, of 'Benidorm Bob'. A day after the coach arrived he began his watch on Manny, saw him link up with one of his Irish colleagues and then visit Rocky's Pub before going on to the Hotel Presidente, where one of the courier teams was staying. They noted that Manny was 'very agitated' and then when they attempted to follow one of his

Irish team they lost their man, who hopped in and out of side streets, a recognised anti-surveillance technique.

Manny had sussed something was wrong.

'I was conscious of being watched. I realised from time to time they would be having a look at us, but that didn't worry me. I thought it would be in connection both with my collecting from couriers and my terrorist background. I didn't realise that even now they did not know about the existence of the bus, because I still hadn't been told about the phone call to Tam's house. Some of the surveillance wasn't the best.

'Generally when we went over to Benidorm I didn't go out on the town, because I didn't like it. I preferred everybody to stay together. I didn't really like anybody leaving the house but one night we went out and were having a couple of drinks when we were approached by a couple of guys who were talking about a bit of this, a bit of that and where could they get a bit of charlie. Right away I was suspicious. Back home we used to identify soldiers and policemen by looking at their shoes and their haircuts and that gave us an indication that they were military or police. And to me these guys were just like policemen. The questions they were asking just didn't fit the scene. So again we tightened up security, but by then it was too late, because they were on to us.'

Yet even at this stage, the police had nothing positive, only innuendo, to link anyone to drug smuggling. Suspicion did not count as evidence. While the police sat, watched and waited, spending considerable time in the pleasant surroundings of the Benidorm bars, just a few yards away the bus, M749 YSM, waited to receive its secret cargo. Then came a remarkable stroke of luck, as far as the police were concerned.

Lauder and Ferguson had been watching the Hotel Presidente on the Avenida del Mediterráneo, close to the seafront, for signs of Manny and spotted him leaving the hotel in a taxi. When the cab returned empty, Brian Ferguson strolled over to the driver and began a conversation in Spanish that eventually turned to his previous passengers. 'I arranged to meet them here but just missed them,' said the customs man.

'No worries,' he was told, 'I took them to the Hotel Don Pancho.'

'Where's that, señor?'

'Just around the corner, want me to take you?'

Two days later, the superintendent drove into the Avenida de Almería to keep an eye on the Don Pancho when he spotted something that made him blink. Parked at the side of the road was a white Mercedes bus, M749 YSM, and on the side was the logo 'BMH Travel, 191 Scotland Street, Glasgow'. Police would always claim this was the first time a bus had come into their investigation – which raises questions as to why it was decided to put this particular vehicle under watch. Had they linked the 'bus' of the telephone call to one being seen near a hotel where Manny was spotted? There were literally dozens of foreign coaches in Benidorm at any one time, many of them from Scotland.

Lauder asked his Spanish counterparts to keep an eye on the coach. Three nights later, just before midnight, it drove off but next morning was back in place. Two days later, as it was watched, two men, John Wood and Michael 'Benji' Bennett, loaded their suitcases inside and then helped a party of children and their parents put their luggage on board. The bus headed off and was spotted at Calais ferry terminal next day. Had it been stopped and examined, the police would have discovered a full illicit load worth over one million pounds beneath the feet of the passengers.

Why had Manny gone from the Presidente to the Don Pancho?

'In Rocky's I'd spotted these guys wearing luminous yellow coats, they looked like a pair of bananas, but I knew right away they were police. People were even cracking jokes about the appearance of the "Banana Men". I said to my friends, "There's something wrong here, something is going on. Get back to the apartment and sit tight."'

He took the taxi to the Don Pancho to warn Benji that something was amiss and was angry when Bennett refused to believe him.

'Fuck you then, mate, you won't see us again,' said the Irishman.

He rang John Healy in Glasgow, who told him, 'You're paranoid.'

'Okay, we'll find out who's paranoid,' came the angry response from Benidorm. 'But I tell you now that we ain't going back. That's how convinced I am the cops are there. We don't need the money.'

When Manny sat down to think, he was sure there was nothing linking him to the bus or to anything that might be hidden inside. After realising the police were in town, he and the others had taken precautions to make sure any check of their rooms would show up – a thread across the wardrobe door and a scrap of paper on top of the door, a hair over a suitcase, a tiny dab of powder on a floor or door to reveal hand or foot marks. The searchers had been clumsy. The hair was not there, the thread broken, the paper on the floor and the powder disturbed, but there was nothing incriminating in the rooms anyway.

So they decided to stay on and act like any other holidaymakers, rising in the mornings, taking breakfast, walking, sitting on the beach or around the Presidente pool, visiting a strip club in the evenings and then returning to their rooms. They wanted to give the impression of being unconcerned. They did not know police were watching the bus but could not connect it to drugs.

It was the day the bus left that panic set in when Jock, who had excellent contacts among the Spanish police, arrived out of the blue to warn Manny the bus had been spotted and put under surveillance. Convinced he was going to prison for a long time, even though the only evidence against him was that of his association with McGraw and the others, he agreed with Jock that it was time to leave, and leave quickly.

Jock and two friends drove the three Irishmen on the back of motorcycles to the local railway station, where they caught a train to Bilbao, in the north. From there, they moved back south-east to the coast and Barcelona, where they stayed overnight, all the time trying to make sure they were not being followed. From Barcelona next day they took another train into Italy and finally caught flights to Dublin, nervously waiting at the Republic airport for a hand on the shoulder that never came. Their journey ended with a final train journey to Belfast, where they waited for the axe to fall.

Back in New Lodge he answered a call from Glasgow and was told the coach had arrived safely, had not been stopped anywhere. He was convinced, rightly as it turned out, this was because the police had no evidence that anything illicit was on board.

'They've let it go through, Tam, only because they'd been fucking watching and knew there was nothing.'

To his astonishment, he was told, 'It's coming over again; you going back?'

He took a moment to recover and thought, 'Cheeky bugger. I'm not putting my head in the noose,' but could only say to his friend, 'No way, Tam, we've had enough. Look, if the guys insist on sending it, make it a dry run. If it's stopped, the police will find nothing.'

His advice was ignored.

In mid-September, the bus set off from Glasgow once again en route for Benidorm with a party of mothers and children, their smiles and waves showing their happiness and expectation of the sun and fun to come. Not everyone was happy to see the bus depart on time, however. On the morning it left, a close friend of the smugglers ran for the coach clutching a bag containing £50,000 in cash, hoping someone on board would use it to buy hash and thus treble his outlay. Unfortunately he arrived just in time to see it joining the motorway. Throwing the bag into the boot of his car, he drove home cursing his luck. Subsequent events would give him cause to thank the driver for leaving on time.

That evening the McGraws were spotted at Glasgow airport. Police wondered if they were bound for Benidorm, but their destination was their old favourite, Tenerife.

Luck was on the side of the smugglers. In southern Spain the police had stopped a van carrying two tons of hashish, and as a result the drug was in short supply. What was available was loaded under the floor of the bus, but it was a pittance compared with previous loads. Detective Superintendent Bob Lauder was waiting in Benidorm. He saw the coach and gave orders for it to be stopped on the return journey. As it neared Glasgow on the evening of 28 September, a posse of police cars and vans, their sirens wailing, forced it to a halt on the M74 motorway. Much to the astonishment of the passengers and the driver, Benji Bennett, under the floor was hashish, but a miserly haul of just 114 kilos, worth £263,000.

27

BIKINI LINE

BENJI WAS THE FIRST to be arrested. He was cautioned when the bus was stopped and then taken off for questioning protesting his innocence.

Then the others followed while all the time McGraw was in Tenerife. An old friend phoned him on the island with the news and he was urged to stay where he was, but McGraw pointed out that would suggest he had something to hide. He returned home in early October, a week after the bus was seized.

Manny had waited in Belfast, taking telephone calls telling him how the others were being picked up and knowing his turn was bound to come.

'When I was active with the IPLO I'd wake up every morning thinking this could be my last day on earth, while now I wondered if each today would be my last taste of freedom for a very long time.'

He was at home when two detectives from Strathclyde Police arrived in Belfast to tell the RUC they were there to arrest him. The announcement was greeted with incredulity. 'You're two cops and you're going into New Lodge to nick him?' asked an astonished RUC man. 'You won't get out alive. We better come with you.'

The Glasgow cops joined a small army of the RUC in plain clothes and uniform and a team of soldiers that pulled up outside

Manny's house. 'In you go,' said the RUC man. As they went to his door, neighbours came out and began pelting the visitors with stones, bottles and cans. Inside, they told Manny, 'We're arresting you,' and told him it was in connection with the importation of drugs into Scotland.

'I told them to fuck off and that I knew nothing about drugs,' said Manny. 'But I had to go in the end and I didn't want anybody else getting into trouble. They said they were taking me to the airport and I said, "Put me on a plane and I'm going to attack the person in the seat in front. I'll strangle whoever it is and then I'll wreck the plane." They had a think, made a phone call and took me to the ferry terminal at Larne instead, where they booked a cabin and handcuffed me to the bottom bunk. During the crossing they were throwing Maltesers at me. Police were waiting for me at Stranraer to drive me to Glasgow.

'It was a rotten day, because I knew I'd never be able to go back to Belfast to live. There would be too many people there, especially IRA Volunteers, wanting to talk to me when it came out what it was the police were saying I'd been involved in. In the car I kept telling the cops I knew nothing about drugs on any buses.'

The police were still struggling to link Tam McGraw to the hash find, but the only evidence they had was circumstantial. There may have been hash there, but nobody had seen it being put in place. It was true he'd been seen in Alicante, but rumour was he was there on a short break with his pal John Malloy. And he had been meeting and phoning Manny. But so what? They were friends, after all, and were the trips to Belfast just en route to Donegal to set up the takeover of the Paradise Bar?

Two weeks later, the McGraws were off again to Tenerife for a fortnight. The day they came back, Tam went off to Malaga for a week. When he returned, he too was arrested.

In England, news of the arrests was read with interest by Paul Ferris. He too was in a prison cell, having been picked up by armed police in London when guns were discovered in his car. It was being alleged they were destined for gangsters in the Manchester area or even the UDA. Like his old enemy 400 miles to the north, he was facing a very long time in jail if he was convicted. He read too of the surprise death of William Manson, the man who had murdered his friends Joe and Bobby. According to Manson's death certificate, the cause of his passing was an overdose of co-proxamol, a painkiller favoured by so many suicides it would come to be withdrawn in 2005. On the streets, the rumour was that Manson's death was no accident, nor was the dose self-inflicted; instead, the word 'poisoned' crept into conversations.

Jails could be dangerous places, as Manny and the other smugglers were about to discover. Back in the Maze prison, Billy 'King Rat' Wright, doyen first of the UVF and then of the more militant Loyalist Volunteer Force, was shot dead by one of Manny's former INLA Volunteers, Christopher 'Crip' McWilliams, who was there for killing an IPLO member and was later given life for the murder of Wright. The prison authorities had, for some reason, transferred Wright to a section of the jail holding fervent nationalists, so his murder came as no surprise. Wright left jail in a coffin. Elsewhere in the Maze, 'Dingus' Magee and Gerard Mackin were among 100 nationalists who wanted out too. They were on the verge of crawling out when the weight of a patrolling warder caused the roof of their 30-metre tunnel to collapse. They only had a few more feet to go to freedom.

But just how really dangerous prison life could be was about to be brought home to Manny. There had been more than 30 arrests, but a group of 11 who the police claimed were the hard core of the smugglers were shuffled around prisons, though mainly held in Barlinnie and in Saughton, Edinburgh. The police were struggling to build a case that would convince a jury. Some officers believed the bus had been stopped too soon, that the surveillance should have been continued until the actual loading of hash could be witnessed. Word leaked out that in the absence of firm evidence, dirty tricks were being used. Lawyers acting for some of the accused formally complained their offices had been bugged. And yet the case was still weak. So a plan B was put into operation.

One day in Saughton, Manny found himself talking to a stranger who told him his name was Kari Paajolahti, that he was from Finland and was awaiting deportation back there after being nicked for failing to pay a hotel bill in the Scottish Highlands. That much was true, but it was about as far as the truth went. Paajolahti was a confidence trickster, but a bright one at that, articulate and intelligent. At the time of his arrest in Scotland he was on the run from a jail in Finland where he had been doing time for fraud. The authorities in Scotland came up with a deal. If he would spy on the bus smugglers and report back to two customs handlers, one of them Brian Ferguson, not only would they put a generous word in for him with the police back in Finland but he would be also welcomed back into the United Kingdom at any time.

Paajolahti's role was to gain the confidence of Manny and McGraw in particular, to note down what they discussed and try to glean their plans for the future. Manny knew all about the art of the spy; he had seen it so many times in Belfast, strangers wanting to join the Republicans, men planted within them by the police with promises of money or being let off long prison sentences for a variety of crimes. He warned the others to be careful. But the Finn was playing a crafty game.

'Kari was listening one day when Tam was talking about smuggling. He seemed to perk up, because he became very intent, but then when Tam said he just wasn't into drugs of any sort, Kari asked, 'Cocaine, heroin, hash?' Tam told him, "It's just not my scene," and Kari seemed to lose interest. Tam could be an old woman at times, gossiping, but he could also be very shrewd. He started talking about smuggling and said there was more profit and far less risk in smuggling cigarettes than drugs. He said you could buy cigarettes dirt cheap in Tenerife and then use a boat to get them back into the UK and make a fortune. He had a mate in Tenerife who could supply as many cigarettes as he wanted. I think Tam was going to say more, but he held back maybe because he wasn't sure of Kari. But it was obvious he'd been thinking long and hard about this. He said it was a three-day boat trip each way.'

This was one conversation Paajolahti omitted to mention to his customs handlers when they met him three weeks later for a debriefing, and they drove him to Edinburgh airport for the start of his journey back to Helsinki and a shortened stay in prison there. But he remembered it, and tucked away in his pocket was the telephone number of the flat in Barlanark to where Manny's family had now moved. He told his customs friends the smugglers hadn't spoken much about drugs or buses but also said he wanted to return to Scotland once he'd served out the rest of his time back home. 'Don't forget to contact us if you do come back,' he was told. 'You won't regret it.'

Paajolahti was not the only individual to be concerning himself with dirty tricks. Manny had never actually fallen out with Paul Ferris. While he awaited his own trial, Ferris had kept in close touch with developments in the drugs case back in Scotland. One morning, Manny opened a letter from his old friend but was not amused by what he read.

'Paul was saying words to the effect, "Beware, there's a spy in your camp, he's a grass," and I knew he was talking about Tam. Well, I could make up my own mind about that. I didn't need anybody else to do that for me. I was the one who would decide, not Paul, and I trusted Tam. Paul kept sending letters on this theme and eventually I stopped writing back to him. We hadn't fallen out, but I didn't need his advice.

'There have been a lot of nasty things said about Tam, a lot of people have said he tried to save himself by stitching up everybody else. But I know for a fact that is a lie. Each of us agreed we would show everybody else copies of what we had told the police. I was one of three who said absolutely nothing, Gordon was another, so our files were pretty thin. Tam's was the size of an encyclopaedia, because he just never stopped rambling on about any subject under the sun, except smuggling drugs. He even talked about his wife's bikini line, at which the police terminated the interview. But he never implicated anybody, did not say a single word that could have landed any of us in trouble.

'It's true Tam took prison badly. He just wanted to be out and home with Mags. He was sharing a cell with a guy who came to us and said, "That fucker never ever stops talking. He's talking when I go to sleep at night and he's on his feet talking when I wake up at four in the morning. I was going to plead not guilty because I'm innocent and I've a really good chance of getting off, but that would delay things and mean I'd have to spend longer on remand locked up with your mate, so just to get away from him I'm pleading guilty." The guy got six months and reckoned it was worth it just to get away from Tam.

'The police and prison service were in cahoots to try to cause trouble among us. They kept Tam and the others separated, as often happens in high-profile cases, and tried to spread suspicion that he was talking to the police, collaborating. The police interviewed all of us regularly but were told nothing. They made a lot of visits to Tam, and one night when he was on the telephone to home I asked him, "Tam, have the police been talking to you?" He took it the wrong way and was shouting into the telephone, "I'm being accused of grassing." When he finished his call, I said, "Tam, nobody is accusing you of anything. We know you're not telling the police anything, but we agreed among ourselves not to keep secrets and we are simply wondering what the police wanted." He said, "They've been asking me about the Paradise Bar, that's all."

'Tam told us, "If the prosecution came along with a deal now offering to let you all go if I take the rap and a 12-year sentence, then I would go for that," and we knew he meant it. We never doubted either his honesty with us or the determination of the police to put him away for a very long time.'

Having believed Manny was the Mr Big behind the buses racket, the police now concentrated on proving the mastermind was Tam, who had been warned that if convicted he would expect at least 14 years.

'If he'd been in any shape or form a police informer, then he would not have been given such a hard time. They were out to get him.'

Manny was angered by an incident that showed the prison authorities in a poor light.

'One day Tam came along to my cell and asked if he could have a word. He looked agitated and angry. He said, "Manny, I'm really sorry, but your brother Patrick has died. These bastards didn't have the decency to come along and tell you themselves and got me to do it for them."

'I thanked Tam and knew he was angry at being asked to be the bearer of bad news for others whose job it had been to tell me. I went to see one of the governors and told him I wanted to attend Patrick's funeral. He told me, "I'm sorry, I can't allow that." When I asked why, he said he couldn't spare the manpower to take me to Belfast for the ceremony. It would also have meant getting the agreement of the RUC, who would put forward the same argument, that they couldn't spare the men'.

'I was furious. "What the fuck kind of justice system is this? I'm on remand. I'm pleading not guilty. I'm innocent in my eyes and in the eyes of the law until if and when I'm found guilty. Others have been allowed out for funerals, why should I be penalised because you drag me all the way here from my home in Belfast?"

' "I've made my decision and there it is," was all this guy would say. To this day that has stuck in my gut. I feel it was a shocking thing to do, especially in the light of how things turned out.'

On the other hand, some prison officers were occasionally more sympathetic.

'At Saughton we were kept apart from mainstream guys at visits. A room was usually kept aside for anybody visiting beasts, sex offenders, who needed protection, but they were shunted off somewhere else so we could use it. One day John Healy and me were in it having visits when this prisoner walked past, looked in and shouted, "Fucking beasts. You're getting it."

'When our visits were over we went back to the hall and suddenly this character who had threatened us showed up, shouting "fucking beasts" again, "I'll fucking kill you." We told him to fuck off, but he was right up for bother, took his glasses off and came striding over to us. John was a really fit, hard man, and as the idiot got up to him and me, John started giving him a doing. I joined in and so did five or six of our pals. We dragged him off to one of our cells and were giving him a real beating when the door opened and screws appeared. We thought we were in real trouble. "You're getting charged," shouted one of the screws and pointed to the guy lying on the floor, his teeth out and his face covered in blood. They dragged him away screaming, "Look what those bastards have done to me," while the rest of the hall fell about laughing. We heard nothing more about it.'

McGraw too was a victim of strange justice. While he waited to go on trial, the authorities in the Republic, always strapped for cash, announced they were confiscating the Paradise Bar, grossly prejudging the outcome of the trial in Scotland by claiming it had been used to launder cash made through drugs.

At one stage it was planned to hold three trials, the accused sorted into three groups depending on the nature and seriousness of their alleged offences. But a decision on whether to proceed with the second and third would only be taken after the outcome of the first was known. If it was a triumph for the police and the prosecution, they would go ahead. If not – well, such an outcome, as far as the Crown was concerned, was unthinkable.

While the first trial got under way at the High Court in Edinburgh in April 1998, 11 men sat in the dock. Michael Bennett, John Wood, Graeme Mason, John Burgon, John Healy, Emmanuel McDonnell, Thomas McGraw, William McPhee, Gordon Ross,

Trevor Lawson and Paul Flynn all denied being concerned in the supply of cannabis resin between January 1993 and November 1997 in a variety of places, including Glasgow, Denny in Stirlingshire, Dover, Manchester airport, Torremolinos, Salou, Malaga, Donegal, Belfast and at Camp Davy Crockett. They further denied they were 'knowingly concerned along with other persons in smuggling cannabis resin'.

28

COUGHING UP

UP TO THE VERY LAST MOMENT, the police did not give up trying to cause a rift between McGraw and the others. Each day in the van taking the accused men to the courthouse, one was held within a cage on his own – Tam McGraw – giving the impression he had asked for protection from the others.

It was not that which caused their hearts to sink, though, but seeing Hannah Martin enter the witness box. 'She's talked,' Graeme Mason whispered to Manny. Sure enough, Hannah had. On the way back to Glasgow, the Land Rover had been stopped by customs officers at Dover. No drugs were found in the vehicle, because it had been sent as a decoy to distract any surveillance from the bus. Hannah had been questioned and released, but the experience terrified her. The police had warned they would want to see her again and she lived in dread of their return. When they did, she had been given a choice of telling what she knew or being charged as an accomplice and probably going to prison for a long time.

Hannah was one of life's losers. She had never had much until the holidays and good times life with Mason brought her. The police convinced her she had been used by Del Boy and that it was payback time. And so she told all she knew, from the carrier bags packed with bundles of notes; the hard faced Irishmen who came to collect money; the rows over the Balmer phone call; and her anger at discovering children had been part of the plot. But the only person she implicated was Mason; she knew the names, she said, of none of the others.

Hannah repeated her bizarre tale to the jury, often looking towards John Healy and hoping for his forgiveness. There was no kindness, though, for Mason. When she finished her evidence, he knew he was doomed.

News of the trial reached those in Northern Ireland through newspapers and conversations with friends in Scotland. That Manny was alleged to have been a vital cog in such a spectacular drug-smuggling enterprise attracted considerable interest. There were two sharply opposing schools of thought: those who felt that by involving himself in drugs he had let the Republican cause down, and those among his many friends who did not feel Scottish justice could be trusted to treat him fairly. However differently these factions felt towards him, both wanted him back in Belfast: one to save, the other to punish.

The IRA sent an active service unit to Edinburgh to study the arrangements for the daily transportation of the men to court from Saughton and to see whether there was a reasonable chance of ambushing the prison van and freeing those inside. When an ambush was deemed impractical, because of the considerable strength of the security cordon, which included a helicopter and armed police, and the clear difficulty of achieving a getaway through the crowded streets of the Scottish capital, other ideas were studied.

The prospect of setting fire to the High Court building was examined; so were the chances of attacking jurors (bribing was regarded as too despicable); and the suggestion that the water supply to the court building could be poisoned was discussed but discounted because too many women and children were sure to be among victims. The idea of a roadside car bomb that would detonate as the convoy carrying the prisoners passed by met a similar fate, given the thumbs down because no one could be sure in which van Manny was. In the end, the decision was simply to let things take their course and have another look at the situation once the outcome of the trial was known.

For Manny, Wood and Ross that came on the 45th day of the trial, when they were told they could go home, that there was no evidence against them. In Manny's case, the prosecution had tried to make much of telephone calls between the accused, saying these reached heights each time the bus left or arrived. Logs listing these calls had to be confirmed with the signatures of British Telecom officials. In Manny's case, detectives had travelled to Belfast, where an official, worried about the possible implications of what would be seen as cooperating with the police against a well-known Republican, would only agree to sign his log with 'Mr X'. When the trial judge was told of this, he ruled Manny's log inadmissible. It had been the only evidence linking him to those alleged to have run the drug buses.

That ruled out any immediate action either on his behalf or against him. Technically he had done nothing wrong; he had not been concerned in any drugs rackets and had not brought any organisation into disrepute. He would still have questions to face, though, about how he came to be caught up in the plot, and it was made clear that the IRA in particular would not allow him back in Belfast.

He continued going back each day for the remainder of the trial to sit in the public gallery, hoping things would go well for his friends, all the time knowing that had they listened to him when he warned they were in danger of slipping on banana skins left by the men in yellow coats, the police would have had little if anything concrete to pin on any of them. In prison, Healy had told him, 'Manny, I apologise, I wish I'd listened to you.'

Manny was especially interested in what would happen to McGraw. The police had been bitterly disappointed when Manny, the man they had at one time thought was the boss of the whole racket, had been freed without a blemish on his character. Now they concentrated on getting a result against Tam. Mags McGraw was so confident her husband would walk free that she had told him she wouldn't even listen to the outcome of the trial on radio or television but would have his favourite meal of mince and tatties ready for his homecoming. McGraw had put his future in the hands of the lawyer whose attention to detail had saved many an accused from wrongful conviction. Liam O'Donnell was skilled and dogged and had urged McGraw not to idly waste his time on remand but to use it to study the police claims.

It was a master stroke, because in going through what the prosecution claimed were implications of guilt suggested by examinations of his thousands of telephone records, he discovered evidence of tampering. Experts introduced by the lawyer confirmed this. O'Donnell had another ace to play. He had persuaded razor-sharp QC Donald Findlay to represent McGraw, and Findlay came up trumps. Much had been made of McGraw's apparent wealth, of his links to Manny and the other accused, and of his trips overseas.

Findlay summed up the case against his man by telling the jury, 'There is not a single scrap of evidence in this whole case which in any way connects Thomas McGraw with the bus, these holidays in Spain or anything else. There is not a single scrap of actual evidence that one penny piece of McGraw's money reached Spain and was given to somebody to supply drugs. The Crown case is based on suspicion and possibilities and that has never been enough to convict someone in Scotland of a crime.'

The jury took two and a half days to make up their minds. When they filed back into court to announce their verdicts, the trial had run for a staggering 55 days. They found Burgon not guilty; Bennett not proven by a majority; McPhee and Lawson unanimously not proven; the case against McGraw not proven by a majority; Mason and Flynn unanimously guilty; and Healy guilty by a majority.

Prosecutors claimed Healy's drug trafficking had earned him around three-quarters of a million pounds. He was jailed for ten years; Mason for eight; and Paul Flynn, a quiet, well-liked Liverpudlian who Manny thought could have done a stage act as an Arthur Askey lookalike, for six years. Paul did not survive long in prison. He had a heart condition and suffered a fatal collapse one morning while taking a shower.

Once the dust had settled, the Operation Lightswitch team assembled in Strathclyde Police headquarters in Glasgow for a mini inquest. It had been, to put it mildly, a disappointing outcome and in no way justified the cost. Certainly the team had pounced too soon, but were they being too hard on themselves? Manny felt the ending of the tale of the buses was down to good police work as much as anything else. And in the end, hash smuggling on such a vast scale had been halted. Without police action, the bus runs, officially thought to have been around 20 but actually double that number, could have gone on considerably longer.

Less than two weeks after the three men were driven away in a prison van to start their sentences, another of Manny's friends was also given a long stretch behind bars. In London, following a trial at the Old Bailey, Paul Ferris was convicted of conspiracy to sell or transfer prohibited weapons, conspiracy to deal in firearms and of possessing explosives and weighed off for ten years – later reduced on appeal to seven.

'I was sorry when I heard what had happened to Paul, because while I'd been annoyed at what he wrote about Tam in the letter, I'd never fallen out with him. And at the end of the day, had it not been for Paul I'd never have met Tam.'

Manny went off to visit John Healy in prison. He'd always liked John but had been surprised by his decision to go into the witness box in his own defence. He felt John did not help himself, but there was no way he was going to abandon his friend. In the visiting room at Shotts jail, the pair spoke in near whispers, not wanting any other visitors or the prison officers who throughout wandered past their table, usually finding some excuse to stop beside them, to hear what was being said. The subject was one of the businessmen who received sensational returns for their regular investment in the bus runs. In a league of earners from the smuggling racket, one of these men would have been near to the top. But some among those who had spent so much time locked up awaiting a trial suspected he had collaborated with the police in order to save his own neck. They wanted him killed. Others felt he would suffer most by being hit in his pocket.

Two days later the businessman was asked to attend a rendezvous in an Asda car park in Glasgow with a friend of one of the drug smugglers; he was too scared to refuse.

'Look mate, you know who I'm here on behalf of,' he was told. 'I'll come straight to the point. We both know you've stepped out of line and the consequences have been pretty drastic. A mutual friend is in jail. He wants you dead, and frankly, I can sympathise with him. In his shoes I'd feel the same, but I've done what I can on your behalf and have a simple message. It's not open for discussion; you give me an answer here and now. Our friend wants £100,000 or you are dead. That's it. You have a choice. Pay up or be whacked. What's it to be?'

'I'll pay,' was the response. 'But I'll need time, a couple of months.' He saw the anger on the other's face and hastily went on, 'Give me a couple of weeks to get enough cash together for the first instalment and ring me.'

He was warned, 'You realise what will happen if you try anything?'

'Don't worry, I won't.'

'Oh, I'm not worrying. Frankly, I think you've got off very cheaply. But others might not be so generous.'

'What do you mean by that?'

'Time will tell.'

Thirteen days later, £15,000 in cash was handed over in a plastic shopping bag. From then on, every week the two met always at a different location. Sometimes the bags would contain £8,000, sometimes £10,000, it came in dribs and drabs, but within two months the debt had been paid in full.

Manny was not the only visitor to Shotts with an interest in John Healy. Hannah Martin had been devastated by the outcome of the trial. She felt no remorse over the fate of Mason but knew her evidence had been instrumental in putting away the two others. Alone at home, she cried. At least once a week she took to going out to the bleak prison car park or nearby, simply to sit and be near the only man she had ever loved.

Manny, meanwhile, was having increasing worries about his loved ones. He knew the issue of his returning to Belfast had to be somehow resolved, and a move was made unexpectedly quickly. After he was freed for lack of evidence he had asked for a meeting with a Republican sympathiser living in Glasgow who, he knew, maintained close contact with members of the IRA in Belfast. This man had even visited Manny in jail while he was on remand to tell him of the aborted moves to disrupt the trial but also, reassuringly, to promise him his support.

'I know what you've given for the cause, Manny,' he said. 'Sometimes people back home don't realise just how difficult the cops over here can be, especially to somebody with your background. I'm doing all I can, but there's a lot of feeling right now. We both know nothing will happen to Sally and the family, but my advice is for them to stay here permanently, or at least until this is all sorted.'

The Glasgow Republican set up a meeting between Manny and two IRA Volunteers who travelled especially over from Belfast. They met at the Celtic Supporters' Club building on London Road, Glasgow, and the visitors told him they wanted to see his case files in order to examine the strength of the evidence against him. 'I'm sure you would,' he told them, 'but at the end of the day it was decided there was no case to answer because there was no evidence against me. So there is no case for anybody to investigate.'

The visitors were unimpressed, and one leaned forward to say, 'Well, we know differently.'

Manny realised some mischief-maker had been at work. 'Well, it doesn't matter what you say, I'm an innocent man, the judge said there was no evidence against me,' he pointed out. The argument went backwards and forwards until the meeting ended in stalemate. 'If I was guilty of smuggling drugs or dealing in drugs, I wouldn't be here today seeing you, I'd be in the nick,' he pointed out. The two IRA Volunteers left, saying they would need to report back to superiors in Belfast.

In fact, while they had been in Glasgow, others in Belfast were making efforts on Manny's behalf. A leading politician contacted him seeking the low-down and after being briefed intervened on his behalf, with the result that Manny received a message giving him clearance to reappear in Belfast. He would make regular visits to his old stamping ground but knew his days as a paramilitary were long gone and decided to remain living in Glasgow for the time being.

As Christmas 1998 neared, he picked up the telephone at his home in Barlanark one day and, out of the blue, heard the voice of Kari Paajolahti asking, 'How are you, my Irish friend? I hear they didn't put you or Thomas in prison. How did you manage that?'

'We managed it because we hadn't fucking done anything,' Manny replied. 'Where are you and what are you up to?'

'Oh, I'm in London, but I have something I know you're going to be interested in. I'm coming up to Glasgow. I want to meet Tam and you. Can you get me a hotel? I'm a little short of funds.'

Manny called McGraw, who told him, 'Okay, go ahead, but watch that fucker. I don't trust him. He's up to something.'

He was right. A lesson in just how devious the forces appointed to uphold law and order in the United Kingdom can be was about to be demonstrated.

Just about the only truth the Finn had told was that he was in London. In fact, he had been meeting his same customs handlers to talk about the entrapment of McGraw and McDonnell and had been handed a formal document that gave him the green light to be a criminal and not be prosecuted. This astonishing paper, signed by the two customs officials, ended up in the hands of a *News of the World* investigator. It began, 'I, Kari Juhani Paajolahti, have been told that I may take part in a particular crime, the importation of controlled drugs, providing the part I play is a minor one when judged against the criminal proposal as a whole.' It went on to stress that he was not to take any major role, but in effect it was encouraging a known fraudster and crook to set up others in criminal acts knowing he would walk away unscathed.

Paajolahti already had a plan of action mapped out. Having failed to net McGraw and Manny once on a drugs scam, the customs men were using the Finn to con the pair into another drugs racket via a scheme in which they already knew McGraw was interested.

Manny met him when he arrived in Glasgow and took him to his hotel, then to the Park Lane pub, on Hope Street.

'Paajolahti said he'd been thinking about Tam's idea of smuggling cigarettes from Tenerife and wanted to help. He had a relative who was captain of a boat docked in London and was looking for business. He wasn't fussy what the cargo would be.

'He then said he had something else he knew we'd want to join. He'd been in Amsterdam and made contact with a Dutch organisation that was bringing in heroin. His idea was to go over to Amsterdam posing as a workman and bring gear back hidden in a length of tubing. He said he would hand the heroin over to us in the Molly Malone bar in Glasgow. He'd need us to put up £48,500 in cash to buy the heroin. I asked how much he'd want for acting as courier and he said £2,500.'

Paajolahti would ultimately admit to a journalist it had been a plan carefully concocted with customs officials. If McGraw and

Manny went along with it, they would instantly be arrested and charged with plotting to smuggle heroin, a serious offence that would guarantee them a double-figure prison term. Paajolahti, on the other hand, would be allowed to disappear but keep the £2,500.

'When I told Tam about Kari, the boat and the heroin, he said right away, "For fuck sake, you need to be careful about that bastard. Tell him we might be up for using the boat to bring in ciggies, but we're not up for drugs." I went back to Paajolahti and passed on the message. I could see he was disappointed, he'd hoped we'd fall for the heroin trick, but tried to put on a brave face. "Okay, Manny, I'll speak to my relative and call you back." That was the last time I ever spoke to him or saw him. He disappeared.'

In reality, Paajolahti contacted the *News of the World* to reveal details of the customs plot. 'I don't want to mess up those people in Glasgow,' he said. 'One of them's an Irish paramilitary, and the Irish kill you, don't they?'

29

BULLETPROOF VEST

MANNY HOPED TO PUT TRAGEDY and murder behind him by moving to Glasgow, but his hopes were soon shattered. With the start of the new millennium just a few weeks off, Gerald Rae, with who he had made friends in prison, was found dead in his car in strange circumstances.

Gerry was doing his best to overcome a drug problem, and alongside his efforts at self-rehabilitation was a long-running battle against Strathclyde Police. Almost ten years before his death, his home had been raided by a gang of men who beat him with pickaxe handles and baseball bats. Gerry maintained the gang were policemen. Three years later in another police raid on his home, he alleged a quantity of drugs said to have been discovered had in fact been planted.

His point seemed to have been proved when a court acquitted him and he alleged seven police officers had committed perjury. During their trial and after he had given evidence, Gerry's body was discovered and it was said he had been clutching a bag of almost pure heroin and had died from a heroin overdose. Police said there were no suspicious circumstances, but Gerry's many friends believed, and still believe, otherwise. All the police officers were cleared.

'I liked Gerry. He had been a good pal and good company in prison. His death came as a total shock.'

Mid-way through 2000, Manny was asked if he would meet members of a well-known east end of Glasgow family, the McGoverns. 'They're worried about a situation and are looking for advice,' he was told by a close friend, who arrived with some of the family members after he agreed to help.

'They were very friendly and polite, and thanked me for seeing them,' said Manny. 'They said they knew of me through Tam and his people and were friendly with Tam. He had suggested they had a chat with me. During our meeting it emerged they believed one or two IRA hitmen had been hired to come over from Northern Ireland to shoot one of them. Although they said they weren't sure which one, I sensed they knew all the same.

'I had the feeling this wasn't the whole story, but it was obvious they had genuine concerns. They wanted to know if I could offer any advice on what precautions to take; was there any way of finding out whether IRA people were already over in Scotland; what was the best way of handling all of this? I said, "Look, I'm sorry to tell you this, but if there are two IRA men either over here or coming here to shoot somebody, yourselves or anybody else, then it's going to happen no matter what you do. The only advice I can give you is to tell you to change your routines, if you're in a car make sure your wives and kids aren't with you, check underneath your car every time it's been parked up, especially outside your homes, be aware of your surroundings and watch who you speak to and what you say. Don't tell anybody your movements. Don't let anybody know where you are going to be at a certain time. That's about all the help I can give, except to wear a bulletproof vest."

'Tam had a bulletproof vest that he'd loaned to me after the stories started circulating about a possible hit on me over the drugs case. I offered to loan it to the family but pointed out it was no guarantee of safety. "Just be very careful," I said.'

Not long afterwards, the brains of the family, Tony McGovern, was shot as he drew up in his car outside the New Morvern pub in the east end of Glasgow. The killer went for his head and lower trunk. Tony had ignored Manny's advice to keep his movements a secret and had announced as he left the bar earlier when he would be returning.

'Was I shocked when I heard Tony had been murdered? Not really. I knew if somebody was set on killing him then there was little or nothing anybody could do to stop that. The day after the shooting, Tam turned up and asked, "Was Tony wearing my bulletproof vest?" and I told him he had. "Nobody's safe," he said.'

The dead man was only 35. He had been involved in a series of violent incidents with a man who had once been his best friend. Sometime later, James 'Bull' Stephenson was accused of the killing, but after spending months in custody was released and the charge dropped.

Freedom was very much in the thoughts of Paul Ferris, and in January 2002 he was finally released, walking out of the gates of top-security Frankland jail – specially built to withstand terrorist attacks – in County Durham shortly after seven in the morning to be met by a phalanx of newspaper photographers and television cameras. Behind the intensity of the interest lay curiosity as to whether his return to Glasgow would spark off a street war. Most suspected the chief opponent would be McGraw, who was saying nothing in public, keeping his own counsel. Those who knew of Manny's friendship with both players wondered whether he would now have to choose sides, but his attitude was that ever since he became a regular visitor to Glasgow he had been pals with both and saw no reason why that shouldn't continue to be the case.

Once the hullabaloo had died down, Ferris and Manny resumed their old relationship, with the former occasionally calling at the Irishman's home for a chat. Ian 'Blink' MacDonald, the armed bank robber, joined Ferris one day and was told they were popping in to see Manny at his Barlanark apartment. Blink remembers it well.

'Manny invited us in and offered us a coffee. He went off to make it, and while he was in the kitchen we heard some muffled shouts, then the noise of Manny moving about, opening a door, talking, closing the door and a couple of minutes later rejoining us. He said, "Did you hear that cunt?" and we said we'd heard voices. "I've kidnapped him," said Manny. "The cunt owes £20,000 and I've told him he's not getting out of here till he pays up. I've had him here four days." We never found out the guy's name but later on gathered Manny was minding this character for somebody who was owed the money.'

The bad blood that had existed between Ferris and McGraw had reached boiling point largely through the former claiming his rival was a police informer – an allegation denied by a senior police officer in his autobiography. McGraw was known in the east end as the 'Licensee', a tag that Ferris claimed was because he had a licence from his police friends to escape prosecution in exchange for information and favours. Friends of McGraw pointed simply to the fact that the nickname was the result of his running, with Mags, the Caravel bar.

The feud exploded into bloodshed one morning in April 2002 when they met by chance as they were driving in opposite directions through Barlanark. There have been many versions of the ensuing fight, but McGraw's claim that he was getting the better of his opponent is backed by a third party, Mark Clinton, who was a passenger in Ferris's motor at the time.

According to Clinton, the vehicles stopped, the drivers climbed out and McGraw emerged from the rear of his holding a golf club – it turned out to be a number seven iron. He proceeded to batter the cowering Ferris until Clinton intervened, stabbing McGraw on the arm and shoulder. The fight broke up when a watching resident screamed that the police were on their way. Both protagonists claimed they were uninjured, but in his biography, *Crimelord*, McGraw admitted he needed hospital treatment for his injuries. Newspapers got wind of the fracas and after stories were published Ferris had his licence revoked. He spent several more weeks in prison in Durham before being freed.

Manny said, 'I knew he and Tam didn't like each other. When Tam beat him up with the golf club I didn't know what to do, because I liked them both. After it happened, Paul telephoned and asked me to meet him. When I did I saw straight away he was marked; it was obvious he'd been in a fight and Paul told me what had happened. It seemed he was asking me to choose sides and I didn't want to do that. It was crazy; I was in a no-win situation, a catch-22, and for a time I fell out with both of them. Even Tam wouldn't speak to me.'

Things were made even more difficult in September that year. In March, one of Manny's co-accused Trevor Lawson, had been knocked down and killed not far from his Dunipace, Stirling, home as he ran across a busy motorway trying to escape a pub fight. Now another of the accused was killed. Handsome Gordon Ross, whose good looks and charm had once pulled a girlfriend from the arms of a world-famous Manchester United footballer, had been in a bar on Shettleston Road in the east end of Glasgow when he was told someone outside wanted to speak to him. He went out the door and was immediately stabbed, dying in the gutter. That meant three of the original 11 in the dock at the drugs trial were dead. Three more had been jailed.

Three months later, Hannah Martin died in hospital after a long and painful fight against liver disease and a struggle to simply survive. Gone for her were the bright lights, beaches and airports. After giving evidence at the smugglers' trial she had been abandoned by the police, and lived in fear of retribution from those against who she had turned. Not so long ago she had carried hundreds of thousands of pounds. Now she had nothing, even sitting in darkness once for a full week because she had no money for an electricity meter.

Manny and McGraw would occasionally exchange a brief word, but their closeness of the past was gone. Yet the Irishman still worried for his friend, and that worry turned to real concern as a result of a series of events kicking off at the beginning of February 2003. John 'Grug' Gregg, a leading figure in the UDA, had a fearsome reputation for violence, one increased by his coming close to once shooting dead Gerry Adams, a murder attempt that brought him a long jail sentence. Just after he reached Belfast docks on his way home from watching his favourite Glasgow Rangers side, Gregg was shot dead. The hit had been ordered by his long-time rival, and master self-publicist, Johnny Adair, who was, at the time, in prison. The murder enraged Gregg's supporters, who, at gunpoint, five days later, ordered up to 100 of Adair's associates, including his wife, Gina, and their family, out of Northern Ireland. Gina fled to Scotland, from where she moved to Lancashire.

A week after the exodus, a newspaper claimed McGraw was a close ally of the Adairs, that he had done drug deals in the past with Adair, helped Gina shop for jewellery, entertained her, and allowed her husband to stay at his Mount Vernon home. These allegations have always been strenuously denied by the McGraw family and their friends.

Manny read the article and immediately feared for his long-time pal. Most of the Republican paramilitaries in Northern Ireland were now trying to encourage the move to peace, but there were enough in Scotland who would be furious at suggestions of McGraw having links to a Loyalist thug. Further, many of those close to him were Catholics.

'I couldn't believe it when I read this,' said Manny. 'I had spent so much time in Tam's company in the past that I was certain that had he been in contact with Adair I'd have known. The name had never been mentioned to me. I contacted Tam and asked, "Are you dealing with Johnny Adair?" He immediately said it was a load of garbage and I never doubted his word. I knew it was untrue. If at any time I'd even suspected Tam had a friendship with Adair I'd have immediately broken off from him, despite the depth of our relationship.

'In any case, I was certain that Tam would never have had anything to do with a cider-drinking, thieving, queer-bashing thug of the likes of Adair, who was regarded as a joke in Northern Ireland. He built himself a reputation as somebody of major influence but was never rated by the paramilitaries. When I was with the IPLO, one of his mates gave us Gina's phone number. I'd ring her and say things like, "Hi Gina, guess where Johnny is, he's up shagging such and such, he's in her house now and if you go up there you'll find him" or we'd say, "Oh dear, Gina, Johnny's having it away with one of his hangers-on. It's a real bum steer for you." She'd shout down the line, "You fucking UVF bastards."

'Adair was so thick you couldn't even shoot him in the head. He was at a UB40 concert in Belfast in 1999 when an INLA unit got to him and blasted him in the nut, but the bullet ricocheted off him. When he wasn't in jail, the IPLO tried to get him. He used to come over on the boat to Scotland, and our staff gave the go-ahead for an operation to bang him when he arrived in Glasgow.

'The plan was to smuggle two gunmen over on a Celtic supporters' coach. We'd watched him a few times when he came across and monitored his movements, who he saw, where he went and what he did. He wasn't very clever at avoiding surveillance. Once he'd been whacked, the active service unit guys would just lose themselves in the crowds of supporters and go home the same way they'd arrived. Adair antagonised so many people with his bragging that we knew the police would be scratching their heads wondering who had taken him out. The operation was tried a couple of times but called off because there were always kids around him, and then he was jailed, which saved his life.'

The killings on both sides of the Irish Sea continued. In March 2003, Billy McPhee was watching a teatime rugby match on television in a crowded bar-restaurant when a man walked up to him and stabbed him repeatedly in the neck, head and upper body. McPhee bled to death despite efforts by customers to save him, while the killer calmly walked away to collect his substantial cash fee from a multimillionaire businessman. Mark Clinton, who had made his peace with McGraw and was friendly with Manny, was accused of the murder, but almost as soon as his trial at the High Court in Glasgow opened, it was stopped and Clinton was freed when the prosecution withdrew the indictment for lack of evidence. Manny had come to know McPhee through their mutual friendship with McGraw, but McPhee's wild and careless partying and antics in Spain had worried him, and even when he was asked to be more discreet, the Scot ignored these requests.

For McPhee, there had been no safety in a crowd. Nor was there for Kevin McAlorum, the killer of 'Yo Yo' Gallagher. McAlorum must have felt he had a charmed life. Sentenced to 16 years in 1997 for having a gun, he was freed three years later under the Good Friday peace initiative. While in jail he had a remarkable escape, as Manny remembers.

'Another of the prisoners was a real card who stood no nonsense from anybody. Some cell doors were opened one night for recreation. Guns and mobile phones were everywhere, and this prisoner had a pistol, which he put to the head of a screw after grabbing him. "You'll take me to McAlorum's cell and unlock it, because I'm going to shoot him," he said. "If you don't take me, I'm going to shoot you." The screw was marched at gunpoint along the landing towards McAlorum's cell but threw his keys out of the window. At that, the guy put the gun on the floor and surrendered.'

McAlorum survived that attempt on his life, but in June 2004, after dropping off a child at a primary school, his car was rammed by two gunmen from an INLA unit, who shot him dead.

30

SACRIFICE

THEY HAD LOOKED FORWARD to this moment. The bar of the luxury hotel was crowded, but they would not allow distractions to spoil the pleasure of this day. An old alliance resumed. Manny and McGraw shook hands and within moments were chatting together as though there had never been a break in their friendship. The reunion was arranged by a mutual friend, who told both it was time to forgive and forget. But, as Manny was to discover, there were some things about which McGraw remained as unforgiving as ever.

McGraw knew of the businessman who had caved in to the demand for £100,000. He had protected this individual from adverse publicity by insisting, while being interviewed for the book that would tell his life story, there be no reference to this man's real role in the scandal of the smuggling buses. Now, he decided, he too was due a share, and in Manny he had just the man to make sure he got what wanted. Sitting in one of their favourite watering holes, the Black Bear, near Uddingston, McGraw turned to the Irishman and told him, 'That fucking guy owes me £20,000.'

'Well, I'll go and see him and pass your message on,' was the reply.

When he saw Manny, the businessman's face fell. 'Every fucking time I see you it costs me a fortune,' he said. 'How much this time?'

'Twenty thousand. And if it's not paid, you know what happens.'

'Why me?' the victim asked.

'How was it you weren't in the dock with everybody else?' he was asked, but he refused to answer. The money was delivered three days later.

The Irish government eventually agreed it had been out of order in seizing the Paradise Bar, which it had subsequently sold at a knock-down price. By the time his lawyers had been paid, McGraw received £23,000, a pittance compared with the original £195,000 he had paid.

Not long afterwards, Blink MacDonald had challenged McGraw and another man to a fist fight, a 'square go'. Of course, no one was picking up the gauntlet. But then Blink received a visit from an old pal, and what he heard left him scratching his head.

'Manny McDonnell's been to see me,' he said. 'He's offered me £15,000 if I'll have a go at you.'

'McGraw?' asked Blink, and his caller nodded and went on.

'Look, I don't want to kill you. What if I just stab you in the shoulder and then I can go back, say you've been whacked and then look shocked when it's announced you're still alive.'

Blink looked at the hitman in astonishment. 'You're fucking kidding me, aren't you?' he asked. 'No way. Get to fuck.'

One mid-July day in 2007, McGraw and Manny met for a lunchtime drink at the Black Bear. McGraw was the first to arrive, and as soon as he saw his friend he walked over, hugged him and kissed him on the cheek. The greeting took Manny by surprise. McGraw wasn't an emotional man.

'What's up Tam?' he asked, and he was shocked by the reply.

'I trust you, Manny. I just have this odd sensation that something's not right.' Then he bought a drink.

The memory of that strange incident came back to Manny two weeks later when McGraw died unexpectedly at home after a heart attack. Mags was by his side.

'I was devastated when I heard he was gone,' said Manny. 'We'd gone through so much together. Tam was such a brilliant organiser, but he wasn't a great leader, and I say that with no disrespect. He tried to accommodate everybody, to please all sides, and that's where I believed he fell short of being totally top-notch. He allowed too many others to make decisions that he should have taken. I once told him, "Tam, you need to take things by the scruff of the neck and make it clear that while you'll listen to the views of others, what you say will go." But he was a wonderful friend.

'Sometimes he could annoy the life out of you. He'd talk about Paul but do nothing. I think Paul had a grudging respect for Tam. But Tam, on the other hand, did not respect Paul. He once told me, "You don't ask for respect, you earn it. Nobody who asks for respect deserves it."'

Manny joined hundreds of others at his friend's funeral.

A few weeks afterwards, he travelled over to Belfast to look up old friends and see old haunts. He was determined to track down dead Billy Kane's brother Eddie and eventually found him living quietly in a coastal village 15 miles from Belfast. The two old paramilitaries sat watching fishing boats returning with their catches, sharing their sadnesses.

'It was always known that if and when I moved on as commander of the IPLO unit, Eddie would take over. But that came about more quickly than had been expected, and when the unit reverted to the INLA Eddie found himself in charge.

'Any time I met Eddie on the street it had been awkward. He knew he should not talk to me about anything the unit was involved in but kept telling me what was going on, as though he was reporting to me, and I would have to remind him to say nothing to me or anybody. Even then I thought there was something wrong with Eddie, something troubling him, something about his body language and even in the way he spoke that pointed to him being unhappy. Then after I moved to Scotland we lost touch for years until I felt I needed to see him again, to find out how he was.

'That day as we watched the boats come and go, I knew this wasn't the Eddie Kane I'd known at the beginning. This was a spent force, a man who was burned out, who had given too much and more. I told him, "Eddie, you're a quarter of the man you once were," and when he started talking I knew why.

'He said, "I lost my da when McGurk's was blown up, then Billy was murdered, my wife left me, taking the family, and I knew I'd lost my ma too – she never said anything, but I was always sure Ma blamed me for what happened to Billy. Those bullets that took him were meant for me, and if I hadn't been in the organisation there would have been no cause to come to our home."

'I knew then that his guilt over the slaughter of his brother was tearing him to pieces. I could see tears starting, and when we parted I felt so sorry for him. So many made sacrifices for the cause, but were Eddie's any less than those of any other? Those who punished him may have hurt him physically, but those wounds were as nothing compared to the terrible burden he carried in his mind and would carry until his dying day.'

In 2009, Manny read that the Irish National Liberation Army, which had declared a ceasefire in 1999, had formally announced it was continuing its fight but through peaceful political means. He thought, 'They gave up their weapons, but in the IPLO we'd never have done that voluntarily.'

Had it all been worth it? He had no doubt the sacrifices of Eddie Kane, Billy Kane and all the others who had given their lives and who, like him, had donated their futures to the cause of fairness had been justified by the outcome. Manny's days of hate are past. One of his closest friends, Thomas 'TC' Coughlan, is a Rangers supporter. In some areas of Glasgow it would be unthinkable for rival supporters of the Old Firm to share friendship and trust, but like so many who fought in the Troubles, Manny knows such trifles as the colour of a man's football jersey are an irrelevance; what matters is knowing with confidence he can place the same degree of faith in Thomas as he once did in those who served with him in his unit.

Yet never a day goes by without his paying for the cost of justice.

'Am I glad to be out of it? Yes, and I'm glad I came through it alive. It was horrendous seeing people blown away. I'm sorry members of the British Army died, that they went home in boxes, because just like us they had mothers and fathers, sisters and brothers, girlfriends or wives, people who loved them and who they loved.

'People thought we were animals without fear, but that was never the case. Others might have deliberately set out to murder civilians, but not us. Ours was a war, fought against those in uniform and enemies totally opposed to all we stood for. It didn't matter if a soldier was a Catholic or a Protestant. We fired the gun at the uniform.

'There were 18-year-olds going home to England in coffins, just as there were children dying by the score in Northern Ireland, but the way we looked at it was that the more coffins we sent home the more likely were people in England to say, "Hold on a minute, what are we doing there?"

'I know that someday Ireland will be united, and when that happens people may look back and wonder why so many had to die. The small area of Belfast where we lived was known as Murder Triangle and 1,700 people died in it. Everybody who died must be remembered, but I hope that when Ireland is free and one, someone will say a special prayer for Johnathan and Tim.'

Till then, the Irish stranger will continue lighting a candle in his grief over two little boys he never knew.